ISLAMIC BRITAIN

'Philip Lewis provides an insider–outsider
account of Bradford, one of the most publicized
Muslim communities in Europe. Sympathetic in tone
and sociological in approach, it will be of interest not
only to community workers, policy-makers and
lecturers in race relations/ethnicity but also to
the informed reader interested in contemporary
British society.'

PROFESSOR AKBAR S. AHMED,
University of Cambridge

ISLAMIC BRITAIN

*Religion, Politics and Identity among British
Muslims: Bradford in the 1990s*

PHILIP LEWIS

I.B.TAURIS PUBLISHERS
LONDON · NEW YORK

Ishtiaq
for friendship
and perspective

Published in 1994 by I.B.Tauris & Co. Ltd
45 Bloomsbury Square, London WC1A 2HY

175 Fifth Avenue, New York, NY 10010

In the United States of America and Canada distributed by
St Martin's Press, 175 Fifth Avenue, New York, NY 10010

A full CIP record for this book is available
from the British Library

Library of Congress catalog card number 94 60695
A full CIP record for this book is available from the
Library of Congress

ISBN 1 85043 861 7

Maps drawn by Russell Townsend
Set in Monotype Baskerville by Lucy Morton, London SE12
Printed and bound in Great Britain by WBC Ltd,
Bridgend, Mid Glamorgan

Contents

Acknowledgements

This work started life as a Ph.D. thesis, and I owe a debt of gratitude to Kim Knott for her unfailing encouragement and supervision. She helped me to see that tradition, a commitment to truth and imagination are, or should be, common to religious and scholarly communities. Anna Enayat and Judy Mabro of I.B. Tauris transmuted thesis into book with exemplary speed. They showed me that the editorial process is itself an art. Colleagues in the Christian Study Centre and the Institute of Islamic Research in Pakistan taught me that collaborative work across religious traditions is not only possible but essential for mutual understanding. Finally my wife and children – Faith, Tim and Naomi – with their irrepressible humour were a welcome reminder that there is life after research.

Introduction

In 1985 an Urdu poster displayed in shop windows throughout Britain invited devotees of a deceased Muslim mystic to a celebration held in his honour in Britain's 'Islamabad' or 'city of Islam'. Islamabad was Bradford. The occasion was organized by a relative and spiritual successor of the holy man, who had worked in a local textile mill for twenty years.[1]

Although for well over two decades Bradford had been home to a growing Muslim community which had made a wide impact on its economic and civic life, most Bradfordians were unaware that their city was the home of a distinguished South Asian religions leader and the centre of a regional order with followers in France, Germany and Holland. But local people were not alone in their lack of information about the spiritual life of their Muslim neighbours. In 1985 the majority of those concerned with race relations in Britain – whether policy makers, community workers, academics or activists – still thought of the religious identity of the country's ethnic minorities as a somewhat marginal issue with only a limited impact on social policy. Even then the matter was subsumed under the category of multiculturalism. Yet within five years Bradford had become known to the non-Muslim as well as the Muslim world as a city of Islam, an infamous place where an enraged Muslim community had burned a novel. From being culturally and politically invisible, Muslims were suddenly projected as a dangerous fifth column, subversive of western freedoms: a trojan horse in the heart of Europe with a deadly cargo of 'fundamentalist' religiosity.

The northern industrial city of Bradford thus affords a unique vantage point from which to reflect on one of the most significant aspects of social change in Britain since the Second World War, the establishment of ethnic minority communities from the New Commonwealth. More particularly, the focus of this book is the Muslim communities, who originated largely from South Asia – Bangladesh, India and Pakistan.

Even before the publication of *The Satanic Verses* Bradford had become a centre of media interest and comment. For the writer Hanif Kureishi 'Bradford seemed to be a microcosm of a larger British society that was struggling to find a sense of itself, even as it was undergoing radical change.' These words were written in the wake of the 'Honeyford affair' in the mid-1980s, when the city became a public arena in which issues of 'race, culture, nationalism and education' were contested.[2]

Ray Honeyford, the headteacher of an inner city school with a majority of Muslim pupils, had challenged the prevailing educational orthodoxy – multiculturalism. He argued that concessions by the education authority to accommodate the special needs of Muslim parents involved a value judgement which gave priority to the preservation of cultural identity over the promotion of social integration. Foolishly he had chosen to publish one of his many articles on this sensitive educational issue in a small circulation right-wing journal, the *Salisbury Review*, committed to the repatriation of ethnic minorities.

Whatever the rights and wrongs of the educational issue – and they were never seriously debated, with the head teacher demonized by the left as a 'racist' and lionized by the right as a doughty defender of freedom of speech – Ray Honeyford exasperated sectors of the Muslim community by his disparaging remarks about Islam and Pakistani society. More generally, he antagonized the anti-racist constituency with his intemperate and stereotypical asides about Afro-Caribbeans and Sikhs. This unhappy episode dragged on for 18 months and was only resolved at the end of 1985 when he was persuaded to take early retirement and given a generous financial settlement.

In retrospect, the 'Honeyford affair' assumed additional importance. It represented 'the first major public campaigning victory of any Muslim community in Britain'.[3] Muslims could no longer be ignored and were attracting national media interest. Throughout the campaign, pictures of angry crowds picketing the school and holding aloft inflammatory placards were flashed

across the nation's television screens. Ominously, the term 'fundamentalist' had also entered the journalistic lexicon to describe
Muslims.

In the short term, however, the impact of these events should
not be exaggerated. In the minds of all those who reflected on
issues of citizenship and ethnicity, questions of urban poverty,
racial discrimination and language disabilities continued to receive
priority. In the shadow of urban riots in the 1980s the key public
and constitutional issue facing the nation could still be framed in
terms of 'whether Toxteth belongs to Britain, whether the blacks
are British citizens – or whether these territories are to be seen
as under the alien occupation of foreigners ... if they are citizens,
then they have equal rights and duties with the white majority'.[4]
Within this tradition of race relations discourse, black or Asian
were still the preferred terms to describe ethnic minorities from
South Asia. There was little attempt to incorporate religion in
race and ethnicity perspectives, either as an important component
in self-description or as a vehicle for the expression and mobil-
ization of collective minority interests. This was surprising because
the early assimilationist phase in race relations, premised on the
notion that migrants were an homogenous collection of individuals, had been discredited. Research in the late 1960s had
already shown that migrants were culturally embedded in communities, displaying distinct patterns of adaptation and group
formation.[5]

Assimilation was formally repudiated as government policy in
1966, when the future Labour Home Secretary, Roy Jenkins,
insisted that the government did not seek 'a flattening process of
uniformity, but cultural diversity, coupled with equal opportunity
in an atmosphere of mutual tolerance'.[6] This led to a belated
acknowledgement of Britain as a multicultural reality. However,
there were ambiguities concealed in the term multicultural. The
Jenkins formula presupposed equal citizenship in the public
domain, such as housing, education and jobs. This, indeed, was
the imperative and logic of race relations legislation. But most
commentators assumed the space in which difference was legitimized was limited to the private domain. Here a diversity of language, culture and religion could be expressed. The 'Honeyford
affair' made it clear that minority communities in general, and

Muslims in particular, wanted public recognition for their unique religious and cultural identities.

The *Satanic Verses* affair was to indicate how intractable such issues of public recognition could become. Bradford was once more at the centre of media attention. For the nation at large the city acquired notoriety with the book-burning incident in January 1989. Henceforth, Bradford was perceived to be the epicentre of British Muslim anger and resistance to the novel, which persisted unabated for more than two years. Following Ayatollah Khomeini's fatwa a month later, Bradford, in the popular imagination, became a centre of Muslim 'fundamentalism', with the city a bridgehead in the West for the establishment of separatist, Islamic enclaves. For Muslim and non-Muslim alike, no city was more important in the construction of a British Muslim identity.

In the immediate aftermath of the book-burning and fatwa, hopes of multicultural harmony and civic stability were replaced by fear of urban conflagration. Scenes of effigies of Salman Rushdie being burned, taunting Muslim crowds and angry banners rekindled memories of the Honeyford affair. Fay Weldon could fulminate against 'these primitive folk up North, these mad fundamentalists' and declare that 'our attempt at multi-culturalism is dead. The Rushdie Affair demonstrates it.'[7] Lord Jenkins could muse aloud in the *Independent* that 'in retrospect we might have been more cautious about allowing the creation in the 1950s of substantial Muslim communities here'; nonetheless, he took some comfort from the fact that 'by far the most unacceptable threat comes not from Bradford ... but from Teheran'.[8]

The Iranian intervention had transformed a national issue into an international crisis, and made it much harder to resolve. With the dismantling of communism and the ending of the Cold War, Western Europe was in danger of re-awakening to an older enmity. Muslim communities across the continent were finding themselves increasingly isolated and friendless. In the autumn of 1989 in France three Muslim girls who sought to wear headscarves in contravention of school rules were portrayed as demanding a privileged status for Islam in the secular space of state schools. This happened at the time France was celebrating the bicentennial of its republican and anti-clerical revolution!

When the Gulf crisis erupted, British Muslims were seen as potential subversives, disloyal to a nation at war. Peregrine Worsthorne thundered in the *Sunday Telegraph*:

> Islam, once a great civilization worthy of being argued with ... has degenerated into a primitive enemy fit only to be sensitively [sic] subjugated ... If they want jihad, let them have it ... [Islam,] once a moral force, has long been corrupted by its own variations of the European heresies, fascism and communism – a poisonous concoction threatening seepage back into Europe through mass migration.[9]

Such sentiments, which legitimized contempt and racism in the tabloid press, sent clear signals to many Muslims in Britain that they were, at best, tolerated aliens.[10]

Fortunately the moral panic subsided, although it left behind a dangerous legacy of mutual suspicion. One of the most worrying aspects of this was the habit of describing British Muslims as 'fundamentalist'. The term fundamentalism presupposes a unitary notion of Islam, spawning militant Muslim activists across the world. Drawn from American Protestant history, it is almost totally useless today for either description or analysis. Its pejorative overtones of religious fascism obscure the diversity of traditions and groupings within Islam. One major concern of the present study is to dispel this parody of the Islamic tradition. The vitality, popularity and persistence of Islamic mysticism in Britain gives the lie to such pernicious misrepresentation.

This is not to argue, however, that there is no movement within the Islamic world which sets its face against the West and seeks to capture political power. This movement is described by participants and scholars alike as 'Islamist'. The Society of the Muslim Brothers founded in Egypt in 1928 by a school teacher, Hasan al-Banna, gave institutional expression to Islamism, and became the model for similar groups across the Muslim world. Islamism was critical alike of the otherworldly excesses of Islamic mysticism and the seductive allure to the Muslim elites of Western, secular ideologies, whether communism, socialism or nationalism. In its place Islamism insisted that the Qur'an, traditions and Islamic law, properly understood and interpreted, should be the basis of the state and society in all its dimensions. Its novelty lay in merging politics and religion.

For the Islamist, Islam is a self-sufficent ideology. Like the role of the Communist Party under Lenin, Islamism exists to mobilize, educate and lead the masses rather than represent them. It remains to be seen whether it can translate its utopian rhetoric into coherent and compelling social, economic and political policy. The Islamist slogan that sovereignty belongs to God alone seems to allow little place for human freedom, still less democracy and dissent.[11] The movement exists in Britain but, as we shall see, is struggling to establish its relevance in a situation where Muslims are a minority.

The heightened awareness of a British Muslim presence has not been entirely negative. A recent annotated bibliography of academic publications about Islam and Muslims in Britain indicates a slowly rising curve of interest since 1985 that increases exponentially after 1988. Two features of the research are particularly welcome. First, the range of academic disciplines seeking to understand Muslim communities has increased. While social scientists still predominate, these have been joined by specialists in such diverse fields as law, politics, geography, education, religious and cultural studies. Second, almost a quarter of the contributions listed come from British Muslim scholars themselves.[12]

Critical discourse about Muslims in Britain is beginning to benefit from such an inter-disciplinary perspective. A recent monograph by the doyen of race relations theory, Professor John Rex, has sought to integrate the importance of religious identity into a revitalized framework for ethnic minority studies. Rex makes the important observation that too often it is assumed that minority communities must either work through the political mainstream or mobilize on a religio-communal basis.[13] It is possible to do both, as the Irish Catholic and Jewish communities in Britain have shown.

Political theorists have begun to look again at the nature and implications of membership of a political community. It is legitimate to expect Muslim communities to acknowledge the authority of the established system of government and its laws. At the same time, of course, as British citizens they enjoy the same rights as other communities to negotiate changes to accommodate their special needs. It is not legitimate, however, to expect them to surrender their specificities of culture and custom when these do not impede the discharge of their obligations as citizens. This is simply 'to confuse the state with the nation, a form of authority with a culture'.[14]

Islamic Britain seeks to build on the insights of such research. More specifically it can be seen as seeking to complement localized studies by anthropologists. These tend to focus on the processes of labour migration, and their impact on social networks, gender roles, caste and leadership. Such monographs have usually focused on one ethnic group, usually the Mirpuris from that part of Kashmir held by Pakistan, Azad or Free Kashmir (as distinct from the rest of Kashmir under Indian control), or have used categories of nationality – Pakistani, Bangladeshi – as an organizing principle. This book adopts a religious studies perspective, more alert to the commonalities across ethnic boundaries generated by belonging to a shared religious tradition. It thus contributes an important case-study of the relationship of religion and ethnicity.

My hope is that the present work, an empirical study of Bradford's Muslim communities, will be of interest to the general reader eager to get behind media caricatures of Islam. It can serve as a microcosm of the achievements and predicaments of these Muslims who have largely abandoned 'the myth of return' that sustained the pioneer migrants, and who are struggling to develop a British Muslim identity.[15]

Islamic Britain seeks to illuminate the dynamics of Muslim community formation, highlight an emerging pattern of pragmatic engagement with the local state, and illustrate the growing confidence exhibited by British-born Muslims. Bradford Muslims are also active in regional, national and transnational associations and organizations. The crises of recent years allow us to see how such multiple loyalties are mobilized and managed.

One critical issue for the future of British Islam is examined in depth: the nature of the intellectual and cultural formation of the religious leadership, which took place largely in South Asia, and their ability to connect with the different linguistic, cultural and educational experience of Muslims born and educated in Britain. Such difficulties, implicit in any migration process, impact most obviously on British Muslim women, many of whom are the first generation to enjoy formal education and to work in the public domain – yet many still find themselves unwelcome in the male domain of the mosque.

I have deliberately spoken of Muslim communities in the plural to underscore the empirical fact that Muslims belong to a variety of linguistic, regional and sectarian groups. The making of a British Islam is an ongoing, unfinished process of experimentation, diversity and debate. I have included material on a variety of sensitive issues troubling Muslims in Britain. Many Muslim elders remain confused as to how to respond to an emerging Muslim youth culture, a hybrid of British and South Asian forms, expressed in music, magazines and local media. Much of this is in English, since a decreasing proportion of youngsters are genuinely bilingual. Schools, youth and community centres are places in which British Muslims enjoy space to experiment with their multiple identities, relatively free from parental control. The perplexity of parents is deepened when aspects of their inherited culture which they took for granted as Islamic begin to be questioned. In addition, I touch on the contested terrain of who will represent Islam to the wider society – Muslim politicians, businessmen or religious leaders.

A Bradford focus is also a reminder that the majority of British Muslims, locally and nationally, originate from South Asia. Indeed, a recent analysis concluded that as many as 80 per cent were from South Asian backgrounds.[16] Too often Islam is seen as a Middle Eastern religion and it is forgotten that the largest Muslim populations and nations are found in Asia. The significance of South Asian Islam is not simply numerical. It has either generated or profoundly shaped three of the most important Muslim traditions today: revivalism, Islamism and modernism – all of which are described in Chapter 2. *Islamic Britain* also maps the variety of adaptive strategies these distinct traditions have utilized in an attempt to take root in a radically different context.

After six years in Pakistan studying Islam and Muslim–Christian relations, and almost ten years in Bradford working in the area of race and inter-faith relations, I have incurred many obligations to Muslim friends, none more than the leadership of the Bradford Council for Mosques. If this study contributes to a more informed understanding of British Muslims, both in their strengths and weaknesses, and begins to dismantle the myth of an undifferentiated 'fundamentalist' Islam, then I will have begun to discharge such debts. This experience has confirmed for me the wisdom of a remark by a great scholar of the Arab world, the late Albert Hourani: 'Nobody can now write with meaning about the world of Islam if he does not bring to it some sense of a living relationship with those of whom he writes.'[17]

1

Britain's Muslim Communities

Britain and the Muslim world have interacted in a myriad different ways down the centuries. At various times Muslims have been treated as a military and ideological threat, political allies, trading partners, objects of intellectual curiosity, ripe for imperial conquest and, latterly, as fellow citizens. The North of England furnishes us with one of the first references in Britain to Muslims in Europe. At his monastery in Jarrow the eighth-century Anglo-Saxon monk, Bede, completed his celebrated *Ecclesiastical History of the English People*. In it he mentions that a 'swarm of Saracens ravaged Gaul with horrible slaughter'. However, 'after a brief interval ... they paid the penalty of their wickedness.'[1] The reference is to the battle of Poitiers (732), when Charles Martel checked the advance of the first great wave of Arab Muslim expansion, which had absorbed the Christian territories of Syria, Egypt, North Africa, Spain and Sicily. Bede mentions it in passing and exhibits little knowledge of Islam.

Fifty years later a disaster befell the rearguard of Charlemagne's army in Spain, fighting the Arabs. On 15 August 778, Roland Count of Brittany was killed. This episode worked on the European imagination and generated a Christian epic which 'cheered William the Conqueror's army into battle at Hastings'. The *Song of Roland*, a tale of treachery and heroism on the borders of Christendom, featured as its backcloth 'the unknown Moslem world, a wonder world of fantasy and evil – a kind of parody of the Christian world'.[2]

By 1588 the major Muslim power with which Europeans related was the Ottoman Empire. In that year Elizabeth I proposed an alliance of Protestant England with a fellow monotheist to contend against a nation of idolaters. The appeal was made to

the Ottoman Sultan, Murad III, against Catholic Spain![3] Commercial alliances with the Ottoman Empire persisted for over two
centuries: first as a bulwark against Spanish and French ambitions and then to check Russian expansionism, which threatened
British India in the nineteenth century. With trade and travel, a
more informed interest in the Islamic world developed. Dr
Johnson expressed such an interest in the eighteenth century:
'There are two objects of curiosity – the Christian world and the
Mahometan world. All the rest may be considered as barbarous.'[4]

A Muslim presence in Britain goes back at least three hundred
years to the activities of the East India Company, when men
from the Indian subcontinent were first recruited into the
merchant navy. Known as 'lascars', these sailors were present in
Britain's ports in sizeable numbers. In mid-nineteenth-century
London some did well and established themselves with 'congenial
common-law wives, like "Lascar Sally" and "Calcutta Louisa"'.[5]
Others were destitute, and to meet their needs a 'Strangers'
Home' was opened in West India Dock Road in 1858.

The lascars formed shifting and impermanent settlements in
London and various ports well into the twentieth century. At the
outbreak of the Second World War seamen from South Asia
accounted for some 20 per cent of the merchant navy. Another
group came from the Yemen, particularly after the opening of
the Suez canal in 1869 when increasing numbers were recruited
into the merchant navy. A recent study has documented the
establishment of their communities in London, Cardiff, Liverpool, South Shields, Hull and Sheffield in the twentieth century.[6]
Cumulatively they number no more than 15,000 but represent
probably the oldest permanent Muslim settlements.

Before 1914 the main centres of organized Islam in Britain
were Liverpool, London and Woking, which attracted a transient
community of businessmen and students, mainly from India, and
a few notable converts. These centres often depended on the
energy and enterprise of one individual and did not always survive
their death or departure. Thus a Liverpool solicitor, W.H.Quillam,
embraced Islam in 1887 after visiting Morocco. He claimed 150
adherents to Islam and was an active writer and essayist. From
1893 to 1908 he produced a weekly, the *Crescent*. He was patronized by many Muslim dignitaries: the Ottoman sultan made him

Shaykh al-Islam for Britain, the Shah appointed him Persian Consul in Liverpool and he was able to purchase a building to act as an Islamic Institute with a gift from the Amir of Afghanistan. However, when Quillam left England in 1908 the 'Liverpool movement seems to have petered out.'[7]

Woking was to prove more significant in the history of British Islam, and was to illustrate the formative influence of Indian Muslims working in collaboration with a small number of distinguished British Muslims. A mosque was built in Woking in 1889, named after its principal benefactor, Shah Jehan, ruler of the Indian state of Bhopal. Shah Jehan had been persuaded by the Hungarian orientalist, Dr Leitner, registrar in the University of the Punjab, to fund what was intended to be the nucleus of an Islamic University. A mosque and a students' hostel alone survived Leitner's death in 1899.

In 1913, after a period of neglect, the mosque became the active centre of Muslim mission. The two guiding lights were Lord Headley, who had worked in India as a civil engineer and converted in that year, and a Lahore barrister Khwaja Kamal-ud-Din. The latter had left a successful practice to come to England to challenge misconceptions of Islam and work for conversions. Khwaja Kamal-ud-Din was to become the leading personality in British Islam until his death in 1932. In 1913 he produced the first number of the monthly *Muslim India and the Islamic Review* – renamed *Islamic Review* in 1921. The one shadow on the horizon was Kamal-ud-Din's involvement with the Ahmadiyyas, whose status as an Islamic movement was increasingly contested.[8] Indeed, on the death of both men in the 1930s the management committee severed its ties with the Ahmadiyyas.

The Woking mosque became a social centre for British Muslims, frequented by visiting Muslim dignitaries, with Kamal-ud-Din referred to in the British press as the Very Reverend, by analogy with the Chief Rabbi. The mosque and the Muslim Literary Society it sponsored involved many of the Muslim luminaries of South Asia and Britain, including the distinguished Indian jurist and Islamic apologist, Syed Ameer Ali (d. 1928), who had retired to England in 1906, and the Qur'an translator Marmaduke Pickthall (d. 1936). 'In 1924 it was reckoned that thirty regularly attended prayers at the Woking mosque, that there were a thousand British Muslims scattered about the country and 10,000 Muslims from overseas.'[9]

An increasing number of the overseas Muslims resident in Britain were students. In 1880 there were some 100 Indian students, in 1910 more than 700 and in 1931, 1,800.[10] Of course, not all were Muslims. However, many distinguished Indian Muslims were to study in Britain and some, like Syed Ameer Ali, spent many years in the country. An oil painting now graces the entrance to the Great Hall and Library of Lincoln's Inn in London. It portrays the most famous Muslim to study law in the nineteenth century: 'M.A. Jinnah, Founder and First Governor-General of Pakistan'.[11]

If the Woking mosque is perhaps the oldest in Britain the most prestigious is the Central Mosque at Regent's Park. The land was donated by King George VI in return for a site in Cairo intended for a new Anglican Cathedral. In November 1944 the King opened the Islamic Cultural Centre. The Central London Mosque Trust, whose trustees were drawn from ambassadors and high commissioners of 13 Muslim countries, set to collecting funds for the new mosque. In 1977 it was finally opened. It would be wrong to think of the Central Mosque as analogous to a cathedral, since theologically Islam does not have priests, still less a hierarchy. However, if all mosques are equal the Central Mosque could be described as 'first among equals'.[12]

In the 30 years that elapsed between the inception and completion of the Central Mosque, the Muslim presence in Britain had changed out of all recognition. The dramatic multiplication and consolidation of Muslim communities is evidenced by the dramatically rising curve of mosque registrations. In 1966 18 were registered, in 1977 136 and in 1985 338.[13]

Location and Size of Britain's Muslim Communities

Statistics for the total number of Muslims in Britain vary from three-quarters of a million to two million. The reason for this discrepancy is that census data do not include religious affiliation. Therefore figures are generally extrapolations from place of birth statistics and Labour Force Surveys – sample surveys of less than 1 per cent of the population. The 1991 census included ethnic and

national categories. Some of these translated reasonably straight-
forwardly into Muslim components – Pakistan and Bangladesh –
but others were more problematic, such as India and Cyprus.[14]

The best recent analysis of all the data, which reviews previous
estimates, evaluates the available sources and identifies the criteria
used, concludes that the Muslim population of Great Britain in
1991 was about one million, and that Muslims with their origin
in Bangladesh, India and Pakistan account for about 80 per cent
of the total.[15] The rest are drawn largely from the Arab world,
as well as Malaysia, Iran, Turkey/Cyprus, East and West Africa.
The public significance of South Asian Muslims in Britain is
further highlighted if we distinguish between Muslims resident in
Britain as political refugees, entrepreneurs or for personal, domestic and recreational reasons, and those who form genuine
communities. The majority of South Asians do comprise communities when defined not merely in terms of residence but with
respect to two additional criteria:

(a) they have worked here, as opposed to merely resided; and
(b) they have to some extent remained in contact with each other
    as fellow emigrants from a particular country through residence
    in a common urban area, work in a similar branch of eco-
    nomic activity and the creation of some kind of communal
    organization.[16]

According to such criteria the large number of Arabs who have
congregated in and around London are residents rather than part
of cohesive communities. Their main country of residence and
work remains the Middle East. The exceptions are communities
of Egyptians, Iraqis, Moroccans, Palestinians and Yemenis. Small
Yemeni communities date from the 1880s, while it is not until the
1980s that substantial communities of Moroccans and Egyptians
working in services and professions became established in London.

The growth and consolidation of South Asian communities in
Britain is evident from Table 1.1, which combines Pakistani and
Bangladeshi populations and gives the percentages of those born
in the UK.[17]

Extrapolating from the 1991 census figures gives us 477,000
Pakistanis, 163,000 Bangladeshis and 134,000 Indian Muslims, in
all a total of 774,000 British Muslims of South Asian origin.[18]

Table 1.1   Britons of Pakistani and Bangladeshi descent and
percentage born in United Kingdom

	Total	% born in UK
1951	5,000	–
1961	24,900	1.2
1971	170,000	23.5
1981	360,000	37.5
1991	640,000	47.0

These communities are not evenly distributed across the country
but are overwhelmingly concentrated in urban areas, whether
London, the industrial cities of the Midlands, the textile towns of
Lancashire and Yorkshire, or Strathclyde. Almost half of the
Bangladeshi community lives in what used to be called Greater
London, with just under a quarter in Tower Hamlets (36,955).
The concentrations of Pakistanis live outside London: almost a
quarter living in two cities, Birmingham and Bradford, numbering 66,095 and 45,280. If the small Bangladeshi communities are
added to these figures such communities account for 8 and 11 per
cent of the total population of Birmingham and Bradford.[19]
However, they are located in a small number of inner city electoral wards: in Birmingham in 8 of the 42 wards, in Bradford in
7 of the 30 wards.

The Pakistani and Bangladeshi communities also have a different age profile to the majority. It is younger, with more than
twice the number of under-16-year-olds compared to the white
community. Conversely, where some 17 per cent of the latter are
aged 65 plus, this is so for less than 2 per cent of those of Pakistani and Bangladeshi origin. The average size of Pakistani and
Bangladeshi households is 4.81 and 5.34, compared to 2.43 for
the majority. On the basis of such figures recent projections of
population growth suggest that the Pakistani and Bangladeshi
communities are set eventually to double in size.[20] This means
that notwithstanding the multi-racial and multi-national character
of Muslims, especially in London and the south, those of South

Asian origin are likely to continue to dominate the public face of British Islam.

Sojourners to Settlers: the Dynamics of Community Formation

The South Asian Muslim communities which have formed in the last 40 years are part of that larger post-Second World War flow of migrants from former British colonies attracted to jobs in industry and services. The primary motive for migration was economic, with 'wages for labouring jobs in Britain in the early 1960s ... over 30 times those offered for similar jobs in Pakistan'.[21] The men were either single or had left their wives at home – indeed, the 1961 census data indicates there were only 81 women among the 3,376 Pakistanis in Bradford. Some 95 per cent of these migrants were of rural origin, and their aim was to maximize savings with which to benefit the extended family back in the village. Additional motives for migration were status competition or, in the case of India, Hindu–Muslim tension.[22]

What is often unremarked in accounts of South Asian migration is that migrants did not come from the poorest areas, but rather from places with a tradition of emigration. In Pakistan they did not come from Baluchistan, but from Azad Kashmir, the Northwest Frontier and parts of the Punjab; the latter prosperous farming areas, irrigated by a network of canals. These areas had long provided recruits for the merchant navy and the British army. With regard to Gujaratis from India, migrants were not drawn from the scheduled castes or tribal peoples, but from villagers in the three districts of Baroda, Surat and Bharuch, a highly literate group, including traders and professionals. They had a long tradition of migration and trading, especially with East Africa.

Of the Bangladeshis in Britain 95 per cent come from Sylhet District in the north-east of the country.[23] Once again, this area had generated a tradition of migration within South Asia as far afield as Calcutta and thence as cooks and galley hands on British merchant ships. There were Sylheti restaurant workers as early as 1873 in London. The lure of the capital became strong in the 1930s, with increasing numbers jumping ship. A recent history of the Sylhetis indicates that in London in 1946 there were some 20 Indian restaurants, in 1960 300 across the country and in 1980 3,000, with the vast majority owned by Sylhetis.[24]

While there were undoubtedly similar push factors operating in all these areas, whether population increase that fragmented landholdings, underemployment or poverty, non-economic factors have probably been underplayed. People growing up in such emigration cultures compete with each other. 'Sending people away from home is an indicator of economic success and enormous social pride for families within their own communities.'[25]

Most South Asian communities in Britain were formed through a four-phase pattern of migration. First the pioneers, then what is known as 'chain migration' of generally unskilled male workers, followed by the migration of wives and children and finally the emergence of a British-born generation. The story of 'Sadiq', a Mirpuri who jumped ship in 1937, provides a typical illustration of the first two phases. Sadiq worked initially as a labourer in Cardiff, lodging with several fellow Mirpuri seamen. Once settled, he wrote to a cousin and a village friend in Newcastle who were living from door-to-door peddling, urging them to join him and try their luck together in Oxford. By 1956, Sadiq had saved enough to finance his brother's trip from Pakistan, and in 1957 they bought a house. This property became the first port of call for five other close relatives and fellow villagers whose migration Sadiq and his brother subsequently sponsored.[26] Chain migration, in which earlier migrants sponsor their kinsmen and help them with housing and jobs, persisted through the 1960s.

Numbers increased dramatically in the early 1960s for two reasons. First, to pre-empt the Commonwealth Immigrants Act of 1962, which closed the door on automatic entry for Commonwealth citizens. The second reason, which explains the increase of wives choosing to join their husbands, was the fear, often fed by rumours, that men had also married a British wife.[27] A total of 17,120 Pakistanis entered Britain between 1955 and 1960, compared to 50,170 in the 18 months preceding the 1962 legislation. This introduced a system of vouchers, which were classified into three types: 'A' for those with specific jobs to come to; 'B' for those with specific skills and qualifications and 'C' for those who were unskilled and without firm promise of work – preference was given to ex-servicemen. In 1965 the issue of further vouchers was suspended. However, since there was still a demand for labour, in the late sixties,

> an increasing number of Mirpuri men began, following one of their periodic trips home, to bring their fourteen and fifteen year old sons back with them to Britain. Young enough to be permitted to enter as dependants – and thus avoiding the bar on males – it would not be long before they left school and started work.[28]

These loopholes were eventually closed and the migration of single men ended with the Immigration Act of 1971. Henceforth, if dependants were to enter, the whole family had to come. Phases three and four of the migration experience now accelerated: the arrival of wives and children and the emergence of British-born communities. Since the late 1960s the growth and consolidation of Muslim communities has been increasingly evident. In Bradford in 1971 the school-age (5–15 years) children of Pakistani and Bangladeshi parents accounted for 4 per cent of all children; by 1981 this figure had risen to 11 per cent, and by 1991 22 per cent. Nationally for the period 1988–90 some 87 per cent of all those under 16 of Pakistani origin were born in Britain, as against a figure of 61 per cent for those from Bangladeshi backgrounds.[29]

While these figures indicate that not all communities have traversed the four-phase pattern of community formation at exactly the same time, another set of South Asian communities collapsed all four stages into one. These were people expelled or who chose to escape the increasingly oppressive nationalist regimes in East Africa. Pressure had been building in Kenya from 1965 and in Uganda from 1969, culminating in Amin's expulsions in 1972. Thus in 1981, 155,000 South Asians of East African origin were living in Britain, of which possibly 15 per cent were Muslims.[30]

Here to Stay: The Reproduction of a Distinct Social and Cultural World

Muslim communities in Britain have been very successful in reproducing much of their traditional social and cultural world.

This is true of Arab and South Asian communities alike. A recent study of Yemenis in Britain described them as:

> a close-knit if internally fissured community, a village-like grouping transposed from their original context into a difficult and often hostile environment. They form an 'urban village' ... living within its own socially, linguistically and ethnically defined borders, and interacting in a selective way with the broader society around it.[31]

These remarks would also hold true for many of the South Asian communities. Muslims from Bharuch in Gujarat, an administrative district where some 15 per cent of the population are Muslim, already live in India in 'remarkably self-contained' enclaves, with their social lives 'dominated' by visits to neighbours and kin and minimal interaction with Hindus. In Blackburn this pattern has been repeated – with the difference that the 'ethnic horizon' of Bharuchi Muslims has become, if anything, 'more closely circumscribed as a result of migration and settlement'.[32] Muslims from Pakistan and Bangladesh, Muslim majority areas, also live in relatively self-contained communities in Britain.

Various factors explain such continuities in social and cultural life. Chain migration meant that village and kin networks were reproduced in Britain. These were further reinforced by transnational arranged marriages, often with cousins from the same areas. In Britain Muslim communities are also sufficiently large and concentrated to generate and sustain a separate institutional and economic infrastructure which embodies and perpetuates religious and cultural norms. The huge investment in and proliferation of mosques is one dramatic indication of both a Muslim commitment to stay in Britain and a determination to pass on to their children their religious and cultural values. The profusion of specialist goods and services, from halal butchers, restaurants, jewellers and book shops, to Urdu and Punjabi video shops is similarly striking.

While such institutional completeness allows Muslim communities to enjoy a large measure of religious and cultural autonomy, their identity is constantly renewed and revitalized by on-going links with South Asia, facilitated by modern communications. A number of Pakistan's most popular Urdu dailies have English editions, Pakistani and Azad Kashmiri political parties have branches in many British cities, and a majority of the religious leaders in Britain's mosques still come from South Asia.

The links which some Muslims maintain with parts of South Asia also 'tend to sustain much tighter and more inward-looking social networks, even in diaspora, than do Sikhs or Hindus'.[33] Three specific areas have been identified as partly explaining the different social and economic patterns that Sikhs and Muslims from adjacent areas of South Asia have traced in Britain.

(i) *In marriage rules*: while Sikhs, like Hindus, are barred from marrying their close kin, Moslems are permitted, and indeed encouraged to do so.

(ii) *In gender rules*: given the conventions of purdah, Moslem women's public mobility is more tightly restricted than is the case among Sikhs and Hindus.

(iii) *In mortuary rites*: while Moslems bury their dead, Sikhs, like Hindus, opt for cremation.[34]

While the logic of the first two points is clear enough, the third needs some expansion. In Mirpur, for example, each extended kin group (*biradari*) has its own carefully tended graveyard, which emphasizes physically the corporate nature of the kin group and its rootedness in a particular place.[35] It is thus still the norm to fly the deceased back from Britain to Pakistan and Bangladesh for burial. In the case of Sikhs and Hindus cremation does not carry with it this sense of belonging to a particular locality.

These remarks, however, should not be interpreted as implying that such cultural norms and practices are unchanging. In Manchester, for example, many British-born Muslim women enjoy a freedom unusual in the Pakistan their mothers left behind, and the constraints of purdah are minimal.

> If their brothers are market traders, they often accompany them on trips to distant markets and assist in selling on the stalls. Many have driving licences. Within residential enclaves they move around freely, visiting school friends ... labour migration has created a new mediatory role for women. On trips to Pakistan they arrange marriages, property investments and other affairs on behalf of their family in Britain.[36]

Further, economic recession, which has hit those of Pakistani and

Bangladeshi descent particularly hard, has also led to a percep-
tible increase in the formal employment of young Muslim women
to supplement the family budget. It needs to be remembered that
they are often the first generation of girls within their families to
receive education and thus to acquire marketable skills. Research
by the Policy Studies Institute indicates that 34 per cent of women
aged between 16 and 24 from Pakistani backgrounds now work,
as against 13 per cent for the 45–64 year old age group.[37]

Residential clustering has also provided a constituency which
ensures the appointment of Muslim councillors. The 1980s saw a
dramatic increase in their number, ensuring that local services
began to respond to their special needs. A recently published
monthly survey, *British Muslims*, indicates clearly the range and
diversity of participation and collaboration now common between
Muslims and many local authorities.[38]

What is sometimes overlooked is the ease with which Muslims
who mediate between their communities and the local state –
councillors, members of Community Relations Councils – operate within two very different cultural worlds. Unlike many of those
with whom they work they are bilingual and bi-cultural. South
Asians sitting on Community Relations Councils are perceived
by non-Muslims to be representatives of their own community.
However, in Pakistan villagers are brought up 'in communities
where the favours of powerful patrons or *biradari* members in
government positions are often vital to secure justice'.[39] In such
an environment the very concept of 'community representation is
alien'.[40] Thus, in relation to their own community many Muslim
representatives on British bodies operate within the more familiar
patron–client mode.

The ability of Muslim politicians to construct distinct constituencies in separate contexts is illustrated in a study of Bangladeshi
activists contesting local council elections in Tower Hamlets in the
mid-1980s. Formal political discourse presupposed a unitary constituency comprising a Bangladeshi community in solidarity as
'black' working class with the white working class. Bangladeshi
electors, however, were more interested in the 'Sylheti backgrounds
and moral worth of the two young candidates' and were mobilized along kinship, village and friendship networks.[41] Working
within the categories of 'black' and 'multiculturalism' the

Bangladeshi activists were, nonetheless, able to win resources for community languages and Qu'ran schools, as desired by their Sylheti constituents.

There is a growing awareness among academics writing about minority communities that they are not simply passive victims of racial prejudice.[42] Rather, they often have cultural capital which can be turned to their advantage, enabling them successfully to circumvent or mitigate the worst effects of racial exclusion. For example, it is evident that Pakistanis in Manchester have created value by trading with each other, by using internal labour, not least that of male and female family members. While most are concentrated in the food, services and fashion industries,

> business enclaves are now emerging – property, hotels and taxi driving being perhaps the most noteworthy recent areas of economic expansion. Pakistanis tend to 'capture' economic enclaves as their experience and success in specific sectors precipitate the entry of fellow migrants into this sector.[43]

The socio-economic profile of South Asian communities in Britain has become a highly controversial subject of discussion. The battle lines are usually drawn up between proponents and antagonists of a deprivationist perspective. This latter sees 'black' and 'Asian' communities as forever the victims of racial exclusion confined to the bottom of the economic pile, as working class or underclass. It is now clear that this reading of the situation is at best partial. It cannot make space for increasing evidence of economic success within these communities. On most indicators the Indian communities are more successful than the ethnic majority.[44] There are also marked distinctions within the minority communities, for example, between the Indian and Bangladeshi communities, with the latter entering Britain much later, at the time of rapid restructuring and recession in the economy.

If we focus on the population of Pakistani origin certain generalizations can be hazarded. Along with other South Asian communities they have borne the brunt of radical changes in the British economy, away from manufacturing to service industries. In this restructuring, textiles and engineering were particularly vulnerable, the very sectors which attracted migrant labour in the 1950s and 1960s. In textiles, nationally, employment has fallen from over 2 million in 1945 to 517,000 in 1986. In engineering one million jobs were lost in the 15 years prior to 1986.[45] Such figures partly explain the very high levels of unemployment among the Pakistani community shown in the 1991 census (28.8 compared to 8.8 per cent for white communities).

However, this is only part of the picture. A 1981 study indicated that between 7 and 10 per cent of Pakistanis live in the most affluent suburbs or in comfortable semi-detached suburbia.[46] Further, when we remember that migrant communities inevitably start at the base of the economic pyramid, a recent analysis of the 1991 census data signalled the real achievements of these communities, none more than the Pakistani population:

> the proportion of Pakistanis in professional occupations exceeds the White norm ... they are slightly underrepresented in the two remaining white-collar categories – the Managers and Technicians. But even though a disproportionate number ... are currently found in manual occupations, they are in no sense comprehensively at the bottom of the pile, for ... they are over-represented in the skilled manual category.[47]

The deprivationist perspective is clearly inadequate and does not begin to do justice to the complex and differentiated picture now emerging. This, however, is not to counsel complacency. It is likely that the minority communities, especially those of Pakistani and Bangladeshi backgrounds, are 'increasingly polarised into those who have already exceeded a certain threshold of success ... and those at the very base of the social pyramid whose lot will have worsened'.[48] Most disturbing are statistics indicating educational disadvantage:

> While a third of all 16–24 year olds in 1988–1990 had a GCE A-level or equivalent or higher qualification, only 18 per cent of Pakistanis and 5 per cent of Bangladeshis did. Moreover these two minorities were the only ones to be significantly out of line with the findings that overall 20 per cent of this age group had no qualification whatever. The proportions of Pakistani and Bangladeshi 16–24 year olds with no qualifications was 48 and 54 per cent respectively.[49]

Bradford Muslims: Their Refusal to Remain Invisible

Muslim communities from the Yemen have been established much longer in Britain than South Asian communities. However, in a revealing aside the author documenting their story noticed that they had,

> remained rather invisible, not only to the indigenous British popula-
> tion but to other immigrants as well. Classified with Indians as 'lascars'
> before the First World War, they now became part of a generic 'black'
> or 'Asian' mass. Yemenis themselves report that they are sometimes
> called 'Pakky' by British workers; on one occasion, in a Pakistani kebab
> shop in Birmingham, the man behind the counter automatically be-
> gan talking Urdu to my Yemeni companion ... at the height of the
> conflict over Salman Rushdie in 1989, Yemenis, who as a whole re-
> mained removed from this dispute, were the objects of anti-Islamic
> abuse.[50]

These comments make clear that the much larger Muslim com-munities from South Asia have largely dictated public percep-tions about Islam in Britain. In this regard no city has featured so centrally and consistently in shaping such attitudes than Brad-ford. It could hardly be said of Bradford's Muslims that they remained largely invisible. Throughout the 1980s they regularly featured in the national media, whether over the issue of halal meat in schools, the Honeyford affair or the very public burning of Salman Rushdie's novel.

Their importance is not confined to headlines. Bradford contains all the major sectarian traditions of South Asian Islam. The city's Council for Mosques, set up in 1981, was able to hold these together, and act as an advocate of Muslim concerns with public bodies. Muslims in Birmingham, the only city with a larger concentration of Muslims, were to fragment into two Mosque councils.[51] In 1981 only three of Bradford's 90 councillors were Muslim. By 1992 it had 11, all Labour, including the deputy leader of the ruling group. These included both a Gujarati woman and a Bangladeshi. This already indicates co-operation across national and regional groupings, since neither could have been elected without the support of the large Pakistani groups resident in those wards. There was also a flourishing and organized Muslim professional and business community.

Like most South Asian Muslim communities, Bradford Muslims are networked across the country with relatives living in other cities, whom they regularly visit on religious and social occasions. Religious leaders in Bradford are also part of regional, national and international associations. Pir Maroof Hussain Shah, a distinguished sufi leader from Azad Kashmir, has devotees across Britain, Pakistan and Western Europe, and ex-members of his organization are now religious luminaries in Manchester and Birmingham.[52] His network of personal and sectarian contacts can be mobilized for celebration or protest. In 1987 and 1988 under the World Sufi Council umbrella he organized celebrations of the Prophet's birthday in Hyde Park, London, which drew crowds of 25,000 people from all parts of the country.

Bradford, then, is an excellent place from which to study how Muslim communities are learning selectively to transcend national, regional, linguistic, sectarian and caste differences in pursuit of a measure of economic independence, political influence and religious and cultural autonomy. It also offers a case-study of how local Muslims are able to work with multiple identities, some imposed rather than chosen, often generated by those working within central and local government funding bodies, as well as educational and race relations bureaucracies. At different times Muslims have been able to negotiate resources on the basis of a shared 'black' identity, a national identity – Pakistani/Bangladeshi – or multiculturalism. They have also been at the forefront in arguing for recognition of that self-ascribed identity which was of importance to them, although routinely ignored by policy makers – namely, Muslim.

Bradford Muslims have also been important in lending or witholding legitimacy to some of the many national bodies purporting to speak on behalf of all Muslims. Most of these organizations have been London based, often the initiative of one individual, which then had 'to work top downwards and establish popular roots'.[53] Bradford Muslims were active in two rival national umbrella organizations representing mosques, both founded in 1984, the Imams and Mosques Council of Great Britain and The Council of Mosques UK and Eire.[54] The latter organization, sponsored by the Muslim World League, based in Mecca, has always had a British Muslim as vice-chairman. Sher

Azam, president of Bradford Council for Mosques for much of the 1980s, held that position from 1986 to 1988. He was also active in the UK Action Committee on Islamic Affairs, UKACIA, formed in October 1988 to press for the banning of *The Satanic Verses*.

The UKACIA has been the vehicle favoured by leading Bradford Muslims to press their demands nationally. It has sought to avoid contentious issues and to identify areas where broad agreement existed. It recently published a well-argued booklet, presented to the Home Secretary, putting the case for new legislation to criminalize vilification and ridicule of religion and to extend to the mainland legislation operative in Northern Ireland against incitement to religious hatred.[55] While supporting the UKACIA, the Bradford Council for Mosques' spokesmen have regularly and consistently distanced themselves from Kalim Siddiqui's pro-Iranian rhetoric and the activities of his Muslim Institute and 'Muslim Parliament'.

The variety of national Muslim organizations and the avowed sectarian diversity of groups in Bradford and elsewhere makes it clear that the term Islam has to be used with caution as an explanatory category. A straight line can seldom be drawn from Islam to social and political policy. However, to argue for a diversity of interpretations, and to challenge the view that Islam is a 'cohesive, homogeneous, and invariant force' is not to suppose that a shared Muslim identity is empty of content.[56] The burden of this book is to delineate how such an identity becomes operative and increasingly important in public life, without subscribing to the essentialist fallacy. This is the notion, not uncommon in popular writing and the media, that it is possible to explain 'all the phenomena of Muslim societies and culture in terms of the concept of a single, unchanging nature of Islam and what it is to be a Muslim'.[57]

2

Islam in South Asia

Many of Bradford's mosques teach Urdu using language text-books produced for schools in Pakistan by the Punjab Text Book Board. This series of eight readers is not for religious education but its content reflects much of the unselfconscious religiosity of South Asia. Most of them begin and end with a prayer and one in six of the stories is explicitly religious. The second reader includes an account of children visiting the shrine, or *mazar*, of a famous eleventh-century sufi, al-Hujwiri, who is buried in Lahore. The children are at the shrine to celebrate the anniversary of Hujwiri's death, which is kept as a local holiday. The word used for this festival is *'urs*, which means wedding, for at his death the soul of a devout sufi is thought to unite with God.

The pages of the story are bordered by vibrant pictures of the activities at and around the large shrine complex. The children play at the local fair, coloured lights adorn the many shops from which devotees buy sweetmeats and flowers – the latter to be placed on Hujwiri's tomb. A huge throng of people, men and women, wait patiently to pray within the hallowed precincts of his tomb. Others queue for the free food distributed on such occasions and are entertained, as they wait, by men dancing to the accompaniment of drums. Hujwiri is known popularly as Data Ganj Bakhsh, the master who gives treasure, and many delightful tales are told of how he acquired this name.

These schoolbooks are full of the heroic exploits of South Asian sufis, variously referred to as 'friend' (of God), 'guide' or simply 'elder' – *wali*, *murshid*, *pir/shaikh*. However, the books have also had to take account of reformist impulses within Islam which are critical of aspects of sufism. Instead of dwelling on Hujwiri's miracles therefore, the books emphasize that he taught non-

Muslims the Qur'an and explained its meaning to them. The narrative omits to mention that Hujwiri wrote a celebrated Persian treatise on sufism, *Kashf al-Mahjub*, (Unveiling the Veiled), and was more at home in initiating devotees into the mysteries of what Reynold Nicholson, his distinguished translator, calls 'Persian theosophy'.[1]

The shrine of Hujwiri is a good reminder that even a universal religion is necessarily clothed,

> in a culture-specific dress. People are not 'religious-in-general', but 'religious-in-particular'. They follow specific religious traditions, with texts, history, rituals, and leaders specific to a group. These are transmitted in a language, with music, persons, and gestures joined in rituals that have meanings in a specific social location.[2]

In order to understand the religious beliefs of South Asian Muslims in Britain it is important to know something of the specific character of Islam in South Asia. This involves some understanding both of the world and presuppositions of sufism and of Muslim responses to the collapse of Mughal power in India and the gradual imposition of British rule.[3] This was the context which generated the array of sects carried to Bradford by Muslim settlers. These sought, alternatively, to defend, reform or reject sufism. To understand the distinctive profile and ethos of these various expressions of South Asian Islam, as well as the social groups attracted to them, is to understand the resources different groups in Bradford could draw on as they sought to root themselves in the radically different environment of a Western industrial city.

The Friends of God: Visible and Invisible

Sufism has been an integral part of Islam from the very beginning and, as Annemarie Schimmel shows in her classic work, *The Mystical Dimensions of Islam*, continues to have an impact across the Muslim world today.[4] Its roots can be traced to the ascetic disciplines developed to counter the allure of wealth and worldliness of an expanding Muslim empire. From its austere beginnings it developed into a thirst for direct experience of God's reality, which went beyond mere command and obedience. By the third

Islamic century (ninth century AD) the accumulated experience of such seekers was beginning to be systematized. In the writings of the ninth-century Baghdad mystic, al-Muhasibi, the quest was spoken of in terms of 'nearness to the Beloved' with 'the heart of the lover ... possessed by the sense of its fellowship with Him'.[5]

Those who undertook this arduous path often wore a coarse garment of wool (*suf*) – the probable origin of the term sufism. Along with a distinctive dress, sufis began to develop particular devotional practices, the most famous of which was *dhikr*, or 'recollection', the repetition of divine names and phrases, and *sama'*, musical concerts. A specialized vocabulary was also fashioned to signpost the religious stages on the journey. Hujwiri devoted many pages of explanation to such terms in his eleventh-century treatise on sufism. He drew an important distinction between '*ilm*, knowledge of the religious sciences, and *ma'rifat*, experiential knowledge of God, a distinction, he claimed, theologians did not allow. Hujwiri argued the need for both sorts of knowledge but considered '*ilm* without *ma'rifat* to be 'stripped of spiritual meaning'.[6]

At the heart of sufism as it developed was the relationship between shaikh and devotee. The shaikh was considered to be close to God and therefore fit to guide the adept. He was to be approached with respect and unquestioned obedience. Hujwiri described the sufi shaikhs as 'physicians of men's souls' and repeated a prophetic tradition that 'He who hurts a saint (*wali*) has allowed himself to make war on Me (God)'.[7]

Hujwiri's treatise on sufism took for granted the existence of sufi hospices with resident novices in attendance on a *pir*. Much of his study was devoted to articulating a code of behaviour for the devotees, as well as the guidelines for hospitality to be extended to visitors. In Hujwiri's day the noviciate was rigorous and could last three years. Companionship was considered essential for novice and shaikh alike. Hujwiri rehearsed a tradition to the effect that: 'Satan is with the solitary, but he is farther away from two who are together'; and God has said, 'There is no private discourse among three persons but God is the fourth of them' (sura 58:8).[8]

One other striking assumption made by Hujwiri was that such sufis were possessed of miraculous powers to validate the truth of the Prophet Muhammad's ministry and were organized into an invisible hierarchy through whose activities the very processes of nature were maintained and Muslim victories against unbelievers won. Three hundred of them enjoyed the 'power to bind and lose and are officers of the divine court'.[9] At the top of the hierarchy stood one called the pole-star, or *qutb*. Such views strikingly parallel the terminology and veneration of imams and religious leaders within Shi'a Islam.[10] However these similarities are to be explained, tension often characterized the relation between sufi and Shi'a.

Hujwiri's treatise on sufism makes plain that most of the building blocks for the later development of sufi orders, or *tariqa*s, already existed in the eleventh century. Such fraternities were to proliferate during the Delhi Sultanate (1206–1555), the creation of Turkish and Afghan armies from central Asia. These new military elites were part of an international Perso-Islamic culture, developed in Iran and central Asia. These areas continued to furnish India with scholars, administrators and craftsmen well into the eighteenth century, and the dominance of Persian as the lingua franca of this high culture only yielded to regional languages and English in the early nineteenth century.[11] The sufis who entered India with the establishment of the Delhi Sultanate were part of the new religious elite, and were to contribute both to fashioning such a culture and to the spread and consolidation of Islam.

The early development of some of the sufi brotherhoods remains obscure. Although many are named after a founder, the relationship between that founder and the developed fraternity is often unclear. Baghdad was the home of two major orders, the Qadiriya and Suhrawardiya, named after Abdul Qadir al-Jilani (d. 1166) and 'Umar al-Suhrawardi (d. 1234). The Suhrawardi became active in South Asia from the thirteenth century, notably in the person of Baha al-din Zakariya of Multan. Bukhara was the home of Muhammad Baha al-din al-Naqshbandi, the fourteenth-century shaikh who gave his name to the Naqshbandiya, a brotherhood present in South Asia from the sixteenth century. However, the most influential order during the Delhi Sultanate was the Chishtiya, whose founder was Muin al-din Hasan Chishti (d. 1233) who followed the Turkish armies to Ajmer in Rajasthan.

These were among the most famous orders in South Asia.

Some were transnational, others were confined to India – the Chishtiya – and others again were regional, such as the Firdausiya, 'scarcely known outside Northern Bihar and Western Bengal'.[12] Yet the Firdausiya produced the outstanding fourteenth-century sufi, Sharaf al-din Ahmad Ibn Yahya Maneri. Throughout the Mughal period (1526–1858) Sharaf al-din's letters of spiritual direction to devotees, *Maktubat-i Sadi*, (The Hundred Letters), were 'prescibed on the syllabus for advanced theological study'.[13]

The various orders differed amongst themselves over such issues as whether to stay aloof from the holders of political power or to seek to influence them; whether or not to accept large gifts and endowments from their devotees; whether listening to music was permitted or not; and what the relationship was between Islamic law and sufi practice. Different shaikhs within the same order adopted a variety of stances on such issues.

The institutional development of sufism can be discerned in the history of the Chishtiya. Initially we may imagine a cluster of devotees around a beloved shaikh, identifying themselves as a single fraternity. Before his death the sufi would designate a spiritual successor, and thus his style of mystical learning would be transmitted in chains of spiritual succession, or *silsila*. The sufi would often give to his chosen successor some prized personal item saturated with his blessing, or *baraka*, a prayer mat, staff or item of clothing, as a sign of transferred authority. The sufi would attract, in life and death, princely patrons, who would enlarge his hospice, embellish his simple shrine with an impressive mauso-leum and secure the works of generosity done there by religious endowments and land grants.

Soon two sorts of successor to the sufi emerged. Alongside the spiritual successor, sent elsewhere to extend the teaching of his master, his lineal descendants became custodians of his tomb and hospice. Already in the thirteenth century disputes could emerge between the lineal descendants and spiritual successor over the control of prized saintly relics. Indeed, such a dispute involved probably the best loved of all the early Chishti shaikhs, Nizam al-din Awliya of Delhi.[14] His recorded conversations, or *malfuzat* – a literary genre peculiar to South Asian sufism – communicate his empathy with the suffering of his fellow men. To the criticism that he was making disciples indiscriminately Nizam al-din retorted,

'there has been an onslaught of humanity beating at the doors of
the masters of the spiritual domain – people of every sort, kings
and princes, men of fame and other sorts. Hence the Shaykhs
have made disciples from the elite and from the masses.' The great
achievement of Nizam al-din was to establish the provincial dis-
persion of the Chishti order. Many of these disciples rooted the
tradition in 'Uttar Pradesh, Rajasthan, Gujarat, Bihar, Bengal and
the Deccan'.[15]

Recent research has illuminated the social impact of another
famous thirteenth-century Chishti sufi, Farid al-din, whose shrine
is located in the ancient city of Ajudhan on the bank of Punjab's
most southerly river. The shaikh, known to his devotees as Baba
Farid, was presented in contemporary accounts as distributing
amulets, or *ta'wiz*, as protection against evil, an agent of healing
and a guarantee of good fortune. Like many Chishtis he himself
held aloof from the court but would write to the Sultan on behalf
of a devotee. Soon after his death his *'urs* began to be held at his
shrine, embellished by royal patronage. On this occasion the
southern door of his tomb, called the 'Gate of Heaven', would be
opened and devotees pass through, thereby 'ritually entering
heaven'.[16]

The shrine would recycle the gifts the devotees brought and
thereby provide for the public kitchen, or *langar*. The shrine complex became the centre of a rich devotional tradition, celebrating
in poetry and song the wonderful deeds of the friends of God. In
short, the shaikh, as well as being a spiritual guide to an elite
who could read his anecdotes and letters in Persian, also functioned as a charismatic personality able and willing to intercede
for his devotees.

Recent research into this shrine has indicated how the pattern
of piety persists to this day. Crowds of devotees still queue to
enter the 'Gate of Heaven' on the occasion of his *'urs*. Baba Farid's
blessed presence is still considered to saturate his shrine and relics.
The shrine also functions as an accessible focus for pilgrimage,
an alternative to Mecca for the majority who cannot afford to go.
Baba Farid's lineal descendants, custodians of the shrine, continue to distribute amulets for healing and well-being. As with
Nizam al-din in the thirteenth century, affiliation remains largely
nominal and no longer involves an exacting noviciate.

The studies of Richard Eaton have also begun to clarify the largely hidden process whereby non-Muslims were drawn into the orbit of Islam. This has been a puzzle, since the regions of most dramatic conversion have often been the most distant from the centres of Muslim political power. Before the partition of 1947 just over 20 per cent of all Indians were Muslim. The areas of highest Muslim density were eastern Bengal, western Punjab, the Northwest Frontier and Baluchistan rather than the upper Gangetic Plain, the heartlands of Muslim political power. The Muslims of the Northwest Frontier and Baluchistan were not converts but Muslim immigrants from the Iranian Plateau. This left the fact of Muslim conversion in eastern Bengal and western Punjab to be explained.

What was surprising was that the writings of the sufis themselves in these areas, or hagiographical accounts by their devotees, generally exhibited little serious interest in Hindus or their religious traditions. Sharaf al-din's celebrated letters seem typical. His translator noticed that, 'The Indian or Hindu context ... is oblique and inferential ... We hear nothing about individual encounters ... [with] yogin adepts, nor attempts at conversion, nor public debates'[17] The published conversations of a famous nineteenth-century Punjabi sufi and poet, Khwaja Ghulam Farid, exhibit the same indifference. His twenty-four recorded conversations show more interest in criticizing Shi'i influence than in Hinduism.[18]

Yet the majority of tribes in eastern Bengal and western Punjab did become Muslims, and Richard Eaton's research has now provided the key to this conundrum. One tribe, the Sials of Jhang, claim to have been converted by Baba Farid. By charting the change in their names from Punjabi secular to Muslim names he was able to argue for a gradual process of absorption into the shrine cult between the late fourteenth and the early nineteenth century. This slow process of conversion was probably largely unconscious since this was a period before 'either British census officals or zealous reformers began urging Indians to place themselves into sharply differentiated religious categories'.[19]

This process of Islamization of non-Muslim tribes was facilitated by the fact that the sufis and their circles often established shrines on sites which had previously been venerated by Buddhists and Hindus.[20] They also generated a rich vernacular tradition of devotional hymns, and these were to root Islam in the hearts and minds of the majority, who were either unlettered or unacquainted with the languages of high Islamic culture – Arabic and Persian. Indeed, such sufis were the creators and custodians of regional languages and culture. While the conversations of Khwaja Ghulam Farid were recorded in Persian, his matchless collection of mystical hymns was in the local language of Siraiki.

The slow process of Islamization of non-Muslim tribes also explains the impatience sometimes exhibited by living sufis at what they considered to be the persistence of un-Islamic behaviour. Little wonder that they often distanced themselves from the religiosity surrounding many shrines. The distinguished seventeenth-century Naqshbandi shaikh, Ahmad Sirhindi, is not untypical in this regard. In one of his letters to a female devotee he drew attention to practices he considered reprehensible:

> women pray to stones and idols and ask for help. This practice is common, especially when smallpox strikes, and there is hardly a woman who is not involved in this polytheistic practice ... they sacrifice animals at the tombs of Sufi saints, even though this custom has been branded as polytheistic in the book of Islamic law. They observe fasts in honour of the saints, though God alone is entitled to this homage.[21]

Such criticisms are intelligible when we remember that not only do 'the most famous shrines ... not invariably house the most worthy shaykhs' but some shrines may not house actual saints at all![22] Historians and anthropologists concur in identifying mythic saints, who are nonetheless the centre of intense devotion.[23] This can happen quite easily since no formal process for canonization exists in Islam. Indeed, religious scholars in Islam are divided as to the very existence of a category of holy men 'to whom one has recourse before and after their deaths, as intercessors ... for obtaining divine graces, even miracles'.[24] In the absence of a formally sanctioned doctrine of this kind, local consensus often becomes the arbiter of sanctity, with paradoxical, if not perverse, results.

Notwithstanding such criticisms, suspect patterns of piety and religiosity persist today. One reason for this is the continued existence of a group who benefit from such practices, namely, the custodians of the sufi shrines and their relics. Control of shrine and relic guarantees to their custodians a share in the generosity of pilgrims and devotees. For this reason their control continues to be disputed and can become the object of unedifying litigation, adding fuel to their critics.[25] The continuing influence of holy men in present day Pakistan and the beguiling corruption to which the whole phenomenon is exposed is sensitively portrayed in Adam Zameenzad's novel, *The Thirteenth House*.

Muslim Responses to Colonialism

The collapse of Mughal power in India in the nineteenth century and the gradual imposition of British control was deeply unsettling for all religions. Hindus, Sikhs and Muslims alike began a process of re-evaluation of their ideals, organization, priorities and practice. The trauma of colonialism for the Muslim elites of South Asia was particularly grievous. For over six hundrd years they had taken power for granted in the region. According to the Qur'an, Muslims constituted 'the best community that has ever been brought forth for [the good of] mankind: You enjoin the doing of what is right and forbid the doing of what is wrong. Had the People of the Book believed, it were better for them' (sura 3:110).

The clear implication of this verse for Muslims was that they should and would prevail over Christians and Jews – the People of the Book. Now history had suddenly gone all wrong. Not only had a proud people been colonized but they had been defeated by a Christian nation. Muslim responses to British power, after the failure of the military option in 1857, ranged along a continuum between isolation and accommodation. This was the period which saw the creation of a variety of new sectarian trends.[26]

For Muslims who had neither the desire nor the economic necessity to learn English, and who could remain outside the new colonial world and its culture, it was possible to opt for a measure of isolation. Although English became the official state language in 1835 and the language of the higher courts, regional

languages still obtained in the lower courts. However, the old
Mughal service elites and the upwardly mobile could not afford
to ignore English and hold aloof from the 'colonial milieu'.[27]

Among the contemporary expressions of Islam in South Asia
that are a product of this colonial encounter, five traditions are
of particular importance, since all have been transferred to Bradford: the reformist Deobandis, the quietist and revivalist Tablighi
Jama'at, the conservative and populist Barelwis, the Islamist
Jama'at-i Islami and the modernists.[28]

The Deobandis

The Islamic seminary (*madrasa*) from which the first group takes
its name was founded in 1867 in Deoband, a small town a
hundred miles north of Delhi. Its founders, Muhammad Qasim
Nanautawi and Rashid Ahmad Gangohi, were acutely conscious
of the extent to which power had shifted away from the Muslims
to a new British and Christian elite, and their aim was, above all,
to preserve and promote an Islamic identity in a changing world.
Although both were classically trained religious scholars, or *'alim*,
they were dissatisfied with the quality of Islamic education then
available.

The Deoband seminary not only re-emphasized traditional
standards through the study of the Hanafi school of jurisprudence,
but sought to use Islamic law as a bulwark against the inroads of
non-Islamic influences.[29] Its curriculum firmly excluded English
or Western subjects. This rejectionist stance towards non-Islamic
knowledge is clearly seen in the comment by the luminary and
rector of Deoband, Ashraf Ali Thanawi (d. 1943), that 'to like
and appreciate the customs of the infidels' is a grave sin.[30] The
seminary also promoted a distinctive ethos, which

> de-emphasised purely local ties in favour of the separate unity and
> identity of the whole group of Deobandis, whatever their geographic
> origin ... fostering a style of Islam that preferred universal practices
> and beliefs to local cults and customs ... and emphasising the diffu-
> sion of scripturalist practices and the cultivation of an inner spiritual
> life.[31]

However, the Deobandis were no mere traditionalists. Besides drawing upon British educational institutions and missionary societies as a source of organizational inspiration for their seminary, they made extensive use of the press, the postal service and the rapidly expanding railway network to spread their message, and to elicit subscriptions, from far and wide. Freed, in consequence, from the obligation to respond to the whims of a few local benefactors – and hence from the vagaries of family control which had reduced so many of its rivals to conditions of crippling dependence – the seminary in Deoband soon began to set new standards of scholarly excellence and institutional continuity for north Indian Islam – a position which was further reinforced by the movement's consistent use of Urdu, rather than Persian, as a lingua franca.

The founders of Deoband were reformist sufis, as well as religious scholars. As spiritual guides to many of their students they saw themselves as exemplars rather than as intercessors. They took their responsibilities as sufi directors seriously:

> The granting of initiation took place only after a period of contact in which the good intentions of the disciple, the spiritual perfections of the *shaikh*, and the personal compatibility of both were shown. Often there would be a prolonged stay with the *shaikh* and substantial instruction in the disciplines and traditions of the order.[32]

As reformist sufis they opposed much of the shrine cult as an unacceptable accommodation to a non-Muslim environment. Ashraf Ali Thanawi, considered one of the leading sufis of his generation, in his encyclopaedic Urdu work *Bihishti Zewar* (Heavenly Ornaments) reminds his readers that to sacrifice an animal, to fast or take a vow in the name of a shaikh, and to keep his photo and recite his name, as an act of devotion, is tantamount to disbelief and the sin of associating another with God. To believe that any place merits respect equal to that accorded to the Ka'aba (the holy sanctuary at Mecca) and to believe that *pirs* can relieve all ills is similarly forbidden. Finally, Thanawi seeks to undercut the function of *pirs* as intercessors by insisting that only those promised by God and Muhammad will unequivocally enter heaven.[33]

While the Deobandis consequently set out on a reformist path, the all-embracing Islamic unity which they hoped to generate proved elusive. It is not difficult to see why. Most of their support came, initially, from well-born Muslim elites, who drew their income from land, trade or government service. Yet a principal target of Deobandi reformist activities was the beliefs and practices of the rural peasantry. In this context the efforts of a twentieth-century revivalist movement, Tablighi Jama'at, were to complement their work.

Tablighi Jama'at

The founder of 'the faith movement', popularly referred to as the preaching party, Tablighi Jama'at, was Maulana Ilyas (1885–1944). A sufi and 'alim, Ilyas had trained at Deoband and taught at the Deobandi seminary in Saharanpur. He was concerned to develop the work of his father, who had sought to preach the basics of Islam to the Meos, Muslims from Mewat, south of Delhi, who had come into the city in search of work. The Meos were little more than Muslim in name, largely ignorant of Islam and shared many Hindu names and customs. Such groups were potentially vulnerable to the efforts of the Arya Samaj movement to reconvert Hindus who had become Muslim or Christian.[34]

Ilyas became aware that neither the traditional sufi hospice nor the Islamic seminary was really organized to touch the lives of such people. Most Meos could not be expected to spend eight years or more in a seminary, and sufis were not in the habit of going out of their hospices on preaching and teaching tours. Disillusioned with the seminary mode of Islamization he resigned his prestigious teaching post at Saharanpur and in the 1920s and 1930s developed his innovative movement, which sought inspiration from the methods used by the Prophet at the beginning of Islam, when neither seminary nor sufi hospice existed.

The aim of his movement was to embody and commend the Qur'anic injunction of sura 3:104, 'that there might grow out of you a community [of people] who invite unto all that is good, and enjoin the doing of what is right and forbid the doing of what is wrong'.[35] In pursuit of this aim, Ilyas eschewed all controversial issues and avoided any political involvement. His emphasis was on individual moral and spiritual renewal, the pre-condition, he contended, for any authentically Islamic endeavour in the public domain.

The striking and innovative feature of Tablighi Jama'at was its expectation that all Muslims should devote time to door-to-door revivalist activity that would contribute to creating an Islamic environment. Its discipline, mutual service, congregational wor-ship, prescribed study and shared activity created the movement's distinctive style of self-reformation, within a supportive and egali-tarian context. Its minimalist six-point programme reflects its sufi ethos.[36] 'Its mobility has provided a medium of religious educa-tion on a mass scale. It may be termed as a unique experiment in adult education'.[37]

Many Muslim scholars have recognized the value of Tablighi Jama'at and involved themselves and their students with the movement. Indeed, the rector of India's prestigious Muslim academy, Nadwat al-'Ulama, Syed Abul Hasan Ali Nadwi, in an address to 'ulama in 1944, warned that if they did not participate in Ilyas' venture they would become 'an untouchable minority to whose culture and way of life the common people would become total strangers; even their language and ideas would be unfamiliar to the general public necessitating a translator between the two'.[38]

It is evident that many listened, although until recently the ethos, methods and impact of Tablighi Jama'at have been largely ignored by scholars of Islam. It is apolitical and does not attract the attention that the self-consciously ideological Islamist move-ment commands. However, its huge following world-wide is be-ginning to be noticed: 'Its 1988 annual conference in Raiwind near Lahore, Pakistan, was attended by more than one million Muslims from over ninety countries ... the second-largest congre-gation of the Muslim world after the hajj.'[39] Its unsophisticated, anti-intellectual yet activist ethos attracts 'semi-educated people from small towns and cities', shopkeepers, teachers and govern-ment officials. Also, 'for many recent migrants from the rural areas to the urban centers of Pakistan ... [it] is not only a com-munity of worship and a source of spiritual nourishment but a badly needed substitute for the extended family left behind.'[40]

The rapid extension of the Deobandi tradition from the more educated and urban to the lower classes and rural settlements

has been commented on by scholars. It is likely, although
unremarked, that the credit for this must go, in part, to the activities of the Tablighi Jama'at. The movement remains within
the Deobandi tradition and shares 'its rejection of popular forms
of religion such as veneration of saints, visiting shrines, and ob-
serving the rituals associated with popular sufism'.[41]

The Barelwis

The Barelwi tradition is the most local and contextual of the
various contemporary expressions of Islam in South Asia. It takes
its name from the home town of its founder, Ahmad Raza Khan
(1856–1921) of Bareilly, Uttar Pradesh. A member of the Qadiri
sufi order, Ahmad Raza used his considerable scholarship to
defend the legitimacy of the popular world of shaikhs and shrines,
where devotees come to seek the help of *pirs* (living and dead), as
intercessors between themselves and God.[42]

Disagreements between Barelwis and Deobandis ultimately
turn on distinct exegetical traditions, which support their very
different interpretations of the nature of God, and the status of
the Prophet and holy men. Ahmad Raza, using well-established
sufi arguments, insisted that the Prophet had 'knowledge of the
unseen' and was bearer of God's light, which the 'friends of God'
also reflected. For the Deobandis, however, such claims were
deemed excessive and encroached on prerogatives belonging to
God alone.[43]

Such theological differences, passionately held, have generated
a luxuriant sectarian literature and, in the early decades of this
century, a fatwa war, whereby Barelwi and Deobandi declared
each other non-Muslim, *kafir*, and sought endorsement of their
respective anathemas from religious scholars in the Hijaz, the
heartlands of Islam in western Arabia.[44] It is hardly surprising
that Tablighi Jama'at activities are banned in Barelwi mosques.[45]
Mutual antipathy between Deobandi and Barelwi can still flare
up into open conflict today.[46]

The Jama'at-i Islami

The Jama'at-i Islami, the Islamic Party, is of rather more recent
origin than the others. It was founded in 1941 by Abul A'la

Maududi (1903–79), a journalist rather than the product of an Islamic seminary. For Maududi, Islam was an ideology, an activist creed and legal system, aspiring to regulate all aspects of life. He criticized religious scholars for obscuring Islam's dynamism with medieval commentary and fossilized law: he argued for the need to move beyond *taqlid* – conformity to the teachings of Islamic law, crystallized in the Middle Ages – and for the exercise of *ijtihad*, scholarly effort, intended to 'ascertain, in a given problem or issue, the injunction of Islam and its real intent'.[47]

In *A Short History of the Revivalist Movement in Islam*, Maududi reviewed previous reform movements in South Asia. While acknowledging their achievements he considered the main reason for their failure was a lingering sympathy for sufism in general, and the master–disciple relationship in particular:

> as soon as *bai'at* (act of allegiance) is performed, the disciples start developing a servile mentality ... [which] does not leave any difference between the spiritual guide and the gods other than Allah. It results in the incapacity of all mental powers of discrimination and criticism ... the disciple is completely obsessed with the guide's personality and authority ... detached from the world of reality they become wholly absorbed in the world of wonders and mystery.[48]

He was no less scathing in his attacks on those who sought to introduce alien, Western ideologies, whether communism, socialism, capitalism or nationalism, into the Muslim world. All these, he argued, threatened to fragment and destroy the transnational Muslim community, the *umma*. For him Westernization was the new barbarism, threatening to return Muslims to the very *jahiliyya* – the emotive term for pre-Islamic paganism – from which the Prophet's message had rescued them.[49]

Maududi's response to these challenges is clear from an article he wrote in the 1970s reviewing his life's work:

> the plan of action I had in mind was that I should first break the hold which Western culture and ideas had come to acquire over the Muslim intelligentsia, and to instill in them the fact that Islam has a code of life of its own, its own culture, its own political and economic systems and a philosophy and an educational system which are all superior to anything that Western civilisation could offer. I wanted to rid

them of the wrong notion that they needed to borrow from others in the matter of culture and civilisation.[50]

To embody this ethos he founded the Jama'at-i Islami, a politico-religious party whose aim was to place trained cells of the righteous in positions of social and political leadership, with the object of transforming Muslim countries into Islamic, ideological states. Maududi's prolific writings have been translated into many languages, including English and Arabic. He has had a considerable following amongst the Muslim Brotherhood and has been courted by the Saudi Arabian government.[51]

In Pakistan, the party appeals, as Islamism does elsewhere, to the products of expanded tertiary education in the cities,

> successful but unsatisfied people. Separated by their education from traditional communities, they are not part of the political elite. Like the uprooted peasants and bazaaris, these strata turn to Islam to symbolize their anxieties, their hostilities to the powers, domestic and foreign, that thwart them, and their dreams of a more perfect future.[52]

This constituency, in Pakistan, initially comprised many refugees from north Indian cities, *muhajir*, with few local roots and thus willing bearers of a trans-regional Islamic identity which they hoped Pakistan would embody. The majority of the theoreticians and intellectuals of the party, academics, lawyers and journalists, come from this group.[53] An additional source of support has come from an expanding 'trader-merchant class ... physically located in the urban areas but ... rooted in traditional rural culture ... antagonistic [to] ... the erstwhile dominant urban class of bureaucrats, professionals and industrialists'.[54]

The trader-merchant class was never part of the 'colonial milieu', and was thus excluded from the anglicized sub-culture of that urban elite. For them, Islam, the public rationale for Pakistan, became a vehicle of repossessing and reasserting their own identity after the religious and cultural dislocation of colonialism, and a stick with which to beat the traditional urban elite, dubbed 'West-intoxicated' by Islamists.[55]

While the party can influence government policy during periods of authoritarian rule it has not done well at the polls.

There are various reasons for this. As an urban-based movement attracting the educated, Jama'at-i Islami has little appeal to most of Pakistan's rural voters, who comprise some 70 per cent of the population. The party has also had to compete with two other self-consciously Islamic parties, one representing Barelwi interests and the other Deobandi. Both gained a larger share of the national vote than Jama'at-i Islami in the free elections of 1970; none did particularly well, though, for between them they polled less than a quarter of the national vote.[56]

The fact that Jama'at-i Islami is opposed by Islamic parties also brings the legitimacy of their politicized perception of Islam into question. Three distinguished members of Jama'at-i Islami – Maulana Manzoor Numani, Maulana Abul Hasan Ali Nadvi and Maulana Wahiuddin – have left the movement, accusing it of being 'overly concerned with temporal power and politics and of neglecting the basic purpose of Islamic da'wa, which is to bring people closer to God and raise their religious consciousnesss.'[57] These three scholars now support Tablighi Jama'at. The mutual rivalry between the two movements is sharpened by the fact that both appeal to similar constituencies.[58]

Islamic Modernism

Reform and revival have been integral to Islam in South Asia and preceded the impact of colonialism. Shah Wali Allah of Delhi who lived and wrote in the eighteenth century was in this respect a figure of unusual importance, and aspects of his legacy were welcomed and appropriated by subsequent thinkers, who had to address the intellectual challenge posed by colonialism and Western culture. Particularly valuable was Shah Wali Allah's sense of history and his defence of the exercise of *ijtihad* in Islamic law, since 'every age has its own countless specific problems and cognizance of the divine decisions with respect to them is essential'.[59]

Among a gallery of thinkers who have sought inspiration from the reformist tradition within Islam in order to respond to the multifaceted challenge of Western civilization, three illustrate distinct, but overlapping responses, developed at different times. Syed Ahmad Khan (d. 1898) attempted to reinterpret Muslim theology to accommodate the 'challenges of Christian preaching, historical criticism and the "new sciences"'.[60] Muhammad Iqbal (d. 1938) in his celebrated lectures, *The Reconstruction of Religious Thought in Islam*, first published in 1934, tried to respond to twentieth-century developments in science and philosophy. Fazlur Rahman (d. 1988), considered it vital to address 'the basic questions of method and hermeneutics' in Qur'anic exegesis.[61] Only thus could modernism be rooted in the Islamic tradition and avoid the excesses and extravagances in interpretation of earlier modernists which had brought the movement into disrepute and furnished its critics with easy targets.[62]

Many modernists share the Islamists' impatience with sufism. Iqbal condemned sufi pretensions to be a spiritual elite enjoying a privileged access to God, rooted in mystic lore and practice, and available only to the initiates. He considered such claims to be the result of the pernicious 'Persianization' of Islam, evident from the tenth century, whereby:

> Muslim democracy was gradually displaced and enslaved by a sort of spiritual Aristocracy pretending to claim knowledge and power not open to the average Muslim ... [which ran counter to] the great democratic Prophet ... [in whose teachings] there is absolutely nothing esoteric ... justifying any gloomy, pessimistic mysticism ... The regeneration of the Muslim world lies in the strong, uncompromising, ethical monotheism ... preached to the Arabs thirteen hundred years ago.[63]

Fazlur Rahman shared Iqbal's concern to present Islam as an activist, ethical tradition and insisted that the Qur'an undercut those who would justify intercession by the Prophet or 'saints'. While he acknowledged that

> the Hadith literature is loaded with references to intercession of the prophets on behalf of the sinful of their communities ... (and in popular Islam 'saints') ... the Qur'an seems to have nothing to do with it. On the contrary, it constantly speaks of how God will on the Day of Judgment bring every prophet as a *witness* over the deeds of his community, a witness whereby the people will be judged.[64]

Syed Ahmad Khan, writing after the failure of the 'mutiny' in 1857, had other more pressing priorities. He envisaged 'the reemergence of a bureaucratic and administrative elite who would guide their fellow Muslims into co-operation with the British–Indian government, and do so on the basis of a mixture of Islamic and Western education'.[65] The institution which carried Syed Ahmad's hopes was the Muhammadan Anglo-Indian College founded at Aligarh (1875). Aligarh and several initiatives it spawned, notably the Muslim Educational Congress (1886) and the Muslim League (1906), certainly lent to the Muslim communities in India a distinct identity. Aligarh embodied the willingness of the old Mughal service elite 'to make adjustments in the education of their sons ... to achieve under altered circumstances [earlier] levels of social prestige and occupational achievements'. An analysis of the careers of Aligarh's alumni over its first 25 years indicates it met such hopes with 'two-thirds of the former students ... government employees'.[66]

Aligarh, with an English principal recruited from Cambridge University in 1883 – the first of a group of able Cambridge graduates to teach there – deliberately used English as the medium of instruction, 'an intentional instrument of acculturation to Victorian values and ideas'.[67] However, neither Aligarh nor the Muslim Educational Congress ever became a vehicle for Syed Ahmad's radical rethinking of Islamic thought. Indeed, support for Aligarh was conditional on Syed Ahmad taking a self-denying ordinance not to be involved in religious education. This was supervised by a separate governing body, intent on avoiding controversy, and thus enshrined a conservative ethos.

The failure of South Asia's premier modern, Muslim, academic institution (it became a Muslim university in 1920) to marry modern knowledge and Islamic study has cast a long shadow. Muhammad Ali (d. 1931), a famous old boy of Aligarh, remembered that the students either played truant during the weekly 'theology hour' or busied themselves by 'writing humorous verse or drawing rude and rough caricatures ... Our communal consciousness was ... far more secular than religious'.[68] Indian politics became the centre of interest and the Muslim League a vehicle for Muslim separatism and the creation of Pakistan.

Given the primacy of English and Western disciplines and the marginalization of Islam at Aligarh, the dilemma was to what extent it was an Islamic college rather than simply a college for

Muslims. Similarly, Pakistan – the struggle for which involved Aligarh alumni – has been bedevilled by the debate as to whether it was intended to be simply a nation for Muslims or an Islamic state.[69]

Because Islamic modernists in South Asia were outside the ranks of the religious scholars (*'ulama*) they were regarded with suspicion by them, and therefore have not been able to influence these custodians of Islamic law. Because neither educational institution nor political party existed to promote Islamic modernism it has always maintained a somewhat fugitive existence. Muhammad Iqbal was, arguably, the only serious student of modern philosophy of whom Islamic modernism in South Asia could boast, and he died in 1938. Fazlur Rahman's attempt to institutionalize modernism, when director of the Central Institute of Islamic Research in Pakistan, from 1962 to 1968, was undermined by opposition from the religious scholars, Jama'at-i Islami political activists and the indifference of a secularized elite.[70]

In Pakistan today the main bearer of modernism is the women's movement. The Women's Action Forum, WAF, came into being in 1981.

> In 1979 the Hodood Ordinance was promulgated, as the first step in Zia's so-called process of Islamization. The Ordinance covers adultery, fornication, rape and prostitution (etc.) … The implications of this ordinance were not to come to light until the autumn of 1981, when a session judge sentenced a man and a woman to being stoned to death and 100 lashes respectively under the provisions of the Ordinance. The case … was the catalyst that galvanized women into forming a pressure group to counter anti-women moves.[71]

Since the process of Islamization was supported, initially at least, by the *'ulama* and Jama'at-i Islami – who allowed themselves to be co-opted into General Zia's government – the WAF felt constrained to oppose these measures within the framework of Islamic discourse. Otherwise, as they belonged to the urban, professional classes and were part of the dominant elite, they could have been dismissed as but another expression of its West-intoxicated secularism. At their second national convention WAF, as part of their struggle for women's rights, decided to 'expose the difference between *maulvis* and Islam as a first step, and between progressives and conservatives as a second'.[72] In their attempt to capture the Islamic high ground WAF has acted as a magnet for a vestigial modernist sentiment and has been able to draw on the researches of Riffat Hassan, Pakistan's pioneer feminist theologian.

In a recent review of the process of Islamization in the 1980s a Pakistani legal scholar contends that all it did was to exacerbate sectarianism within Islam and expose the intellectual bankruptcy of the *'ulama* and Jama'at-i Islami. He concludes by insisting that, 'The future of Pakistan, therefore, seems almost inescapably linked to a reassertion of the Aligarh spirit and the reformist Islamic movement that can be traced from Shah Wali Allah to Syed Ahmad Khan to Iqbal.'[73]

Conclusion

Islam in South Asia is characterized by continuing vitality and much perplexity. The diversity of contemporary expression is witness to the many ways Muslims have sought to repossess a tradition which fractured under the impact of colonialism and modernity. At present there exists a clamour of competing, even contradictory voices. For Tablighi Jama'at the need of the hour is for personal renewal. For the activist member of Jama'at-i Islami the imperative is to capture political power for the righteous. The anguished voice of modernism, not yet silenced, hopes for an honest and energizing dialogue with contemporary culture. However, for traditional Islamic scholarship, in both its Barelwi and Deobandi forms, much energy still seems to be expended on inter-sectarian debates, and there is little serious engagement with the modern world.

Akbar Ahmed, a distinguished Pakistani anthropologist, in his deeply moving personal study, *Discovering Islam, Making Sense of Muslim History and Society*, can still look to the great sufis of South Asia, whether Hujwiri or Mu'in al-din Chishti, for inspiration. Yet he is under no illusions about the challenges facing Muslims today:

> The book reflects the times which Muslims live in. The few voices which speak with learning and courage are isolated. The intellectuals

are bankrupt; the saints invisible. We will find answers to the questions [of modernity] ... only by inquiry and scholarship – and that side of Muslim civilization appears to be dead. The modern Muslim intellectual exists in a state of despair, torn between an ideal world he cannot order and a reality he cannot master.[74]

3

Bradford: Britain's 'Islamabad'

Britain has for centuries been a nation of traders and empire builders. While economic migration is a familiar feature of Christian history, migration and settlement are far from straightforward and unproblematic for many religious traditions. A recent study of Hinduism in Great Britain maps some of the difficulties which those within a traditional Hindu worldview had to negotiate if they were to come to Britain with an easy conscience.

> The centre of the Hindu universe is Brahma's abode and the periphery is formed by gods who defend the materialization in time and space of Brahma. Beyond the periphery lies the Black Sea, and the small island of Vilayat where live a race of barbarians who call themselves Englishmen. The English eat the flesh of Mother Cow, and have no 'social order' (that is, no caste).[1]

Various stratagems were devised to render life tolerable in such an inauspicious place. Some migrants chose to settle and to this end they 'ritually consecrated the alien land so that it became part of the auspicious land'.[2] Others, like the Gujarati traders working on the east coast of east Africa, 'kept their families and ancestral deities in their natal villages in western India. Marriages were contracted there; life-cycle rituals were performed there; and at the end of their working lives they returned to Gujarat from where they dispatched their sons to succeed them in business overseas.'[3]

This chapter considers some of the difficulties South Asian Muslims encountered in shifting from a sojourner status – sustained by the myth of return – to final settlement in Bradford. The ethos and character of Islam is also seen unselfconsciously at work as Muslims established communities, generating separate

49

residential zones and a network of businesses and institutions, religious and cultural, to service their special needs.

Migration, the Nation State and Islamic Law

The Urdu term for migrant, *muhajir*, is from the same Arabic root which gives us the word *hijra*, the migration of the Prophet Muhammad from Mecca to Medina in AD 622.[4] This obligatory migration involved abandoning property and blood ties in Mecca to support the nascent community of Muslims in Medina. This event resonates through Islamic history, with the Muslim calendar measuring the passage of time from that event, AH, the year of the Hijra. Muslims across the centuries have readily identified themselves with this prototypical migration. The very existence of Pakistan is rooted in a convulsive migration experience, in part, re-enacting the Prophetic example.

A recent study of the dynamics of migration within the Islamic tradition has isolated three persistent features, consistent with Qur'anic teaching: '(1) ... an obligation of physical movement towards self-definition in the nascent Muslim society; (2) *hijra* was closely associated with *jihad* (armed struggle); and (3) *hijra* established a bond of relationship among Muslims.'[5] The important question which subsequently exercised Muslim thinkers and jurists was to identify situations when the *dar al-Islam*, the House of Islam – where Islamic power and law prevailed – ceased to be so and thus made jihad or hijra mandatory.[6]

Such questions were far from being academic. Within 30 years of the Prophet's death, during the caliphate of 'Ali (AD 656–661), the rebellion against him by a group named *khawarij*, (those who go out), established 'the third major political trend in early Islam ... a rejection of both Sunni and Shi'i positions'.[7] Their rebellion was rooted in an uncompromising adherence to the letter of the Qur'an, a repudiation of arbitration in a dispute where right and wrong seemed clear, and an egalitarianism governing the election of rulers. In this context their act of withdrawal was tantamount to declaring the area from which they withdrew was no longer *dar al-Islam*.

Events soon outstripped Islamic jurisprudence. Islamic law had been developed within the early imperial phase of Muslim history, when it was plausible to suppose the Islamic imperium might one day include all the lands of the infidel, and 'The People of the Book', and thus a division of the world into *dar al-harb*, the domain with which Islam was (potentially) at war, and *dar al-Islam*, into which it was to be incorporated, made some sense.[8] Colonialism compounded the difficulties facing Muslim thinkers. India during the British Raj sharply focused the discontinuity between theory and practice.

A historian of the Muslims in British India highlighted this disjunction:

> Muslim jurisprudence could offer no clear prescriptions ... where a large Muslim population lived permanently under a non-Muslim government ... where the balance of power was permanently tilted in favour of the infidel; where there was no generally accepted *imam* or *khalifa* (to focus opposition and declare whether the conditions were propitious for an armed struggle) ... and where ... a large non-Muslim majority [was] ready to take advantage of any mishandling of relations with their foreign rulers.[9]

While Muslims in India had recourse, at different times, to both jihad and hijra, 'the Hanafi majority view has been that if Friday and the religious holidays can be observed, the land is *dar al-Islam*.'[10]

The political situation in the twentieth century has further complicated the labours of Muslim jurists: in a world of nation-states, some of which have Muslim majorities, others Muslim minorities, what and where is to count as *dar al-Islam*? The modern world is not the *dar al-Islam* of the middle ages. It is no longer possible for a Muslim to travel, migrate or settle in any part of the trans-national, Muslim community, the *umma*. Even countries which have Muslim majorities may have a secular constitution, be repressive regimes, indifferent to Islam or uncongenial for Muslim minority sects.

If the proliferation of nation-states has made the issue of what is to count as *dar al-Islam* problematic, the emergence of a new type of hijra has raised yet more issues for Islamic jurisprudence. Should Muslim economic migrants in the West see themselves as international commuters, intent on returning to their homeland, when they have earned enough money, or should they choose to settle in *dar al-kufr*, the house of unbelief?[11] A distinguished Muslim scholar in Britain acknowledges that 'Muslim theology offers, up to the present, no systematic formulations of the status of being in a minority.'[12]

Since Islamic history and Islamic law offer so few practical guidelines for Muslims living as a minority in a country like Britain, we should expect to find experimentation and some confusion as, over time, they have attempted to negotiate a *modus vivendi* with the majority, aimed at preserving and transmitting an Islamic identity to their children. It is better to speak, initially, of Muslim communities, in the plural, since it is evident that Muslim migrants were bearers of a diversity of languages, cultures and conflicting histories.

It is wise to stress the novelty and the complexity of the issues which now confront Muslim minorities in the West.[13] This, of course, can lead to some exasperation when those Muslims who operate happily within a traditional Islamic worldview seek simply to restate the received wisdom. Ahmed Deedat, a popular Muslim preacher and controversialist from South Africa, in one of his recent visits to Bradford, insisted that the justification for migration and settlement as a minority in Britain must be 'neither easy living nor the dole but *jihad* or *da'wa*, invitation to Islam'.[14] Since jihad was thrown in for rhetorical effect, given his love of military metaphor, Deedat was arguing that the only rationale for migration to a non-Muslim state was the desire to invite others to Islam.[15]

This contrasts with the stance and publications of Shabbir Akhtar, a Bradford Muslim, who has little patience with an Islamic chauvinism which refuses to engage with the intellectual and social realities of British society. He can turn on its head the traditional Islamic prohibition from entering *dar al-kufr* – the presumption that Muslim life, property and religion is not safe – by claiming that 'the freest Muslims live in the West and in Iran. Everywhere else, Islam is an outlawed political force.'[16]

Other Muslims, impatient of the disparate histories, experiences and expectations of Muslim communities in Britain, seek to create and institutionalize an elusive, national unity. Thus Kalim Siddiqui, in his inaugural address to the 'Muslim Parliament', boldly declares that 'Western civilization ... is the modern world's sick man ... destined for oblivion ... [with Islam] the antidote to a morally bankrupt world'. The hand-picked members of his 'Muslim Parliament' – including five from Bradford – are urged to draw inspiration from the Prophet, who 'showed us how to generate the political power of Islam in a minority situation and how to nurse ... it until the creation of an Islamic state and the victory of Islam over all its opponents.'[17] Such heady rhetoric is accompanied by a desire to rewrite the actual history of Muslim migration into Britain, by locating it within a particular, Islamic perspective.

Siddiqui's grand aspiration and inspirational style contrasts markedly with the sober analysis of the situation facing Muslims in Britain given by Ishtiaq Ahmed, the information officer of Bradford's Council for Mosques, at a recent conference on 'Racial Equality in Europe'. In it he reminded his listeners that,

> the majority of British Muslims are economic migrants. They have come to this country in order to escape the harsh socio-economic realities in their countries of origin. They have come here in search of a better economic deal and improved life opportunities. This simple fact frequently gets overlooked and instead all kinds of hidden agenda ... are attributed [to us] in order to explain our presence in this country and ... in Europe. Allow me to emphatically state that most of us do not harbour any thought of colonising Britain and Europe. We are not here on a mass conversion spree. We do not seek to dismantle the political, socio-economic fabric of this society. We have no such grand hidden ambition or grand plan. We entertain no such illusion.[18]

Deedat, Akhtar, Siddiqui and Ahmed – preacher, intellectual, ideologue, and pragmatist – exemplify some of the voices heard within Bradford's Muslim communities today. An empirical study of migration, settlement and community formation will enable us to understand the changing contexts within which such discourse occurs. The four speakers are concerned to identify priorities the communities should pursue, locally and nationally, if a future is to be secured for a Muslim presence in Britain. That such issues are being discussed, in English, in a variety of public forums, indicates that many Muslims in Bradford are no longer sustained by the myth of return but see their future in Britain.

Migration, Settlement and Mosques

In Chapter 1 the push and pull factors underlining the specifics of Muslim migration from South Asia were identified, along with the reasons why particular areas, and particular villages within these areas, were involved in the phenomenon of chain migration. Bradford's history of settlement is no different in outline. The first Muslims in the city were seamen, who had jumped ship, and pursued a precarious existence as door-to-door pedlars in the late thirties. Their economic situation improved with labour shortages during the war.[19] In 1941 other ex-seamen were 'directed from seaports such as Liverpool, Middlesborough and Hull to munitions factories and essential wartime industries in the Bradford and Leeds areas.'[20]

The presence of a few South Asians excited little interest in the city. In Bradford in 1953 migrants from South Asia, the West Indies and West Africa numbered no more than 350. This figure increased tenfold over the next five years, with Pakistanis in the majority, numbering some 2,500. Most came to plug the labour shortages in textiles and transport. Bradford City Transport began appointing South Asians in 1954 and by 1959 they comprised more than 15 per cent of all the bus conductors.[21] The educated gravitated to the buses while those without formal education, the majority, worked the night-shifts in the textile mills. Most were wool combers; a dirty job, traditionally done by women, who were excluded by factory legislation from working the night-shift.

The 1961 census indicated that there were some 3,376 'Pakistanis' in Bradford – which, of course, included both West and East Pakistanis. East Pakistanis would be described as Bangladeshis as from 1971, when what was then East Pakistan seceded from West Pakistan. The majority of the 'Pakistanis' were unskilled, male workers; the census counted only 81 women.

This largely male world was invisible to the majority of Bradfordians. In 1959 the only public concession to their presence was telephone kiosks with instructions in Urdu and Hindi. A picture of what life was like for these economic migrants can be gleaned from interviews conducted in the late 1980s.[22] Most lived in two inner city areas (Manningham and Little Horton), crowded into mutiple occupancy houses. These were usually shared with relatives and friends from their own villages. It was not uncommon for ten or more men to live in one house; some worked the day-shift, others the night-shift. In some cases as many as 30 men lived in one house.

Such communal living had many advantages. It enabled a new arrival to be fed and looked after until he found a job. It minimized expenditure, leaving men free to remit to their families up to a quarter of their earnings. There would usually be someone in such households with some education who could fill in insurance and taxation forms. Social life revolved around a few cafés, with traditional South Asian food and music, and three cinemas, which showed South Asian films and served tea, kebabs and samosas.

A unique collection of photographs of South Asian men taken in a Manningham studio between 1955 and 1960 offers an oblique and poignant commentary on their lives. These photographs were generally sent home to reassure families that they were successful and at ease in an alien environment. The all-male group would feature brothers, cousins and uncles. Such photographs 'flattered by a special kind of misrepresentation'.[23] Affluence was indicated by watches, five-pound notes and radios. The influence of South Asian film stars was evident in the dark glasses sported by some of the younger men. Their status was affirmed by smart, Western suits, briefcases, umbrellas and rows of pens lining their top pockets. These 'symbols of prestigious clerical employment' were displayed by men who, in most cases, worked in the mills or on the buses.[24] Very occasionally photographs featured couples, but in this early period 'the women are always white'.[25]

The numbers of South Asian men in Bradford increased in the early 1960s, initially to pre-empt the Commonwealth Immigrants Act of 1962, which closed the door on automatic right of entry for Commonwealth citizens and introduced a system of work vouchers. Nonetheless, chain migration of single men was to continue until the Immigration Act of 1971. However, the new feature of the migration process in the 1960s was the arrival of Pakistani wives and daughters, some 70 per cent of those enumerated in the 1971 census coming after 1967.[26] In Bradford in 1971 out of 12,250 Pakistanis, 3,160 were women.

Local authority figures suggest that by 1981 there were 32,100 people whose family origin was in Pakistan and Bangladesh and by 1991 there were 48,933, or one in nine of the population of the City of Bradford Metropolitan Council. The following provides an estimate of the relative sizes of the different Muslim communities in 1991. The largest originate from Pakistan: 29,000 from district Mirpur in Azad Kashmir; 5,500 Punjabis, mostly from Jhelum, Gujar Khan and Rawalpindi; 9,000 from the Attock district of Chhachh; 1,780 Pathans from Bannu, Chhachh, Hazara, Kohat, Mardan and Peshawar. Bangladeshis from Sylhet number 3,653. Indians and East Africans from Surat district in Gujarat number 1,800 and 900 respectively.[27]

The critical shift from all-male households to the establishment of Muslim communities followed the arrival of wives, fiancées and children in the late 1960s. Their arrival created a need for mosques and religious teachers. Earlier, religious sentiment had been expressed in avoiding non-halal meat, but for the rest the men were preoccupied with 'survival' which left little time for religious devotions.[28] When the Bangladeshi men originally migrated, most

> suffered an almost total lapse of religious observance; yet migration was not perceived as a threat to their heritage. It was possible to live on the margin of British society, avoiding any deeper involvement than work necessitated ... The migrant lived and worked in Britain on behalf of his family, who, it may be surmised, prayed on his behalf.[29]

This now changed. The establishment of mosques and supplementary schools indicated a shift within the migrants' self-perception from being sojourners to settlers. The investment needed for a mosque, and an imam to lead prayers and teach children, both reflected and precipitated community formation.

A seminal article on Bradford's Pakistani communities, based on research done in the early 1970s, outlined a two-stage process of community formation whereby an initial tendency towards fusion – in which pioneer settlers associated together regardless of their regional, caste or sectarian origins – gradually gave way, as numbers grew, to fission and segmentation; in this second stage of fragmentation ties of village-kinship and sectarian affiliation grew steadily more significant as the basis of communal aggregation.[30] This process, which was illustrated with reference to

Table 3.1 Estimate of Mosques and Supplementary Schools by Sect
in Bradford in 1989

Sect	Mosque	Supplementary school
Barelwi	11	7
Deobandi	12	2
Jama'at-i Islami	2	
Ahl-i Hadith	1	
Shi'a	2	
Ahmadiyya	1	
Non-aligned student	1	

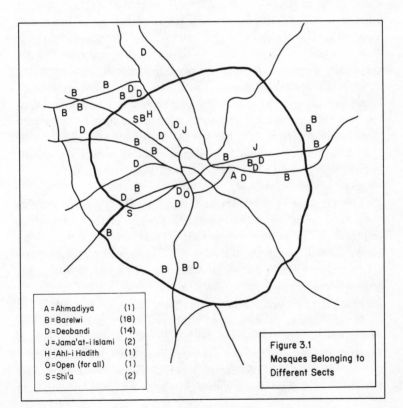

Figure 3.1
Mosques Belonging to
Different Sects

A = Ahmadiyya   (1)
B = Barelwi   (18)
D = Deobandi   (14)
J = Jama'at-i Islami (2)
H = Ahl-i Hadith   (1)
O = Open (for all)   (1)
S = Shi'a   (2)

housing settlement in the 1960s, can also be seen in the proliferation of mosques and supplementary schools.

In 1959 the city's first mosque was opened in a terraced house
in Howard Street. It was run by the Pakistani Muslim Association, and its trustees included both East and West Pakistanis from
a variety of sectarian traditions. Fusion gave way to fission over
the next few years as the Howard Street mosque came to be
dominated by settlers from the Chhachh, a district on the borders
of the Punjab and the Northwest Frontier Province of Pakistan.
The appointment of a Pathan trained in the Deobandi tradition
as its first full-time imam, in 1968, also gave it a clear sectarian
character.

Fission was proceeding apace. In 1961 the Bradford Muslim
Welfare Society – most of whose members were from villages
around Surat in Gujarat, India – established their own Deobandi
mosque. Soon afterwards, Pir Maroof Hussain Shah, from district
Mirpur in Azad Kashmir, formed Jami'at-i Tabligh al-Islam, the
'Association for the Preaching of Islam', and in 1966 opened the
first mosque in the Barelwi tradition. Table 3.1 classifies by
sectarian allegiance the number of mosques and supplementary
schools in existence in 1989. These include a mosque open to all
students and not aligned to any one sect, another belonging to
the Ahl-i Hadith tradition and one Ahmadiyya mosque, a hetero-
dox sect whose right to belong to the Muslim *umma* is hotly contested, and whose activities in Bradford have been the focus of
protest.[31] Figure 3.1 plots the location of these mosques according
to sectarian identity.

The creation of mosques and supplementary schools reflects
the growth, location and differential settlement patterns of distinct
regional and lingusitic communities. Table 3.2 makes this clear
by enumerating both the number of mosques and supplementary
schools formed each decade and the number controlled by each
regional group.[32] Figure 3.2 locates and identifies such mosques
and supplementary schools on the basis of regional control.[33]

These data on mosque formation enable us to hazard some
broad generalizations about community formation. The Indian
Gujarati community did not delay settlement and already had its
two mosques by 1962. A second group of Gujarati Muslims, also
from Surat, arrived from Kenya in the late 1960s following its

Table 3.2 Estimate of Mosques and Supplementary Schools Per Decade by Regional Group Controlling Them

Period	Mosque	Supplementary school	Total
1960–69	5		5[a]
1970–79	11	2	13[b]
1980–89	14	7	21[c]

[a] Mirpur (1), Punjab (1), Chhachh (1), Gujarat (2).

[b] Mirpur (3), Punjab (3), Chhachh (4), (East African) Gujarat (2), Bangladesh (1).

[c] Mirpur (14), Punjab (1), Chhachh (2), Bangladesh (3), Student mosque (1).

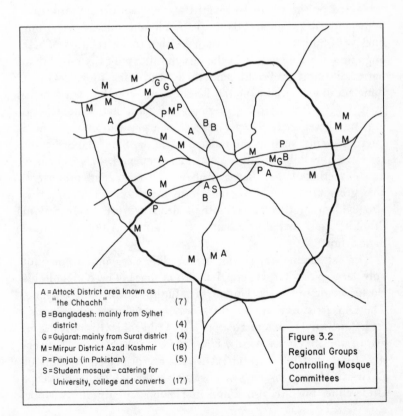

A = Attock District area known as
    "the Chhachh"   (7)
B = Bangladesh: mainly from Sylhet
    district   (4)
G = Gujarat: mainly from Surat district   (4)
M = Mirpur District Azad Kashmir   (18)
P = Punjab (in Pakistan)   (5)
S = Student mosque – catering for
    University, college and converts   (17)

Figure 3.2
Regional Groups
Controlling Mosque
Committees

independence in 1966. While they initially worshipped with the Gujaratis from India, they soon sought to give institutional expression to their different histories and caste identities.[34] In 1971 and 1978 they established two community centres, which included supplementary schools.

The Bangladeshi community has been slower to shift from male settlement to family consolidation: it had no mosque until 1970 and its other three mosques had to await the 1980s (1984, 1985 and 1987). Family consolidation of the Mirpuris has also been an extended process. While their first mosque was functioning in 1966, the bulk of their centres (14 out of 18) did not open until the 1980s. The bulk of the Punjabi and Chhachhi centres were complete in the 1970s.

The more protracted process of Pakistani and Bangladeshi family consolidation compared to that of the Gujaratis is partly explained by the relative strengths of links with their respective homelands. Pakistani and Bangladeshi migrants maintained strong links with their homelands – both Muslim majority areas. These ongoing links are evident in the fact that the majority enjoy dual nationality and prefer to send their dead back to Pakistan or Bangladesh for burial. Gujarati Muslims, however, had less attachment to Hindustan/India, originating from a state where Muslims numbered only 8.5 per cent of the population and where internal events, such as the judgement in the Shah Bano divorce case and the Babri mosque saga, had deepened their insecurity and exacerbated their sense of being an embattled minority.[35] The greater emotional distance from their country of origin is also evident in the fact that their dead are usually buried in Bradford, and that the Indian government does not allow dual nationality.

The settlement trajectories of the different communities not only vary, somewhat, in time, but also in space. The Bangladeshis cluster in three wards, Undercliffe, Little Horton and Bowling. The Gujaratis overlap with them only in Bowling, and have also settled in University and Heaton. The Chhachhis/Pathans live in five of the inner-city wards: Undercliffe, Little Horton, University, Toller and Bowling. The Mirpuris are dispersed throughout six wards, living in the same wards as the Chhachhis, except Undercliffe, but are also found in Heaton and Bradford Moor.

Table 3.3 Mosques/Supplementary Schools, Muslim Councillors and Percentage of 'Asian' voters in wards where Muslims are clustered (1991)

Ward	Mosques/ Supplementary schools	Muslim councillors	Asian voters (%)
University	11	3	49
Little Horton	6	2	22
Toller	4	2	36
Bradford Moor	4	1	40
Bowling	7	1	16
Heaton	4	0	18
Undercliffe	3	0	11

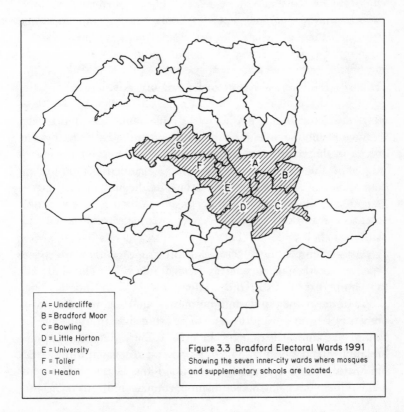

A = Undercliffe
B = Bradford Moor
C = Bowling
D = Little Horton
E = University
F = Toller
G = Heaton

Figure 3.3 Bradford Electoral Wards 1991
Showing the seven inner-city wards where mosques and supplementary schools are located.

The Punjabis are scattered throughout the city, since they are active in sectarian traditions, such as the Shi'a, which only has two centres in the city, or those with only a single centre – Ahl-i Hadith, UK Islamic Mission and the Ahmadiyya.[36]

All 30 mosques and nine supplementary schools are located within a radius of 1½ miles from the city centre, within seven inner city wards (Figure 3.3). Since a majority serve local constituencies – their proliferation reflecting the need for accessible centres for young children to attend Qur'anic school in the late afternoon – this suggests that suburban drift is not yet a major feature of Muslim communities. Only one mosque is purpose-built, with three others under construction, and the rest in converted terraced houses, disused mills, cinemas or churches. Five of these seven wards returned Bradford's nine Muslim councillors in 1991 (all Labour), and all seven have large concentrations of the different Muslim communities. Table 3.3 correlates the location of mosques/supplementary schools, Muslim councillors and the percentage of 'Asian' electors in each of these seven wards.[37]

Economics and the Creation of a Distinct Cultural World

The proliferation of mosques and supplementary schools reflects a huge economic investment by Muslims in the city. The priority given to the creation of religious institutions is an unambiguous signal of a determination to pass on the Islamic tradition to their children and grandchildren. This task has been facilitated by the creation of substantial Muslim residential zones, where people feel secure and can continue to practise a measure of social control over their children. These residential enclaves have spawned an astonishing array of businesses providing goods and services specific to Muslim cultural and religious needs. These provide the immediate focus of this section.

A study in 1985 of 'Asian' businesses in Bradford traced their dramatic rising curve. In 1959 there were five; in 1970, 260; in 1980, 793; and at least 1,200 in 1984.[38] Their rapid growth correlated with the dramatic contraction and recession in the textile industries, which saw the loss of 61,000 jobs in the period 1961–91.[39] Unemployment had a disproportionate impact on 'Asians', who in 1980 accounted for 8 per cent of the labour force but 20 per cent of all textile workers. It is evident that many of the newly unemployed sank their personal savings into small businesses, often at great risk: only one in seven had any relevant experience before going into business. Concentration in the declining sectors of the manufacturing industries partly explains the higher levels of self-employment amongst those of Pakistani and Bangladeshi backgrounds: 23.9 and 18.6 per cent compared to 12.8 per cent in the white workforce.[40]

The profile and analysis of these businesses is instructive. Some 75 per cent were in retailing, within which category over half sold food, less than 20 per cent sold fabrics and 10 per cent were newsagents. Services was the next largest category, within which over half were restaurants and takeaways. Two-thirds of all businesses were located in seven inner city wards, set amidst the 'Asian' residential areas, where commercial properties were cheap. These businesses generated jobs for about 15 per cent of the economically active 'Asians' in the city. Over half of the proprietors employed their wives; indeed, over half of those employed belonged to the owner's family.[41]

Many of the first-generation settlers worked 'long hours on all-Pakistani night shifts (in textile mills)', thereby having 'minimal contact with the indigenous population'.[42] Their children often found employment in 'Asian' businesses, which similarly involved little interaction with those outside their communities. This was especially so where these provided services specific to the 'Asian' communities, such as halal butchers; shops providing Punjabi, Hindi and Urdu audio and video cassettes; specialist goldsmiths, jewellers and cloth retailers.

One specialist service of interest is that provided by a local *hakim*, Mazhar Rana, who offers 'the most effective Unani herbal remedies along with diet information'.[43] The *hakim*, a term from an Arabic word meaning wise, is trained in the principles of classical Greek medicine, *unani tibb*; according to these principles of humoral physiology, developed in the works of Hippocrates, Aristotle and Galen, and elaborated by the great Muslim polymath Ibn Sina in the eleventh century, illness results from an imbalance between the four humours, related to four primary qualities: blood (damp and hot), phlegm/mucus (damp and cold), yellow bile (dry and hot) and black bile (dry and cold).[44] The task of the *hakim* is to help the patient conserve or restore his own inner symmetry.

The methods of diagnosis include taking the pulse, physical examination of urine and the taking of a case history. Once the humoral imbalance is identified, a treatment of herbs and appropriate diet is prescribed to restore balance. The *hakim* is part of Islamic culture, where medicine is understood as 'an ancillary dimension of religion'.[45] The distinguished Islamic seminary of Deoband has a department of *unani tibb*, and many large and famous sufi shrines – such as that of the thirteenth-century Chishti mystic, Muin uddin Chishti at Ajmer, near Delhi – include a herbal medicine clinic.[46]

Born and educated in Bradford, Mazhar Rana now runs the family business, founded by his father, a Pakistani *hakim*, who came from Sialkot to Bradford in 1964. After taking 'A' levels Mr Rana gained a diploma in herbal medicine and homeopathy from an 'International College, Natural Health Science' in London. He imports herbs from South Asia and his clientele are South Asians in diaspora in Britain, Europe, the USA and Canada. Local *'ulama* both buy herbs from him and refer patients to him. The *hakim* has certain obvious advantages over a Western GP: he will spend longer with the patient – 20 minutes to an hour, when the average for GPs is five to seven minutes; he shares the world of assumptions and language of the patient; he can offer a holistic therapy including diet, herbs and religious advice. Since he is able to diagnose a variety of ailments by, *inter alia*, feeling the pulse, and thus not requiring the removal of clothes, his methods are especially congenial to Muslim women. In conversation Mr Rana broadly analysed the complaints he dealt with as 35 per cent gastric, 15 per cent skin, 15 per cent arthritis, 10 per cent depression (mainly women) and 15 per cent psycho-sexual.

Mazhar Rana, a British Muslim, has thus managed to translate into Britain alternative 'systems of medication and diet ... tried and tested for centuries' in South Asia.[47] He exemplifies a new generation of British Muslim professionals, bilingual and bicultural – his promotional literature is in Urdu and English – who can operate in both cultures. He will refer patients to allopathic practitioners for certain complaints, e.g. syphilis, since it can be cured free on the National Health Service with a course of penicillin. Mr Rana's service means that Muslims in Britain can, as in South Asia, continue to 'participate in a pluralistic medical system, and choose among health professionals representing different secular, as well as religious, medical traditions'.[48]

Many Muslims from South Asia consider a knowledge of Urdu is vital for the preservation of religion and culture, not least because it remains the lingua franca of the majority of South Asian Muslims. It is the language in which an enormous amount of Islamic literature is written, and into which a large part of the rich store of Islamic scholarship in Arabic and Persian has been translated. In this context any initiative which seeks to keep knowledge of Urdu alive is of great importance: three local commercial ventures are significant in this regard. In 1974 an Urdu magazine was launched in the city, the *Ravi*. After a precarious start it was taken over in 1976 by a Pakistani migrant from Gujrat in the Punjab, Shaikh Maqsood Ellahie. In that year about 500 copies fortnightly were printed. By 1992 it had a print run of 8,000 copies – since 1979 it has been a weekly – of which a quarter are sold locally and the rest are distributed to Pakistanis in Britain, Europe, the Middle East and America.

While *Ravi* is a weekly offering news and comment, a monthly Urdu-language literary magazine, *Ujala*, was launched in 1989. The Urdu word means day-break/splendour, and the magazine is self-consciously in the South Asian progressive writers' tradition. This tradition can be dated to 1935, when a manifesto was issued by the Progressive Writers' Movement insisting on the need for literature to be socially relevant and a vehicle to combat the evils of 'hunger, poverty, social backwardness and slavery'; the more radical wing of the movement also 'ridiculed in strong terms the oppressiveness of religion and tradition'.[49] The production of *Ujala* was possible since the development of printing technology had enabled the launch of a firm of the same name, in 1982, which offered a service of translation, typesetting and printing in South Asian languages. Some 2,000 copies are printed, of which a quarter are distributed locally. The proprietor of the firm, Fazal Mahmood, is involved in both ventures.[50]

The third and final commercial venture which needs to be mentioned as a vehicle and expression of the continuing vitality of Urdu in the city is Bradford City Radio. The Independent Radio Authority granted the franchise to a group of local investors in June 1989 to set up a commercial radio station aimed at the ethnic minority communities in the city. Its programmes are in Urdu, Hindi, Punjabi and English.[51]

Along with these local initiatives, the London edition of the Pakistani Urdu daily *Jang* is also read in the city, and Yorkshire Television is beginning to cater for the distinct linguistic and cultural traditions of South Asia: in May 1991 it launched a season of 'Asian' films with sub-titles and it also produces an 'Asian' music and culture show, 'Bhangra Beat'.[52] Since the early 1980s the Local Education Authority has found funding for some 35 teachers of 'community' languages in some of the middle and upper schools of the city. The libraries have specialist librarians to provide a service in vernacular languages. In all, it would seem that Urdu has a continuing constituency and future in the city, able to sustain a variety of commercial ventures.

A walk around the Muslim areas of the city also indicates many outlets of Pakistani firms and South Asian goods: Pakistan International Airlines, Habib Bank, two large book shops selling books and magazines in Urdu and English, imported from Pakistan – much of it explicitly Islamic. All the goods and services one would expect to find in any British city are also provided by members of the Muslim communities, who because they are often bilingual naturally attract members of the 'Asian' communities, e.g. the Muslim lawyers in the city have their practices in largely Muslim areas.[53]

It is evident that many of the commercial enterprises that sustain and develop a separate cultural and religious world were often created and supported by the children and grandchildren of the first settlers. This fact should qualify the view of an earlier researcher that there would be increasing disaffection amongst Bradford-born and educated Muslims resulting from the differential participation by parents and children in three distinct, social arenas: the homeland, the Muslim communities in the city and the majority society.[54] Such disaffection clearly does exist and is rooted, in part, in a communication gap between parents and children – an issue explored in Chapter 7. However, it is reasonable to suggest that where parents and children can communicate in a common language, Urdu, the impact of inter-generational tensions are minimized.

Community Organizations, State Funding and Cultural Integrity

Writing about South Asians in Bradford in 1972–3 an anthropologist concluded that the community was 'fragmented with no "grass-root" organisations'.[55] It would not be possible, 20 years later to say the same thing: while the mosques represent the largest investment by the Muslim communities to preserve religious, cultural and linguistic distinctiveness, there has also been a proliferation of often complementary and overlapping associations and organizations reflecting diverse linguistic, cultural, and political allegiances. Some appeal mainly to the elders, others to youth, and many straddle both groups. This dense network of voluntary community initiatives – some funded in partnership with local and central government – both support and express a measure of cultural autonomy.

To glance at lists of organizations affiliated down the years to the local Community Relations Council – renamed Racial Equality Council in the autumn of 1991 – or those seeking funding from the local authority is a revealing index of the plethora of such voluntary associations. They vary from localized groups with a narrow focus, such as the Gujar Khan burial society, collecting regular subscriptions from those originally from that area of the Punjab in Pakistan to enable them to send their deceased back for burial, to the two day-centres for the elderly run by the Council for Mosques. There are Urdu cultural groups who meet to read poetry, and a variety of regional self-help associations such as the Attock Cultural Association, the Azad Kashmir Muslim Association, the Bangladesh Porishad (for Sylhetis), the East Africa Muslims Society, and the Pukhtoon Cultural Society (for Pathans).

In 1979 the Bradford Council for Voluntary Services and the Local Authority, Youth and Community Department both appointed community development workers for the 'ethnic minority' communities in the city. They were able to tap into central government 'Urban Programme' money to finance, *inter alia*, a range of youth and community centres, which benefited the different Muslim communities in the city: the Karmand Centre and Grange Interlink Community Centre were opened in 1982, the Pakistan Community Centre in 1984, and the Frizinghall Community Centre in 1986 – all include youth provision. Three youth centres, largely catering for Muslims, also began functioning in the 1980s: the Bangladesh Youth Organization in 1982, al-Falah in 1985 and Saathi Centre in 1986. The latter was initially hospitable to the pan-Asian, anti-racist Asian Youth Movement (AYM), founded in 1978. However, AYM's anti-racist stance, from its early days, had to contend with the powerful centrifugal pull of Hindu, Sikh and Muslim identities, and the tension between 'Asian' and Afro-Caribbean communities.[56] AYM did not survive the return in the late 1980s to community consolidation around separate Hindu, Sikh and Muslim identities.[57]

Most political parties in Pakistan and Azad Kashmir have branches in the city. The Pakistan People's Party (PPP), formed in 1970 as a bearer of 'Islamic socialism', established a branch in Bradford in the same year. The Pakistan Muslim League (UK) also has a branch in the city, along with Tehrik-i Istiqlal, The Movement for Stability. The All Jammu and Kashmir Muslim Conference (UK), the party which campaigns for Kashmir to join with Pakistan, opened an office as early as 1966. There are also a few members of the Jammu Kashmir Liberation Front in the city, who want Kashmir to be independent of both Pakistan and India. The party which toppled Benazir Bhutto's PPP in October 1990, Islami Jamhoori Ittihad, Islamic Democratic Alliance, has had its Bradford satellite since the autumn of 1989, when one of its leading members, General Zia's son Ajaz al-Haq, visited Muslims in the city. On 24 October 1991, designated 'Kashmir Day', the Kashmir Centre UK was launched in a meeting at the city's Pakistan Community Centre. Its aim was to support the fundamental right of self-determination 'brutally and savagely denied to the ... people of Kashmir by the illegal and oppressive Indian military forces of occupation'.[58]

South Asian and British politics interact in various ways. To the bemusement of political commentators, a Pakistan People's Party candidate stood for the local Manningham ward elections in 1970, although 'what the policy of the PPP would be in Bradford's City Council ... was something of a mystery'![59] In the early 1970s, with the memory of civil war between West and East Pakistan still very much alive, it was not surprising that West Pakistanis in Manningham twice voted against co-religionists from Bangladesh and frustrated their hopes of election.[60] Bradford's first Muslim councillor was to be Bangladeshi, Munawar Hussain, co-opted as an alderman in 1972. This category of alderman was allowed to fall into abeyance in 1974 with local government re-organization, whereby Bradford from being a county borough was metamorphosed into a metropolitan district council.

By 1981 the city had three Muslim councillors, all Labour. One of them, Councillor Hameed, was also president of the Bradford branch of Tehrik-i Istiqlal. By 1991 the city could boast nine Muslim councillors, who were thus in a position to adopt an advocacy role on behalf of their communities. They included Councillor Ajeeb, the city's first 'Asian' Lord Mayor in the year 1985–6. Seven of the Muslim councillors were from Azad Kashmir, thereby reflecting their numerical dominance in the city; one was an East African, originally from the Punjab, and the other was a Bangladeshi, elected in 1991, in a largely Pakistani/Azad Kashmiri ward. This latter indicates that a new generation of younger politicians was beginning to develop tactical alliances across regional and linguistic divides.

Two of the same young councillors who can engineer such alliances are also involved in the management of the Kashmir Centre UK. Its secretary, Councillor Rangzeb, organized a visit to Kashmir by a delegation including two local MPs, representing the Conservative and Labour parties, in February 1992.[61] With a general election in the offing neither political party could afford to appear indifferent to an issue in South Asia of great concern to a majority of their Muslim constituents. We have moved a long way since 1970 when a member of a Pakistani party could seek election in Bradford. Twenty years on local MPs cannot afford to be ignorant about Pakistani and Azad Kashmiri politics.

Education has always been a possible source of friction between the Muslim communities and the local authority. Muslim anxieties about aspects of the educational system were evident as early as 1973. In that year Riaz Shahid, standing as an independent candidate in a local election, was pressing the local authority to provide more single-sex girls' schools. He defeated the Labour candidate in the ward election, and just failed to pip the Conservative candidate.[62] A researcher writing about Bradford at that period lamented that, 'Mainstream schools ... are essentially monocultural and mono-lingual. The culture and language of ethnic minority children is not taught and, in most schools, not acknowledged or recognised as an additional skill to be valued.'[63] A geographer who mapped the social and ethnic geography of Bradford in the 1970s, musing on the 'cultural self-sufficiency' of the Muslim communities, noted that 'education ... constitutes the principal "leak" in an otherwise fairly closed system'.[64] Worries about education were to be a main trigger for the creation in 1981 of the Bradford Council for Mosques.

By the early 1980s the local authority was sympathetic to Muslim concerns to consolidate their religious and cultural identity. This was a reflection of an emerging political will, nationally and locally, to identify and ameliorate the deprivation underlying the earlier explosion of urban violence across the country. What is important to notice here is that the local authority did adopt a series of educational measures to honour the pledge given in its 1981 twelve-point race relations initiative that every community in the city had 'an equal right to maintain its own identity, culture, language, religion and customs'. From 1979 the policy of dispersing 'Asian' children throughout the city's schools ('bussing'), intended to assist their acquisition of English by avoiding mono-lingual 'Asian' schools and ensuring some mutual contact between them and indigenous children, was dropped, under pressure from parents, local politicians and a Commission for Racial Equality investigation.[65]

Local educational authority memoranda, under the new educational banner of 'multiculturalism', sought to respond to Muslim concerns about dress codes for girls, single-sex swimming and physical education; they showed flexibility over extended visits to South Asia, introduced halal food in some schools, renegotiated the agreed religious education syllabus in 1983 and funded a pioneer Interfaith Education Centre in 1986, with teaching assistants from all the city's faith communities. Capitalizing on generous subventions from the Home Office to meet 'special needs' of ethnic minority children (section 11) the authority had, by 1989, some 280 language support staff, 97 nursery nurse posts, 40 home–school liaison posts, 18 bilingual assistants, and 34 community language teachers. While there were few 'Asian' teachers among the authority's 5,000 staff, a variety of initiatives, not least by the local Bradford and Ilkley Community College in setting up bilingual access courses, has seen their number increase to about 130 in 1991.

These measures, intended to reassure Muslim parents that the state sector of education could accommodate most of their 'special needs', were dogged by dispute. An educational researcher has reviewed the controversy in the city in the mid-eighties sparked by articles written by a local headteacher, Ray Honeyford. This research suggested that the local authority on such issues as single-sex education and extended leave for children to visit South Asia 'indicated a value judgment which gives priority to the preservation of cultural identity over the promotion of social integration and cohesion'.[66] Whatever the truth of such a contention, a local teacher writing in 1987 pointed out that Muslims in the city would have less 'inter-cultural contact' than would have been the case a decade earlier. 'The cultural boundary may be conceived of as moving in time and space, ten years ago it was arrived at on beginning school, now it is met when the child leaves the middle school – and home area – to attend upper school.'[67]

This statement is true but potentially misleading: only 15 per cent of 'Asian' children were ever bussed;[68] as soon as schools are not seen as a vehicle of social engineering then, inevitably, first and middle schools approximate to neighbourhood schools, and thus reflect the composition of those areas. It is not altogether surprising that by 1989 some 45 local schools had an 'Asian' intake of 70 per cent plus, of which ten were middle schools and four upper schools. A survey of pupils transferring to upper school from middle school in 1991 showed some 672 Muslim pupils concentrated in four upper schools, whose total intake was 80 per cent or more Muslim, while 603 were distributed between 17 other upper schools.[69] This indicates that just under half the Muslims transferring to upper schools in the city do *not* attend the four, largely Muslim-intake, upper schools adjacent to their core residential areas.

Other educational vehicles of social interaction include the prestigious, private Bradford Grammar School, with at least 5 per cent of its 1,200 pupils Muslim, and the new City Technology College, opened in September 1990 and drawing from inner-city wards, with more than 15 per cent of its students Muslim in 1992. In all, we need to allow for a larger measure of 'inter-cultural contact' than earlier research might lead us to postulate. However, for the present argument, the important point is that the city's schools have sought with a measure of success to reflect the concerns of many Muslim parents, who themselves can choose the pace at which the primary socialization of family, mosque and Muslim peers can yield to the secondary socialization of schooling amongst non-Muslims.

The institutional completeness characteristic of Muslim communities, observed in the mid-sixties, has persisted and been enhanced by the proliferation of culture-specific goods and services, organizations and an education system which, with local authority encouragement, has similarly sought to support rather than subvert religious and cultural distinctiveness. Such institutions continue to make explicit the Muslim communities' 'refusal to adopt local norms or to surrender its ... identity' except as part of a process of local negotiation.[70] The conclusion to a recent study of Muslims in Manchester also holds true for Bradford's Muslim communities:

> the stress on cultural independence is not a permanent barrier to participation in the outside world ... it constitutes a protection from stigma and external domination ... The one-way deterministic approach which defines immigrants as 'victims' is unable to account for the dialectic process which interaction between the immigrant group and the state generates. This process results in the increasing integration into wider structures while, simultaneously, it fosters a separate cultural institutional identity.[71]

Multiple Identities and Criss-crossing Loyalties

It is apparent in Bradford that the Muslim communities have a multiplicity of centres of influence – nine Muslim councillors in 1991, a Council for Mosques and an emerging business and professional elite. A later chapter will seek to identify more closely the respective spheres of influence and tensions between these groups.

However, it is important to illustrate how Muslims can belong to a variety of religious, political and cultural associations, as well as change allegiances within the kaleidoscope of such groupings, and yet still contribute to strengthening a distinctive multi-layered cultural and religious tradition. This is particularly important for an understanding of the constraints within which the city's religious leadership and Muslim activists have to operate.

Three examples will suffice to illustrate the range and diversity of these cross-cutting allegiances. Ishtiaq Ahmed came to Bradford from Gujar Khan in 1967 when he was ten years old. He attended a mosque in the Barelwi tradition, to which his father belonged. In upper school in Bradford he joined the Islamic Youth Movement (IYM), founded in 1974, the youth wing of the Jama'at-i Islami tradition in Britain. He later became its national general-secretary.

In 1979 he was appointed the Bradford Council for Voluntary Services' first community worker charged with developing 'ethnic minority' services. In the mid-1980s he was active in race relations, employed in the race relations department of a neighbouring council (Calderdale) and a founder-member, with a Bangladeshi, Mohammed Salam, of 'a radical group called the Black Workers Collective (BWC) which was set up in Bradford to organize black workers and defend their interests and democratic rights.'[72] In 1987 he and Salam were dubbed 'young Turks' by the local media, when they were appointed chairman and vice-chairman, respectively, of the Bradford Community Relations Council, replacing some of the better known elders. By 1990 he was information officer of the Bradford Council for Mosques and had returned to his Barelwi roots, representing one of their mosques.

Ahmed is an example of an educated Muslim who is bilingual and bi-cultural, and whose progress turns on considerable natural abilities, allied to a keen strategic sense, eager to forge alliances across linguistic, sectarian and religious divides. Our second example, Raja Najabat Hussain, operates more self-consciously within a regional and *biradari* network.

Hussain came to Bradford in 1977 from Azad Kashmir when he was already 22 years old. In Azad Kashmir he had organized a new students' group, the Muslim Students' Federation, an activist group favouring a united Kashmir, allied to Pakistan. In England he became the general-secretary of the All Jammu and Kashmir Muslim Conference. In 1988 he was a member of the Barelwi Jami'at-i Tabligh al-Islam executive committee in Bradford 3, which controlled six mosques and supplementary schools; he sat on the Council for Mosques, was chairman of the Karmand Centre and Bradford Moor Conservative Party, and vice-chair of the Bradford Law Centre. His power base was unashamedly the Rajput *biradari*, possibly the largest in the Muslim community.[73] In 1988 all members of the Bradford 3 Jami'at-i Tabligh al-Islam executive belonged to the same *biradari*, as did the president of the Council for Mosques that year and the chairman of the Pakistan Community Centre.

While Mr Hussain is proud of his *biradari* and their extensive influence, as director of the Kashmir Centre UK he is quick to point out that its advisory group includes members of other *biradaris* – high-status jat and low-status artisan castes alike: many of the latter have availed themselves of the educational opportunities in the city to acquire professional qualifications and some have become councillors. The advisory group, in fact, cuts across *biradari*, sectarian, regional and generational differences. Amongst its younger members it numbers two councillors, a social worker, a college lecturer; the elders include the Deobandi secretary of the Council for Mosques, from Chhachh, and two Punjabi businessmen, one of whom is the president of the Islami Jamhoori Ittihad, Islamic Democratic Alliance, at present the ruling party in Pakistan.

The membership of the Islami Jamhoori Ittihad is our third and final example of the labyrinthine alliances which criss-cross the different Muslim communities in the city. In Pakistan the party is a coalition of different religio-political groups, which joined together to topple the Pakistan People's Party (PPP). These same groups joined it in Bradford. The Muslim League was represented by its president, Raja Hamid Rashid, one of the two Punjabi businessmen involved in the Kashmir Centre UK, himself a Barelwi, active in the Hanafia mosque in the city and a member of the Council for Mosques. The UK Islamic Mission – a vehicle of the Jama'at-i Islami tradition – was represented by their president, a Punjabi, Umar Warraich, a retired health inspector in the city. The Ahl-i Hadith was represented by another

Punjabi businessman, Mr Awan and the All Jammu and Kashmir Muslim Conference was represented by the ubiquitous Najabat Hussain, an Azad Kashmiri Barelwi. What is significant about this group is that membership of distinct, sectarian traditions, often with a history of mutual antipathy, does not prevent individuals co-operating on a different platform.

The reproduction in Bradford of much of the commercial, political, linguistic and institutional world of South Asia allows for a large measure of religious and cultural autonomy. This is not to suggest that the Muslim religious leaders endorse it all uncritically. Nor is it assumed that all Muslims are devout. Yet, for all that, Islam is part of their cultural and ethnic identity. As to whether Islam or, perhaps, Pakistani nationalism will be given particular salience, this depends on context: during the Rushdie affair youngsters rallied around Islam as a vehicle of ethnic identity; after Pakistan won the cricket world cup in March 1992 many youngsters celebrated by driving through parts of the city in high spirits, waving Pakistani flags, some a little too enthusiastically.[74] The religious leadership, of course, hopes that the explicitly 'Islamic' component in identity will assume greater importance.

4

Islamic Institutions in Bradford

We have already looked at the specific character of Islam in South Asia. In this chapter we will describe the different sectarian groupings in Bradford and explore their ethos, leadership, networks, institutional embodiment, resources and priorities. The only dimension of contemporary Islam which will not be addressed here is modernism. This continues its somewhat fugitive existence, with no formal institutional expression, and will be considered in Chapter 7, where a modernist sentiment is identified among some young British Muslims.

The critical question facing the various sectarian traditions in the city is the extent to which each has begun to address the needs of the burgeoning young Muslim population, British born and educated. Here, four issues are especially important: First, which traditions have produced material in English? Second, which have succeeded in establishing Islamic seminaries in Britain? Third, which groupings are hospitable to youth work? Finally, which have the resources and willingness to utilize the electronic media for transmitting aspects of the Islamic tradition?

This last point, the necessity of mastering the world of modern media, is crucial. The print media in the nineteenth century and the electronic media of the twentieth – radio, television, audio and video cassettes – have wrought a revolution in religious consciousness and sensibility. To understand these media and to use them creatively can also facilitate communication across a crucial divide opened up by education and literacy. The difference between an oral culture, where only a minority are literate, and one shaped by universal education, where most are literate, is an issue many religious leaders in Bradford are now having to address seriously for the first time.

Between Orality and Literacy: The Dilemma for the Muslim Educator

Tariq Modood characterizes South Asian Muslims in Britain generally as 'a semi-industrialised, newly urbanised working class community that is only one generation away from rural peasantry'.[1] This is certainly true of Bradford, where most of the first settlers came from the least developed areas of Indo-Pakistan and had little if any formal education. A majority came from Azad Kashmir, an area which, pre-partition, was under the control of the Maharajas, by whom it was 'shamefully neglected', and which 'contained hardly any schools'.[2] Even today, for Pakistan as a whole, according to M. Afzal, General Zia's Minister for Education in the 1980s, 'educational statistics are appalling: 8 per cent of its population are educated up to primary, 2 per cent secondary and 0.02 per cent university level ... (official statistics are 'padded' and inflated).'[3]

In such an environment, sound rather than sight is crucial for the transmission of a religious tradition. Printed books remain scarce and the teacher has to be attuned to the oral–aural dimensions of literacy – dimensions to which typographic cultures tend to be insensitive, given their assumption of the primacy in language of written or printed words. Walter Ong has helped us understand the lineaments of an orally constituted sensibility and tradition. In such an environment mnemonic tricks are essential, in order 'to solve effectively the problem of retaining and retrieving carefully articulated thought ... [whether] heavily rhythmic, balanced patterns, in repetitions or antitheses, in alliterations and assonances, in epithetic and other formulary expressions ... in proverbs which are constantly heard by everyone so that they come to mind readily.'[4]

In an oral culture words are recalled rather than looked up. With knowledge hard to come by, and therefore a valuable commodity, those who specialize in conserving it are highly valued. Orality also 'fosters personality structures that in certain ways are more communal and externalized, and less introspective than those common among literates. Oral communication unites people in groups. Writing and reading are solitary activities that throw the psyche back on itself.'[5]

These comments can illuminate the persistence of three features common to traditional Islam in South Asia, where literacy has been confined to the few. First, the omnipresence of the Qur'an as 'spoken word, a recited word, a word that makes itself felt in personal and communal life in large part through its living quality as sacred sound'.[6] Indeed, Qur'anic recitation – *qira'a* – is a basic discipline of Islamic studies rooted in the Qur'anic imperative of sura 73:4: 'chant the recitation carefully and distinctly'.[7] Bukhari, the most prestigious collection of prophetic traditions, includes one which states that 'when the Qur'an is recited, there descends with the reciting the divine presence (*sakina*).'[8] Little wonder that throughout South Asia – and in Bradford today – many youngsters will devote years to committing to memory the entire Qur'an and thus acquire the coveted title of *hafiz*. Second, respect is accorded to the bearers of Islamic knowledge, with authoritative knowledge transmitted from person to person. A student in an Islamic academy sits at the feet of his teacher, who would,

> dictate the text to his pupils, who might write it down, or frequently would commit it to memory ... Subsequently, there might be an explanation of the text ... the completion of the study of the book would involve a reading back of the text with an explanation. If this was done to the teacher's satisfaction, the pupil would be given an *ijaza*, ('to make lawful'), a licence to teach the text. On that *ijaza* ... would be the names of all those who had transmitted the text going back to the original author. The pupil was left in no doubt that he was trustee in his generation of part of the great tradition of Islamic learning handed down from the past.[9]

Third, in popular piety *qawwali*s, devotional songs, committed to memory, have brought consolation and spiritual nourishment to Muslims in South Asia for over 600 years.

> Under the guidance of a spiritual leader ... groups of trained musicians (*qawwals*) present in song a vast treasure of poems which articulate and evoke the gamut of mystical experience for the spiritual benefit of their audience. Through the act of listening – *sama'* – the Sufi seeks to activate his link with his living spiritual guide, with saints departed, and ultimately with God ... The music serves to kindle the flame of mystical love ... There is no Qawwali experience more vivid

and profound than the *'urs* ... the commemoration of (a sufi's) final union with God on the anniversary of his death.[10]

Qawwalis, with their devotion to particular sufis and their shrines, remain a treasured component of South Asian Islamic piety.

These three traditional features of the transmission and expression of Islamic knowledge – the essential orality of the Qur'an, a highly personalized transfer of knowledge through accredited teachers and the popularity of *sama'* – although persisting, have increasingly been exposed to scrutiny, and their adequacy and appropriateness challenged. The introduction of lithographic printing in nineteenth-century India began a process, yet to be completed, whereby human consciousness was affected by the shift from oral to written speech, from an emphasis on sound to sight.

The reformist Deobandi tradition, with its popularization of teaching emphasizing correct belief and practice, as an antidote to more localized, customary expressions of Islam, is inconceivable without printing. Printing also facilitates a shift from rote learning to an emphasis on understanding. This is evident in an encyclopaedic Urdu work for women, *Bihishti Zewar* (Heavenly Ornaments), first written in 1906 by Maulana Thanawi – a book which has undergone innumerable revisions and been translated into English and which is used in some Deobandi mosques in Bradford. The author of a partial translation and commentary on it noticed that Thanawi urged a teacher using it to make sure that the girls 'should always repeat the lesson in their own words ... and if there are two or three of them they should ask each other questions. The teacher is to teach only what the girls can grasp ... This is far from technical reading aloud in an unknown language or rote memorization of fixed texts.'[11]

The *'ulama* who used the printing presses assumed that the printed book could 'reinforce learning systems that already existed, to improve them, not to transform them'.[12] Indeed, for Thanawi the bewildering range and suspect nature of much printed material made a teacher essential. He himself went as far as to prescribe and proscribe lists of books he considered either worthwhile or harmful. *Bihishti Zewar* was intended, after all, 'for an oral, public world. It was to be read aloud, discussed openly, taught in groups ... his proscribed list ... perhaps intended to discourage ... the privacy of reading silently, of creating a private world of one's own inner voice by losing oneself – a terrible image, in Thanawi's view – in books like novels.'[13]

In the long term, however, print challenged the monopoly of the 'ulama as custodians and privileged bearers of the Islamic tradition. The printed book could render the reader independent of the need for an authoritative teacher and impatient of their necessary conservatism: 'By storing knowledge outside the mind ... print downgrade[s] the figure of the wise ... repeaters of the past, in favour of discoverers of something new.'[14] New trajectories of Islamic thought and practice were developed by those who were not accredited 'ulama, who simply by-passed their time-honoured disciplines of study. Such are the majority of modernists and Islamists.

Modernists and Islamists alike created their own separate institutions of Islamic study and research. The modernist scholar Fazlur Rahman completed his formal study in Western universities, institutions outside the control and often beyond the comprehension of many of the 'ulama. In 1962 he was appointed director of the Islamic Research Institute, a modernist centre set up by the Pakistan government in 1960 as an alternative to their centres of study.[15] Jama'at-i Islami, the movement generated by the Islamist Maulana Maududi, established its own rival Islamic Research Academy in Karachi in 1963.[16] Jama'at-i Islami, which appeals to many educated Muslims, is also 'a product of print culture ... in significant measure sustained by print, [and] a large part of its income comes from the sale of Maududi's works'.[17]

The characteristic products of print, whether newspapers, tracts or books, began to replace the 'oral, mobile, warm, personally interactive lifeworld of oral culture' with a 'community in anonymity', or perhaps better 'communities in anonymity', given the inevitable pluralism of voices claiming to speak and write within an Islamic perspective.[18] The irony now is that the emergence of the electronic media has created what Ong has called an age of 'secondary orality'. Secondary orality bears some resemblances to primary orality in its 'participatory mystique, its fostering of a communal sense ... but [it] generates a sense for groups immeasurably larger than those of primary oral culture'.[19]

Some Muslims from within a traditional Islamic culture have not been slow to understand and exploit the potential of the electronic media. Ahmad Deedat, the popular preacher from South Africa, a frequent visitor to Britain, invariably makes videotapes of his debates, as well as producing written pamphlets. Since these are also in English they are enormously popular with Muslim youth. In Bradford few of the self-consciously Muslim groups are without their stock of his videos. Similarly, the tapes of respected and much loved *qawwals* from Pakistan are very popular in Bradford, whether Nusrat Fateh Ali Khan – a regular visitor to Britain – or the Sabri brothers. In November 1989 BBC2 broadcast a programme entitled 'Rhythms of the World', which featured Nusrat Fateh Ali Khan in concert in Birmingham, where he had been invited by local Muslims to celebrate *milad*, the Prophet's birthday. Video copies of this programme were soon circulating among Muslims in Bradford.

The challenges facing the Muslim religious leadership in Bradford are awesome. How are they to provide personnel, develop appropriate organizations and generate resources to meet the needs of communities with often conflicting expectations? On the one hand, there are the elders in the community, the majority of whom are rural people from South Asia, who are without formal education and who speak a local 'oral-based' dialect, dubbed a 'restricted linguistic code' by linguists; and on the other hand, there are educated, literate, 'text-based' English speakers, who use an 'elaborated linguistic code'.[20]

Pir Maroof and Barelwi Initiatives

When a definitive history of Muslims in Britain is written, the contribution of 'pioneer' religious leaders like Pir Maroof Hussain Shah should not be overlooked. Pir Maroof's energy and range of initiatives are extraordinary. Born in Chak Swari, in the district of Mirpur in Azad Kashmir in 1936, he came to Britain in 1961. At the same time as working for almost a quarter of a century in textile mills he sought to respond to the religious needs of his community.

In 1963 Pir Maroof established the Jami'at-i Tabligh al-Islam, Association for the Preaching of Islam. Membership forms for the association identify as its aims the spread of Islam among Muslims and non-Muslims in the light of the holy Qur'an, Hadith, the consensus of the community and the Hanafi law. The association was also committed 'to follow the spiritual teachings/ mysticism (*tasawwuf*) of the majority of the leaders of the Qadri, Chishti, Naqshbandi and Suhrawardi orders'.[21] By 1989, of the eleven mosques and seven supplementary schools in the Barelwi tradition in the city, eight mosques and six schools belonged to his association.

While Pir Maroof directly controls the association's central mosque at Southfield Square, his relation to the others, which have their own mosque committees, is to provide appropriate mosque personnel and the syllabus to be studied, to arbitrate in disputes, and to organize the major religious festivals which punctuate the Muslim calendar. In the late 1960s he also set up centres in Sheffield and Oldham – often raising interest-free loans to help the local mosque committee buy the appropriate properties. At the same time, he set about establishing *dar al-'ulum*, seminaries, to train *'ulama*: one in his birthplace, Chak Swari, in 1965; another in 1968 near the location of the family shrine in Dogah Sharif, Gujrat, Pakistan. To complete the prescribed course of study for an *'alim*, Pir Maroof himself had had to go outside Azad Kashmir to the large urban centres of Jhelum and Rawalpindi in the Punjab. Therefore, he wanted to provide local centres of training in areas starved of such institutions.

Pir Maroof's first love is *tasawwuf*, Islamic mysticism, and he has a fine library of standard works in Arabic, Persian and Urdu. He himself writes devotional poetry in praise of God and the Prophet. In 1985 on his brother's death he succeeded him as a spiritual guide in the Qadiri, Naushahi order, which traces its ancestry back to the founder of his order in Gujrat, Pakistan, Haji Muhammad Nausha (d. 1654), and thence to the Prophet Muhammad. In all, Pir Maroof is thirty-fourth in a chain, *silsila*, including the Prophet's son-in-law Ali and great sufis like Abdul Qadir Jilani (d. 1166), buried in Baghdad. Nationalism may have fragmented the Muslim world but through such vivid spiritual networks its transnational character is kept alive. As early as 1961 he organized a Naushahi circle for devotees. Pir Maroof is critical of free-wheeling, self-styled spiritual guides and insists on the importance for any *pir* to belong to an order, to have his own spiritual guide and to have his permission to initiate devotees.

With this range of responsibilities Pir Maroof has a punishing schedule involving up to five months' travel a year: some four months are spent in Pakistan visiting his devotees and two seminaries; a month is spent in Holland, France, Belgium and Germany visiting his followers among the Pakistani diaspora and organizing the festivities which surround the birth of the Prophet, the anniversary of the death of the founder of his order, and that of his brother, Pir Syed Abul Kamal Barq.

As a spiritual guide Pir Maroof performs a range of pastoral tasks. On one occasion he mentioned to me the sort of anxieties and questions which led people to seek his advice. A marriage registered under British law is dissolved and the wife is given a divorce without the husband's approval – uncertainty will then remain as to whether such a divorce is Islamically valid. His prayers and a *ta'wiz*, amulet, are sought to offer relief for a range of pressing anxieties, whether an important examination or an immigration case – the latter, particularly, can assume the nature of an unpredictable lottery given the vagaries of British immigration law.[22] A few come complaining of being possessed by an evil *jinn* – most, he insists, are really cases of hysteria (in women), or possibly epilepsy or even high blood pressure; Pir Maroof will usually pray for them, offer a *ta'wiz* and, where necessary, refer them to a GP. Some *murid*s come worried by persistent dreams and seek his interpretation of them.[23] Increasingly, families are split over the issue of arranged marriage and he seeks to mediate between parents and children. Education is a source of continuing worry to parents – is the food halal, what should their stance be on sex education?

Pir Maroof is also involved in a wider political and religious arena. In 1973, while on pilgrimage to Mecca, he created the World Islamic Mission (WIM), an umbrella organization for Barelwi dignitaries, with its head office located in his mosque at Southfield Square in Bradford. Pir Maroof was its founder and vice-president, with its first president Maulana Noorani, leader of the Barelwi political party in Pakistan. Under WIM's auspices two important works of Ahmad Raza Khan (d. 1921) – founder of the Barelwi tradition – were translated into English. The first of these was his Urdu translation of the Qur'an, which has a preface written by Pir Maroof, and the second was his famous *durud sharif*, litanies in praise of the prophet, known as *salaam* – each verse in Urdu ends with that word. The *salaam* is often read at the conclusion of Friday prayers in their mosques.

It is worth rehearsing some of the verses from the *salaam*, which give us an unrivalled insight into the status of the Prophet in this devotional tradition.

> Blessed be Mustafa, mercy for mankind,
> God's light, the right way to find.

> Blessed be the splendour of the next world,
> Dignity, justice and grandeur of this world.

> Blessed be the source of knowledge divine,
> Outstanding and the last in the Prophet's line.

> Blessed be the point of Life's hidden unity,
> And also the centre of its visible diversity.

> Blessed be the giver of blessings diverse,
> On whose account God created the universe.

> Blessed be the prime cause of creation,
> The final medium of salvation.[24]

Such devotion to the person of the Prophet both explains the passion which informs rivalries with other Muslim groups, who in Barelwi eyes do not adequately esteem the Prophet, and prepares us for the anger which fuelled and sustained the opposition to *The Satanic Verses*. The World Islamic Mission is clearly intended as a counterweight to the Mecca-based Muslim World League, a vehicle for those whom Barelwis scornfully dismiss as Wahhabi, whether Deobandi, Jama'at-i Islami or Ahl-i Hadith. The chairman of the Muslim World League in 1982 delivered a fatwa declaring the event and devotions surrounding the Prophet's birthday, *milad*, to be an 'evil innovation'.[25] An English translation of this same ruling was displayed on the notice board of one of the Deobandi mosques in Bradford in 1990.

The issues dividing Barelwi and Wahhabi were made very clear at the Hijaz Conference, a large gathering organized by WIM at the Wembley Conference Centre in May 1985. In the presence of a galaxy of dignitaries, including Pir Maroof and Maulana Noorani, the conference attracted more than 3,000 participants from all over Britain. Formal resolutions were passed: condemning Saudi officials for confiscating and allegedly destroying translations of the Qur'an by Ahmad Raza Khan and devotional books; complaining about the draconian measures to which Muslims in Medina and Mecca were exposed when they sought to celebrate the Prophet's birthday; seeking assurances that remaining sites associated with the Prophet, his family and companions would be respected and maintained; objecting to the fact that the Muslim World League, ostensibly intended to foster Muslim co-operation, was staffed almost entirely by Wahhabis, who accounted for only 2 per cent of the Muslim community world-wide.[26]

A back-handed compliment to the Barelwi influence was a book published the same year in Arabic and English, entitled *Bareilawis: History and Beliefs*, by a leading Pakistani Ahl-i Hadith scholar, Ehsan Elahi Zaheer. This polemical work was written in Arabic to alert Muslims in the Arab world to the beliefs of this 'superstitious and innovating sect' whose 'activities are on the increase' – explicit mention is made of their activities in England.[27]

Local and national gatherings and processions on the occasion of the Prophet's birthday (*milad*) continue to be the central event in the Barelwi calendar. Pir Maroof organized the first public procession through the streets of Bradford on the occasion of the *milad* in 1984. Such regional gatherings are often advertised in the national Urdu press, and Pir Maroof's procession in 1988 was promoted in the Urdu daily, *Jang*.[28] In 1987 Pir Maroof was chosen by the World Sufi Council to be its representative in Britain. The council was headed by Sheikh Shams uddin al Fassi, a Saudi Arabian belonging to the Shazili sufi order.[29] In autumn 1987 and 1988 under its auspices Pir Maroof organized enormous *milad* gatherings in Hyde Park, London, comprising some 25,000 people. *Jang* carried a report and pictures of the 1988 gathering on its front page.[30]

Pir Maroof's many initiatives have been bedevilled by economic difficulties, as well as personal and political rivalries. In February 1986 the foundation stone of an ambitious purpose-built mosque was laid, 'expected to take two years to build … [at a] cost of around £8.5m'.[31] By 1990 the scheme had to be pared back to £1 million: the rapidly increasing numbers of young children in the community meant that priority had to be given to building local, accessible mosques and supplementary schools, while promised Arab sponsorship proved elusive – Dr al Fassi only gave £20,000 of the £120,000 promised. Although over £400,000 had been spent on the mosque by 1992, it was still years away from completion.

Money was not the only problem. As early as 1974 Pir Maroof's leadership was challenged by a rival Barelwi group, the Hanafia Association, many of whose members were local businessmen and either devotees of another Azad Kashmiri Pir, Alauddin Siddiqui, or supporters of the Pakistan People's Party. They were therefore antagonistic to Maulana Noorani's party in Pakistan and critical both of Pir Maroof's choice of him as president of WIM and the platform offered to Noorani to speak at WIM's first big gathering in Bradford in 1974. The Hanafia Association also announced its plans to build another purpose-built mosque close to Pir Maroof's chosen site. Mutual recriminations grew steadily more vicious and led to a 'stabbing incident' between rival factions.[32] Since then Pir Maroof's pre-eminent position has been further eroded by the establishment of two more large Barelwi mosques, each owing allegiance to other *pirs*: Suffat ul Islam (UK) Association was established in Bradford in 1985, and Sultan Bahu Trust in 1986.[33]

Although Pir Maroof's supporters still control many mosques and supplementary schools, limited resources and disputes between *'ulama* and *biradari* – a 'localised intermarrying caste group', who often control the mosque committees – have meant that Pir Maroof has had considerable difficulty in keeping his best *'ulama*.[34] Maulana Arshad al Qadri and Maulana Azmi, vice-president and general-secretary of WIM India and UK respectively, both stayed for three years only, leaving in 1976 and 1979 – the latter moved on to a mosque in Manchester; a third *'alim*, Maulana Nishtar, joined the rival Hanafia Association in 1982.

Finding trained and competent religious leaders for the mosques continues to be a major headache. In 1989, of eight trained *'ulama*, fourteen *huffaz*, and ten part-timers working in the Jami'at-i Tabligh al-Islam centres, the general-secretary of the association considered only four to be really competent scholars in Arabic, and not many more knew English.[35] Pir Maroof, as

well as depending on three of his cousins and three of the products of his seminaries in Pakistan, relied on eight Gujaratis, a
situation widely acknowledged to be less than ideal since the
mother tongue of most of the children was Punjabi rather than
the Urdu which the Gujarati *'ulama* know.

The worst effect of intra-Barelwi rivalries has been the failure
of Pir Maroof's vision to see his Islamic Missionary College, set
up in 1974, develop into a fully-fledged Islamic seminary, capable
of training a new generation of English-speaking *'ulama* and
thereby freeing the mosques from the need to depend on South
Asia for personnel. The three *'ulama* listed earlier who left Jami'at-
i Tabligh al-Islam were all well-trained and respected scholars
and were, respectively, principal and governors of the Islamic
Missionary College. Other reasons for the failure of the college
are also instructive: it was short of sponsorship; parents were reluctant or unable to finance their son for the six or seven years
of study required; the college could only take students after they
completed their state education – for it did not have the resources
to establish a preparatory private school – by which time the gap
between the world of Western education and that of a traditional
Islamic seminary was almost insuperable. Finally, the salary they
could command as an *'alim* was little more than £70 a week in
1989, probably one-third of what they might earn in a mill.

The general-secretary of Jami'at-i Tabligh al-Islam considers
that teachers in mosques and supplementary schools have three
essential tasks with regard to the youngsters: to teach them to
read the Qur'an in Arabic; to teach them Urdu – thereby giving
them access to Islamic literature as well as facilitating communication between parents and children – and to furnish them with
essential knowledge of Islam. The literature available and in use
in the mosques turns on the preferences and competence in
English of the teachers. Generally, where a textbook is used for
Islamic knowledge it is an Urdu work, *Hamara Islam* (Our Islam).

Our Islam takes for granted the vocabulary and tradition of the
Barelwis: in answer to the question, 'What is the sign of love for
the Prophet?' the importance of remembrance of God, *zikr*, *durud
sharif*, *milad* and the recitation of *salaam* are all mentioned.[36] The
importance of the intercession of the Prophet on the Day of
Judgment is emphasized; attending the shrines of the sufis and

participating in their 'urs as a vehicle of blessing is stressed; the miracles of the sufis are detailed – walking on water, flying in the air, revealing what is happening far away, raising the dead; an important distinction is made between good and ruinous innovations in religious practice with the former, bid'at-i hasana, deemed acceptable.[37]

For teaching Urdu most of the teachers use the books produced by the Punjab textbook board in Lahore for Pakistan's schools. These reflect the unselfconscious religiosity of Pakistan as illustrated in Chapter 2. Muslim youngsters brought up in Bradford, who have never seen a shrine, still less experienced its carnival atmosphere, must find the taken-for-granted religious world of their parents and teachers inaccessible to them, unless they have personally visited South Asia. A few of the mosques use Urdu books produced for Bradford schools which draw on the imagery and experience of British children.

If parents are literate in English they can supplement the teaching in the mosque with material from the The Islamic Times, produced in Stockport. This monthly magazine, started in the autumn of 1985, has a limited circulation in Bradford – the editor is a murid of Pir Maroof. The magazine is clearly in the Barelwi tradition, with extensive selections from Ahmad Raza Khan's voluminous writings, translated into English. It also includes material for children and women. While it began in English only it soon became bilingual, English and Urdu. On the magazine's fifth anniversary the editorial thanked its readers for their continuing support and noted that its independence and 'Islamic integrity' remained intact since, unlike most other journals, it was not funded by 'foreign Middle East governments' and thus could reflect and analyse the problems of the British Muslim community rather than be the 'mouth-pieces of ... foreign governments ... not bothered about the Muslim community in Britain'.[38] This is an accusation often heard in Barelwi circles.

The Barelwi tradition is not unsympathetic to the need for some youth provision. The difficulty is that there are few in the community with any understanding of organized youth work. Maulana Azmi encouraged the formation of the Muslim youth group for boys, al-Falah, in 1979, and this group continues to draw on the support of 'ulama in the Barelwi tradition. Its new building was opened in 1985 and the plaque celebrating this fact bears the name of a Pakistani sufi, Naqeebullah Khan Shah, who usually visits Britain annually. Many of the management are his *murid*s. The centre has good recreational facilities and a library of Islamic books and videos – Barelwis are quite prepared to utilize the electronic media, where resources permit. The range of activities al-Falah can offer tends to depend on the vicissitudes of local authority funding.

Provision for girls/women, outside supplementary schools, remains very limited. A major factor is that many of the house-mosques have neither space nor resources to build the additional, separate, ablutions facility and prayer hall needed to render their premises usable by women. Only two of the Jami'at-i Tabligh al-Islam mosques have a prayer room for women. However, both Barelwi purpose-built mosques under construction include space for women to pray and to participate in Friday prayers. Maulana (or 'Allama) Shah Muhammad Nishtar is unusual in that he teaches a separate class of girls Arabic to GCSE level. The situation is well described in an editorial in the *Islamic Times*:

> The young boy from his childhood may be sent to the madrassah for Islamic education, he will be expected to pray ... talk to the Mullahs freely, join Islamic groups, attend Islamic conferences or summer camps ... As for girls, apart from some parents sending their girls to the madrassahs there is hardly any other form of participation in Islamic activities.[39]

Deobandi and Tablighi Jama'at Institutions

The management of Bradford's 14 Deobandi centres is much more ethnically diverse than that of the Barelwi mosques and supplementary schools. Seven are controlled by Pathans and Punjabis fron Chhachh in Pakistan, four by Suratis from Gujarat in India – two of which by Suratis who migrated to East Africa – and three by Sylhetis from Bangladesh. Within the Chhachh constellation of mosques, and indeed outside it, the Howard Street mosque – known formally and constitutionally as the 'Muslim Association of Bradford', but popularly referred to as 'Howard Street' – enjoys a certain primacy: it was the first mosque to be established in 1959; it developed an expertise in dealing with local bureaucracies, particularly necessary if planning permission was to be successfully achieved; it helped raise interest-free loans for property; it has burial facilities, which some of the others do not have; it circulates its timetable of prayer times to half a dozen mosques.

Howard Street's first *'alim*, Maulana Lutfur Rahman, was president for some 20 years of a national umbrella organization for Deobandi *'ulama*, the Jami'at-i Ulama Britannia (JUB), founded in 1967; its mosque committee includes Sher Azam, a successful local businessman, who assumed national prominence during *The Satanic Verses* affair as president of the Bradford Council for Mosques. Finally, Howard Street also functions as the centre in Bradford for the revivalist activities of Tablighi Jama'at.

The Twaqulia mosque enjoys a similar pre-eminence amongst the Bangladeshi centres, and for broadly similar reasons.[40] Mention has already been made in Chapter 3 of the separate institutional expression given to the East African Gujarati community in Bradford, in contrast to those from India. Although the management of the mosques is generally controlled by one of these distinct regional and linguistic groups, the congregations using them are by no means so exclusively defined. Punjabis and Mirpuris regularly worship in large numbers at the Gujarati mosques. Some 10 per cent of the children at the Twaqulia mosque also fall into this category, and a provision is made there for Urdu to be taught to them – while Bengali is taught to the other children. The interaction between Gujarati and Pakistani is facilitated by the use, in the mosque and in the education of the children, of Urdu, the lingua franca of the Deobandis.

These links between Deobandi mosques, controlled by different regional groups, are being strengthened. Most significant is the relationship developing between the mosques and the two flourishing Deobandi seminaries; one was set up in 1975 at Bury, 50 miles from Bradford, and the other in 1982 at Dewsbury, 10 miles away. The Dewsbury institute is also the European centre for the revivalist Tablighi Jama'at, which every Christmas hosts a huge gathering from all over Western Europe, comprising as many as 8,000 people. Virtually every Deobandi mosque now has students at one or both of these seminaries. Three of the largest mosques

– the Chhachhi-controlled Howard Street, the Sylheti Twaqulia and Surati Blenheim Road mosque – have ten or more students each at the two centres. Blenheim Road mosque has eleven students at Bury and seven at Dewsbury. Many of the mosques also send groups to the weekly, Thursday evening Tablighi Jama'at teach-in at Dewsbury and host the monthly groups coming from Dewsbury, who lead revivalist activities over a week-end.

The importance and range of interactions between Bury and Dewsbury and the Bradford mosques cannot be exaggerated: Maulana Lutfur Rahman, the President of JUB, is also a *murid* of the principal of Bury, Yusuf Motala. The present vice-president of JUB – Maulana Naeem, imam of the Abu Bakr mosque in Bradford – also teaches part-time at the Dewsbury centre. In the autumn of 1989, Howard Street mosque appointed its first English-speaking *'alim*, the son of Maulana Lutfur Rahman, and the first graduate from Bury to be appointed to one of the city's mosques. In 1990, Blenheim Road mosque appointed the first graduate from Dewsbury to be employed in the city. In Bury and Dewsbury the Deobandi mosques have institutions which are beginning to free them from their dependence on mosque personnel from South Asia. The local education authority supported this development and from 1984 and 1985 began to fund students going to Bury and Dewsbury. In 1990 15 students at each institution were being financed to complete their respective courses of study – six years for Bury and seven for Dewsbury.[41]

Both centres are managed and largely staffed by Gujaratis. This testifies to the importance of this comparatively well-educated community, used to living as a small minority in the non-Muslim environment of India. There are close links between Bury and Dewsbury. The principal of Bury, Yusuf Motala, is a product of the Deobandi seminary of Mazahir-i 'Ulum at Saharanpur, 20 miles north of Deoband. He was directed by his shaikh, Maulana Zakariya (d. 1982), the leading luminary of the institution, to establish a *dar al-'ulum* in England. Maulana Zakariya was one of the most influential figures in the Tablighi Jama'at and author of its hugely influential textbook, *Tablighi Nisab*, the Preaching Course. Although Mazahir-i 'Ulum has a similar syllabus to the seminary in Deoband, its ethos can be considered 'less intellectual and more Sufi in orientation'.[42] A visitor in the

mid-1980s discussed the differences with its treasurer, who insisted that: 'Deoband was intended to resist the British by non-
violent methods, the military option having been tried fruitlessly
in 1857. But the Mazahir-i 'Ulum had, since its very inception,
opted out of this world (*dunya*); it had remained committed only
to the faith (*din*).'[43]

Bury, then, owes its inspiration, much of its syllabus and its
ethos to Saharanpur. *Tablighi Nisab* is recited every day as part of
shared devotions. Its students attend the huge Christmas gathering
at Dewsbury, while a few of the students from the latter establishment spend their last year studying the authoritative collections
of prophetic traditions at Bury, since Dewsbury does not have
staff to teach them. The main mechanism for recruitment for
both centres is the informal Tablighi Jama'at networks, nationally
and internationally. The same teacher, Mr Minhas, advised both
on devising the syllabus for a private boys' school for those 13 to
16 year-olds attending both *dar al-'ulum*, to conform to the dictates
of British law. The main differences between Saharanpur and
Bury/Dewsbury are the need to provide some minimal British
syllabus for those under sixteen years old – in South Asia one
can start an *'alim* course at nine years old – and the absence of
Persian.

The main difference between Bury and Dewsbury is that study
is subordinate to revivalism at Dewsbury, where students are
expected to spend a week-end every month, some of their holidays and a year at the end of their studies, engaged in such
activities. In Bury, they are free to join Tablighi Jama'at groups
during their holidays. The last year at Dewsbury is spent, for the
majority who do not go to Bury, in a Karachi or Delhi *dar al-
'ulum* to complete the study of prophetic traditions. Many students
from Bury after completing their curriculum go on to further
studies at Azhar in Egypt or Medina University in Saudi Arabia
to study Arabic; Hadith, Prophetic tradition; or *fiqh*, the science
of Islamic jurisprudence. The priority for Bury is education, and
the seminary is part of a larger world of Islamic scholarship than
Dewsbury.

The focus here will be on the ethos and curriculum of the
private boys' school. The content of the *'alim* course will be
considered in the next chapter. Since the schools of Bury and

Dewsbury are similar, attention will be directed at the latter only. Dewsbury has some 300 students, the majority of whom are from outside Dewsbury and live as boarders. One hundred and forty of these students attend the private school. The priority for most of those attending is the *hifz* class, to learn the Qur'an by heart in Arabic, without at this stage understanding its meaning; for most of those who stay on to complete the *'alim* programme, understanding the Qur'an begins in the third year of their seven-year course of study.

In the three years at the private school they will also learn correct pronunciation of the Qur'an (*tajwid*), develop competence in Urdu and study a basic Urdu text on Islam, entitled *Ta'lim al-Islam*, Lessons in Islam, written by the distinguished Deobandi scholar, Mufti Kifayatullah (d. 1952). Urdu is the medium of instruction for Islamic studies, taught in five morning lessons. Mastery of Urdu is considered of crucial importance. It is the *sine qua non* of transferring to the *'alim* course, since it is the medium of instruction and textbooks are studied in Urdu. When translation of the Qur'an from Arabic is undertaken the language into which it is translated is also Urdu.

Much of the afternoon is devoted to what are described as *duniawi*, worldly, subjects, to conform to the dictates of British law. By 1989 maths, history, English, science, geography, social studies, law and Urdu were time-tabled, of which four were offered to GCSE level: English language, general science, maths and Urdu. The medium of instruction was English, and separate staff taught this curriculum (one Bengali, three Pakistanis, three Gujaratis and one non-Muslim Englishman). All the other staff, with one exception, were Gujaratis, seven teaching *hifz* and ten teaching the *'alim* course. The day is organized around the five daily prayers, which all attend. This can mean a long day: getting up in the summer before 5.00 a.m. and then going back to bed for a couple of hours.

The buildings are new and comfortable, with teaching methods traditional. Most pupils wear traditional South Asian Muslim dress, and sit on the carpeted floor, with a low bench for books. There are no televisions or videos, since they are deemed to trangress the Islamic prohibition against representation of living creatures. Radio is not allowed since it is seen as a possible

distraction from study and the student might be tempted to listen
to music, frowned on within the Deobandi tradition.

What seems evident is that the students, in the morning and
afternoon, live in two unrelated linguistic and cultural worlds.
There seems to be neither co-ordination nor consultation between
the staff who teach the *duniawi* syllabus in English in the afternoon and those who teach the Arabic/Islamic course in the
morning through the medium of Urdu.[44] An example may illustrate this: in the morning they will study *Lessons from Islam*, in
Urdu, by Mufti Kifayatullah and read about the miracles wrought
by the Prophet, including 'splitting the moon', based on sura 54:1
of the Qur'an. This is interpreted literally.[45] In the afternoon
they will study general science in English. A possible discordance
between these two worlds is neither acknowledged nor addressed.

The methods of teaching remain heavily influenced by the
traditional oral emphasis of Islamic studies. This was picked up
in an HMI report on the school in 1985, which remarked, that,
'Arabic and Islamic studies are tested orally ... many lessons take
the form of exposition by one teacher of subject matter from a
textbook. Pupils are encouraged to understand but not usually to
question or discuss critically.'[46]

The traditional method of teaching, practised at Bury and
Dewsbury, is for the student to master a series of set texts. Thus
a group studying a selection of Prophetic traditions from the
famous twelfth-century collection known as *Mishkat* will in turn
read out aloud the Hadith in Arabic, then translate it into Urdu.
The teacher will correct the Arabic or the Urdu translation, where
incorrect, and give his interpretation of its meaning. This latter
will be taken as normative and when the students are examined,
orally or in writing, the teacher's interpretation will be reproduced. The emphasis is on mastering a given corpus of works
and reproducing accredited interpretation rather than engaging
in individual speculation. This was not understood by the HMIs,
who worried about the absence of individual expression evident
in the centre, whether the absence of 'individual lockers ... posters or decoration of any sort ... [or guidance for] imaginative
and personal writing ... [and argued for] the value of allowing
boys more independence'.[47]

The impact of Bury and Dewsbury on the Deobandi mosques

of Bradford is multifaceted. Mufti Kifayatullah's *Lessons from Islam*, in English and Urdu, remains the favoured Islamic textbook in supplementary schools. A new generation of English-speaking *'ulama*, products of the two seminaries, suggest that this will continue to be the case – the two *'ulama* trained by these centres now working in Bradford both use this textbook. Even more significant for understanding the ethos of Bury and Dewsbury is the importance each attaches to daily public readings from Maulana Zakariya's *Tablighi Nisab*, the Preaching Course – the set text of Tablighi Jama'at – in the religious formation of all students. If for many of the Barelwi mosques the recitation of the devotional *salaam* at the end of Friday prayers offers a unique window into their ethos and priorities, for many of the Deobandi mosques in Bradford the equivalent text is *Tablighi Nisab*. This work is daily recited in most of the mosques for between ten and twenty minutes after the afternoon prayer of *'asr*.

Tablighi Nisab is largely a compilation of Qur'anic verses and Hadith belonging to the genre of *faza'il*, merit/blessing literature, as distinct from *masa'il*, problem literature, which concerns itself with the application of Islamic law in society – the preserve of the trained *'alim*. This compendium includes the booklets of Maulana Zakariya and begins with 'Stories of the [Prophet's] companions' (1938), 'Blessings of the Qur'an' (1929), 'Blessings of [the five daily] prayers' (1939), 'Blessings of zikr' (1939), 'Blessings of tabligh' (1931) and a book by Maulana Ihtesam al Hasan Kandhalwi (d. 1944) *Muslim Degeneration and its only Remedy*.

The tone and content are earnest and eschatological. The first chapter of book one is entitled, 'Steadfastness in the face of hardship', and begins by rehearsing the suffering and abuse the Prophet encountered in Ta'if as he sought to engage in preaching. The episode ends with the exhortation:

> We get so ... irritated over a little trouble or a mere abuse ... does [this] become the people who claim to follow the magnanimous prophet ... [who] after so much suffering at the hand of the Taif mob ... neither curses them nor ... works for any revenge, even when he has the full opportunity to do so?[48]

The second chapter – 'Fear of Allah' – includes a sub-section, 'the prophet reprimands the Sahabah's [his companions'] laughing'. Chapter three is entitled 'Abstinence and self-denial of the Sahaba'; chapter six, 'Sympathy and self-sacrifice'; chapter nine is 'Pleasing the Prophet'; and chapter twelve, 'Love for the Prophet'. The importance of prayer, obligatory and superogatory, is stressed: it is 'the first and foremost item to be reckoned with on the Day of Judgment' and remembrance of God, *zikr*, is considered superior even to giving in charity.[49]

Kandhalwi's booklet, although written in 1938, continues to resonate with Muslim minorities in the West. Kandhalwi worried that,

> The Muslim youth ... affected and influenced by the so-called modern trends or the Western way of life, take pleasure in laughing at the very ideals of Islam and openly criticize the sacred code of Shariat as being out of date and impractical ... we seem to possess a hidden inferiority complex towards our religion and faith.[50]

The answer he offered was to reaffirm the 'wisdom and guidance' of the Qur'an, to seek to conform one's life to Islamic law, 'the path of true success and righteousness', and not to worry about the absence of state power.[51] Further, and this was the central innovation of the movement, was an insistence that preaching was not simply the task of the religious professionals. 'The first and foremost thing to do is to change the aim of our life from material motives and acquisition of wealth to the propagation of ... Islam.' In pursuit of this, controversy was to be avoided, *tabligh* to be engaged in, and leisure spent either in reading good books or in the company of pious and learned companions.[52]

It would be wrong to suggest that these pietist and politically quietist notes are the only ones heard in Bradford's Deobandi mosques. The JUB, the umbrella organization for Deobandi *'ulama* in Britain, to which at least half the Bradford mosques are affiliated, has a more active and combative stance on certain issues.[53] The priorities of the JUB are listed in its 1987 calendar: to press for the acceptance by Parliament of Muslim family law; the establishment of separate Muslim girls' schools as an immediate priority and 'the elimination of the evil Qadiani beliefs, shirk and bid'at' (Qadiani refers to the Ahmadiyya sect).

JUB organizes conferences, regional and national, on the Life of the Prophet – hosted in Bradford by the Bangladeshi Twaqulia mosque in 1988 and the Gujarati St. Margaret's Road mosque in 1989; gives seminars on the practice and meaning of pilgrimage and Ramadan; produces posters and calendars, and has developed a network of trained *muftis*, able to answer questions about the application of Islamic law. In the autumn of 1989 they organized at Birmingham Central Mosque the fourth international 'Tauheed and Sunnah' conference on the topic of jihad: the imam of the prestigious Haram Sharif mosque in Mecca attended and speakers were invited from South Africa, Pakistan, India, Azad Kashmir and Afghanistan, to talk about the Islamic movements and their struggles in these countries. The posters of the JUB, often in English and Urdu versions, adorn many of the Deobandi mosques: the three in evidence in Bradford in 1989 were 'Ramadan – do's and don'ts', 'The heretic beliefs of Shias' and 'The ugly face of Qadyanism'.

The passion and vehemence which continue to inform sectarian differences can be seen very clearly with regard to Deobandi attitudes to Shi'ites and Ahmadiyyas. The traditional reasons for antipathy to Shi'ite Muslims are clearly laid out in a book entitled *Khomeini, Iranian Revolution and the Shi'ite Faith* by a leading Deobandi scholar Maulana Nomani (b. 1905).[54] The work includes an introduction by another distinguished Indian scholar, Syed Abul Hasan Ali Nadwi (b. 1914) – both active supporters of Tablighi Jama'at.[55]

The reasons given for such a study, originally in Urdu and translated into English to maximize its circulation, are illuminating: 'the importance of beliefs is declining dangerously in the eyes of our new generation'. Instead of evaluating Muslims by reference to the Qur'an and Sunna, criteria for praise or blame turn rather on 'the establishment of a government in the name of Islam, acquisition of power and throwing challenges to western powers'; thus Khomeini is eulogized and 'the object of hero-worship ... in the same manner as ... Kamal Ataturk of Turkey and ... Nasser of Egypt'; further, Khomeini's beguiling appeal for different Muslim sects to bury their differences in the name of Muslim unity blinds many to his ambitions to export Shi'ite revolution and to destabilize the Arab countries. Khomeini's writings are cited, indicating his 'perverted assertions and diabolical beliefs', whether elevating the Shi'ite imamate 'to the place of divinity ...

and rank [higher] ... than the Prophets [or] his outrageous condemnation of and vituperation against the Companions'.[56]

The Ahmadiyya movement is usually disparagingly referred to by Muslim critics as 'Qadianis' or 'Mirzais', after the name and birthplace of their founder, Mirza Ghulam Ahmad (d. 1908), a landowner from Qadian in the Punjab. Opposition to them has often destabilized Pakistani politics.[57] The main reason for the anger they arouse is the personal claims made by their founder, which seem to compromise the finality of Muhammad's prophetic status. In Pakistan the movement in opposition to them has been led by the Deobandi 'ulama. In 1984 physical and legal harassment of the movement led to the present leader's flight to Britain, where he established his headquarters.[58] In Bradford the small community has had a centre for worship since 1980.

While the Barelwis met at Wembley in 1985 to criticize the Wahhabis, the Deobandis met in the same place in the same year to organize an annual international conference to condemn the Ahmadiyyas. The vehicle for this opposition, although organizationally separate from the JUB, nonetheless involves their chief officers. The 1988 conference, reported in the British Urdu press, was under the presidency of the JUB vice-president, Maulana Abdul Rahman. This conference rehearsed the litany of observations and demands routinely made at such conferences: 'Qadiani' activities and literature in British schools, universities and colleges, where they continue to 'masquerade as Muslims', should be exposed; the political asylum given to them by West Germany for 'alleged' persecution in Pakistan was regretted; the actions of Pakistan, Saudi Arabia, Egypt, Libya, Iraq and United Emirates declaring them *kafir*, and thus a non-Muslim minority, were applauded; the Pakistan government was requested to remove them from key civilian and military posts, to confiscate their presses and to impose the shari'a punishment against them for apostasy.[59]

Opposition to the Ahmadiyyas in Bradford spilled over into the public domain in 1986. Civic and religious dignitaries had been invited to attend a 'Religious Founders' Day' at the city's central library in September. The theme of the meeting – religious understanding – seemed admirable, as did the publicity by the organizers, the Ahmadiyya Students Association. However, the phrase 'Peace Be Upon Him' – used after the names of Islamic Prophets – had been appended to the names of Ram and Guru Nanak, figures revered in the Hindu and Sikh traditions. This detail plus the Ahmadiyya insistence on organizing the meeting as 'Muslims' enraged many local leaders. Therefore, the Bradford Council for Mosques led a demonstration against the meeting which resulted in its cancellation, and in the ensuing mêlée some 17 protestors were arrested.[60]

Deobandi mosque personnel in 1989 comprised some 19 'ulama and nine huffaz, of whom four and six, respectively, had good English. The higher percentage in the latter category is explained by the success a large mosque like Howard Street has enjoyed in training English-speaking youngsters to complete a course of hifz and to co-opt some of them to continue teaching in the mosques. The fact that the majority of 'ulama are still not confident in English explains why the books used in most Deobandi mosques tend to be in Urdu, even where there is an English translation of the study, as is the case with the Islamic textbook used by almost all the mosques, Lessons in Islam – the same work taught to the students at Dewsbury.

Like the Barelwi textbook, Our Islam, the Deobandi choice reflects their priorities and concerns. There is no mention here of such a category as good innovation, bid'at-e hasana, rather innovation is deemed the gravest sin after unbelief, kufr, and polytheism, shirk. Needless to say traditional Barelwi practices and beliefs are mentioned as falling within all three categories: the claim that the Prophet has 'knowledge of the unseen', asking for the intercession of a sufi, circumambulating the shrines of such a shaikh/pir as one might the Ka'bah at Mecca, constructing elaborate graves for them and decking them out with coverlets and holding fairs at their shrines.[61]

Inevitably, given their date and provenance, such works reflect the world, imagery and problems of a largely pre-industrial, rural India. Thus five pages are devoted to an exploration of what renders water in a well unclean and therefore not usable for ritual ablutions. While some of the mosques use the same Urdu textbooks that are used in the Barelwi mosques and produced in Pakistan, others use those produced by Bradford local education authority, supplied by a supplementary schools officer, in an attempt to harmonize mosque and school Urdu lessons; others, again, produce their own worksheets, without illustrations.

What is also evident is that some of the larger mosques are beginning to build up a lending library of books in English for the children. These are mainly produced by The Islamic Foundation in Leicester, whose publications will be considered in the next section, where the focus is the Jama'at-i Islami tradition. There is no equivalent magazine in English/Urdu to the Barelwi *Islamic Times* to act as a forum for addressing problems in Britain within a Deobandi perspective. Such scarce resources as are available have been allocated to funding a full-time specialist in Islamic law. In 1988 a Gujarati, Mufti Ismail Kachholvi, was appointed in Bradford to run an Institute of Islamic Jurisprudence UK – his activities complement the labours of two other local muftis who also teach at the Dewsbury and Bury seminaries.

Another pressing priority identified by the JUB – the provision of separate education for women – has also begun to be addressed. The Howard Street mosque manages the small private Muslim Girls' Community School, which they set up in September 1984. Virtually all the girls come from the Pathan/Chhachhi communities. The school's intake used to be about 70, but was halved in the autumn of 1989 when the fees were raised from £450 to £700 per annum.

A parallel initiative was the creation in September 1987 by the Bury *dar al-'ulum* of a boarding school and teaching block for girls – the Madinat al-'Ulum al-Islamiya – at Shenstone, Kidderminster. It takes girls from 11 years old, who, in tandem with a British school curriculum, can enter the five-year course of training to qualify as an *'alima*, and thus teach girls and women Islam. Once again the contribution of the Gujarati community is paramount. All ten female staff in 1990 were Gujaratis who taught on a voluntary basis – one of whom was from Bradford. The school transferred to Bradford in the autumn of 1992, where an old hospital building was bought for £500,000 – negotiations with the local authority were conducted on behalf of Bury by Sher Azam, the ex-president of the Bradford Council for Mosques.[62] The move was made for a number of reasons, not least the advantage of having the school in an authority sympathetic to Muslim concerns, and also located much nearer Bury, which would be able to supervise it more closely; such scrutiny was necessary after a very critical HMI report in 1991, which attracted considerable adverse national publicity.[63]

Only two Deobandi mosques have separate prayer facilities for women. This is in line with their traditional perception that women are better advised to pray at home and are not obliged to join in Friday congregational prayers. Thus the influential, detailed textbook on prescribed Islamic behaviour written by Maulana Thanawi, *Bihishti Zewar* (Heavenly Ornaments) repeats the prophetic tradition that 'the best mosque for women is the inner part of the house.'[64] This was also the position of Sher Azam in an interview given to a national newspaper, where he reiterated another prophetic tradition to the effect that 'the reward for women is 27 times greater if they pray at home and 27 times greater if men pray at the mosque.'[65]

Traditional Muslim scholarship is convinced that the woman's place is at home, where she is in less danger of transgressing Islamic norms by finding herself in the company of non-related males. That such a perspective is widely shared is evident from a resolution passed in a national conference of Muslims held in Bradford and organized by the Bradford Council for Mosques. The resolution sought 'exemption from the community charge for those single Muslim women who choose not to register for welfare benefits/employment *for religious reasons* and who ... are wholly dependent on parents'.[66]

The Deobandi tradition, heavily influenced by the ethos of Tablighi Jama'at, with its prohibition of television and video, music and dance, its sobriety and seriousness, is not sympathetic to youth work outside revivalist activities. The only exception in Bradford is the East African Gujarati Muslim caste association, the Khalifa society. As well as their two centres in Bradford, they are networked through the Federation of Gujarati Muslim Khalifa Societies of UK to centres in 12 other cities in the country. The federation arranges caste marriages, has national football and cricket tournaments, limits the size of marriage dowry and has developed arbitration mechanisms for disputes in the community. Its two centres in Bradford have a range of recreational and cultural activities for both sexes.

The UK Islamic Mission and the Struggle to Establish a Viable Youth Movement in Bradford

The main bearer of the Jama'at-i Islami tradition in Britain has been the UK Islamic Mission. A review of the mission's history and diverse activities, celebrated at its twenty-fifth annual conference held in Manchester in August 1988, offers a useful window into its achievements and priorities. It began in 1963 with a group of students and young professionals mainly from Pakistan. Their first conference in 1964 was addressed by the Indian scholar Abul Hasan Nadvi, who urged the importance of *da'wa* – invitation to Islam – and creating a Muslim identity; in 1965 one of two guests at their conference was Professor Khurshid Ahmad, one of Maulana Maududi's trusted lieutenants.

Also in 1965 they invited Maulana Alvi from Pakistan to give leadership to the young group – he became director of the UK Islamic Mission. The dependence on Jama'at-i Islami personnel from South Asia is a constant in the history of the mission and related groups in Britain. With the personnel came their 'ideology', the very term ideology used of Islam is central to the Islamist tradition with its activist thrust and comprehensive ambitions. Thus the first sentence in a brochure introducing the mission's work reads:

> The UK Islamic Mission is an ideological movement. It stands for the establishment of the will of Allah in the life of the individual as well as society. Islam is a faith and a way of life, a world view and a socio-political order ... a complete and all embracing order of life based on the unity of God.

In his presidential address to the twenty-fifty annual conference Maulana Ahmed insisted that whether in Europe, America or other non-Muslim countries: 'If the Muslim settlers ... want to safeguard their progeny, property, businesses ... the only way, safe and certain, is to convert the indigenous population to [a] Muslim majority.'[67]

A priority of the mission from the start was the identification of young leadership, their education and the provision of appropriate literature in English. Thus in 1965 it decided to offer '10 scholarships per year ... to outstanding students engaged in

Islamic movements', which within a decade would produce a nucleus of committed young people prepared to work for the establishment of an Islamic way of life in the *dar al-kufr*, house of unbelief.[68] With money from King Fahd of Saudi Arabia in 1967 they established, in co-operation with the Federation of Student Islamic Societies (FOSIS), a students' hostel.

The mission was also instrumental in the creation of several important institutions: the first chairman of the Muslim Educational Trust (MET), set up in 1966, was a member of the mission. MET produces Muslim literature in English and personnel to teach Islam in schools. Its textbook *Islam: Beliefs and Teachings*, written by Ghulam Sarwar in 1980, has been repeatedly revised and reprinted, and had sold more than 100,000 copies by 1992. It is in use in the two mosques in the Jama'at-i Islami tradition in Bradford.

Islam: Beliefs and Teachings inhabits a different world from either of the Deobandi or Barelwi textbooks considered earlier. Sufis and sufism do not feature in the index; mention of *zikr* or any other devotional exercise is conspicuous by its absence; the *mi'raj* is the only miraculous event allowed in the life of the Prophet.[69] Instead we have chapters devoted to the economic and political systems of Islam – this firmly locates Ghulam Sarwar within the Jama'at-i Islami tradition.[70] There is also material on women, including a discussion of the issue of polygamy, since 'the fact that a few Muslims have more than one wife has become a matter for propaganda against Islam.'[71] This, then, is a textbook written in English, self-consciously apologetic in content and tone, seeking to address some of the questions and anxieties of Muslims in Britain.

The mission also produced an Urdu monthly *Paigham* – The Message – and in the 1970s was active in the establishment of *Impact International*, a monthly magazine in English which continues to cover developments within the Islamist movement worldwide. The mission claimed that the Islamic Foundation, established in 1973, owed its inspiration to their members. The Islamic Foundation is the publishing and research wing of Jama'at-i Islami in Britain. Two of Maulana Maududi's most trusted supporters are involved in it: the chairman of the foundation is Professor Khurshid Ahmad and Khurram Murad was its director in the period 1978–86. Among the established Pakistani leadership these were 'the only two well known Jama'at leaders ... known to have had a foreign education'.[72] Murad studied engineering and Ahmad economics at the University in Leicester, the town where the Islamic Foundation is located.

The foundation has a huge multilingual publishing business. Its English publications include many of Maulana Maududi's works in translation, as well as studies by Khurshid Ahmad, Khurram Murad and others. Its new centre was established at Markfield in Leicester in 1989. Set amidst '9.3 acres ... with a network of buildings, capable of housing all the research, educational, training and youth activities ... [it] is bracing itself to play its part in leading the Muslim communities of the UK and Europe to face the challenges of the 1990s and the approaching 21st century.'[73] It has an audio-visual unit, which has produced innumerable audio cassettes of stories for children based on the foundation's books, video cassettes on the Prophet's life and *da'wa* in the West, a cassette-slide programme introducing Islam and an audio-cassette course on *'ilm al-tajwid*, the science of reading the Qur'an. The foundation is also the home of Young Muslims UK, the youth movement in the Jama'at-i Islami tradition, and their present glossy magazine, *Trends*. Farooq Murad, the son of Khurram Murad, was the national leader of Young Muslims UK in 1988.

The UK Islamic Mission took pride in the 3,000-plus children it had taught in its 38 branches, which include 22 mosques and Islamic centres nationally, and in the 300 non-Muslims of various nationalities who had embraced Islam through their labours in the previous 25 years. The mission also derived satisfaction from 'the systematic work carried out by the Young Muslims [which] gives fresh hopes and opens new avenues ... among youth ... in 17 cities'.[74] Young Muslims UK is linked constitutionally to the mission: the latter's executive appoints an adviser to the Young Muslims and the UK Islamic Mission's president and central council can remove the president and disband the central council of Young Muslims for grave violations of their constitution.[75]

In 1977–8 the mission conceded to the request of its Bangladeshi members to be allowed to form a separate organization, Dawat al-Islam, to promote work among that community.[76] As one would expect there is considerable overlap in membership of the Islamic Foundation, UK Islamic Mission, Dawat al-Islam and Young Muslims UK. One researcher has estimated that in 1987/8, excluding Khurram Murad and Khurshid Ahmad, of the 12 members of staff of the Islamic Foundation, 5 were members of the mission and 2, including the acting director-general, were members of Dawat al-Islam.[77] The executive committee in 1987–8 of the National Association of Muslim Youth (NAMY) – another initiative in the Jama'at-i Islami tradition, founded in the early 1980s with DES funding – included Farooq Murad as chairman, the national leader of Young Muslims; Dr Munir Ahmed as general-secretary, the *amir* of the Bradford branch of Young Muslims; Ataullah Siddiqui, the mission's adviser to the Young Muslims and member of the foundation; and a bevy of other Young Muslims. This indicates the importance those in the Jama'at-i Islami tradition attach to youth work in Britain.

The career trajectory of another activist, Mashuq Ally, illustrates the priorities and ethos of the Jama'at-i Islami tradition in Britain. He was an active member of the Islamic Youth Movement (IYM) – founded in Bradford and the predecessor to the Young Muslims UK in the 1970s – and on the editorial board of *The Movement*, the IYM magazine, which prefigured *Trends*. He was later involved with the Islamic Foundation, did research at the Centre for the Study of Islam and Christian–Muslim relations, Selly Oak College, Birmingham, became a vice-president of UK Islamic Mission and then course superviser of a joint honours degree in Islamic Studies at St David's University College, Lampeter. He featured in *Trends* as a member of the Islamic Studies faculty.[78] Certainly Mr Ally's promotion from youth movement to UK Islamic Mission executive and thence to a career in education, where he is able to present a sympathetic Islamist perspective, is a route which the mission envisaged many ex-members of the IYM/Young Muslims would follow. This expectation, however, proved difficult to realize in Bradford.

In South Asia, Jama'at-i Islami has drawn the bulk of its supporters from the products of modernization, teachers, lawyers and engineers, amongst whom Maududi's scathing criticism of the ignorance and obscurantism of many of the *'ulama* struck a resonant chord. Since most of the Muslim settlers in Bradford were of

rural origin, they provided little in the way of a natural
constituency for UK Islamic Mission, people 'for whom [its]
ideological rigour and studied rejection of Western ideas [was]
attractive and popular'.[79] Thus, although a circle was established
as early as 1968 and ran classes for children in the 1970s from 17
Marlborough Road, the first UK Islamic Mission mosque in Bradford had to wait until 1981, to be followed in 1985 by another
organized by the Bangladeshi Dawat al-Islam.

The Bangladeshi mosque is the larger. It caters for some
hundred male worshippers on a Friday, of whom approximately
40 per cent are Pakistani. It has three full-time Bangladeshi *'ulama*,
one of whom studied in Medina University in Saudi Arabia and
is funded by a Saudi *da'wa* organization. The mosque has its own
separate youth group for boys and some recreational facilities.
The UK Islamic Mission draws on a smaller, largely Mirpuri,
constituency and has had constant difficulties finding a permanent *'alim*, having had four up to 1988. Their present *'alim* is a
well-educated product of the Jama'at-i Islami seminary in Lahore.
Unfortunately, he has little English and thus has limited access to
the rich vein of materials in English produced by the Islamic
Foundation. The situation has not been helped by the failure of
the UK Islamic Mission to sustain a viable Islamic seminary: an
abortive attempt was made in Manchester in 1985, but it had to
be closed in 1987.

The situation with regard to youth work has proved more prom-
ising. In 1971 the Muslim Educational Trust (MET), seconded a
Pakistani member of Jama'at-i Islami, Ahmad Jamal, to study in
Bradford and to begin part-time youth work and Islamic teaching
in schools. By July 1972 the local education authority yielded to
MET pressure and allowed Muslims to give religious instruction
in the city's secondary schools after school hours.[80] Through the
schools Ahmad Jamal recruited a core group to form a youth
movement. The Islamic Youth Movement was born and liaised
with other groups in the country. The Bradford group held weekly
study circles, imbibed the works of Maulana Maududi and other
Islamist activists like Syed Qutb, networked with other groups in
the country, enjoyed national camps in the Lake District, and in
1976 started their quarterly magazine, *The Movement*.

To read excerpts from *The Movement* is to find oneself in the familar Islamist world of discourse. Relationship with Allah, it is stressed, is not a process which,

> confines our lives to the mosque and isolates us from the society at large ... [nor] demands that we live a life of passiveness and timidity, but on the contrary it fosters an attitude of greater concern for the society and mankind so that it may be saved from the fire of hell ... *zikr*/remembrance of Allah ... need not ... of course be done in a traditional way ... in its simplest form it involves the carrying out of every act in Allah's name and thus to remind oneself whether the particular act will please or displease Allah.[81]

Thus the group cleverly co-opts *zikr*, a word heavily freighted with devotional meanings within traditional Islam, to serve an activist end.

In another article, entitled 'Muslim youth and cultural dilemma', several themes are enunciated which were to be repeated during the next 15 years:

> The increase in the number of Muslim youth running away ... [is rooted in] the stubborn and often senseless rituals ... carried out in the name of Islam ... Muslim youth ... fail to see ... why 'drainpipes' are better than flares ... [they are exposed to] meaningless Arabic lessons under tortuous maulvis ... The challenge of the host community, which stands for free thought and takes pride in democracy, does not allow the Muslim youth to blindly follow rituals which is not Islam. It demands an explanation or it imposes a sense of inferiority and cultural backwardness which ultimately suggests assimilation ... The existing Muslim community does not represent Islam ... think of the [Hindu-influenced] exuberant marriage social ceremony in a Muslim home and a host of other social customs ... Islam [does not] ask for any specific style of trousers – Islam simply wants certain parts of the body to be covered.[82]

Unquestioning obedience to an *'alim*, learning the Qur'an off by heart – the stuff of oral culture – are no longer acceptable to these literate and able young men, exposed to the challenge of a questioning and confident culture. IYM gave them space to retain pride in their Islamic identity, while able to distance themselves from and critique aspects of Pakistani culture in the name of Islam. Most came from Deobandi and Barelwi backgrounds and were attracted to an Islam which was intelligible, accessible through English and gave them a feeling of being part of a worldwide Islamist movement, which in God's time would prevail over a Godless West.

However, by the end of the 1970s the Islamic Youth Movement was almost moribund in Bradford. Far from providing the next generation of leadership for UK Islamic Mission, three of the four key activists who had remained in Bradford – including the national president and general-secretary of the movement – never joined the mission, and the one who did eventually left. All four still speak warmly of the IYM. In retrospect, they continue to value the confidence and organizational skills it encouraged them to develop, and the movement's aspiration to relate Islam to society at large. Nonetheless, the reasons for their leaving the Islamic Youth Movement and distancing themselves from UK Islamic Mission are instructive. The rhetoric of an Islamic state, on which they were nourished, while within the realm of practical politics where Muslims are in a majority, began to pall when the Jama'at-i Islami tradition was but one small component of a Muslim minority in Britain. The movement was seen as elitist and dismissive of the traditional world and values of their parents, and could cause divisions in the family.

They also began to notice that Jama'at-i Islami, while rejecting as unIslamic the uncritical devotion of a *murid* to a shaikh/*pir*, was in danger, paradoxically, of elevating the person and works of Maulana Maududi to a similar status. Yet Maulana Maududi's scholarship was open to question.[83] By the late 1970s Bradford members of IYM were expressing some disillusionment with the parent body in Pakistan. With the overthrow of Pakistan's Prime Minister, Zulfiqar Bhutto, in 1977, Jama'at-i Islami had thrown in their lot with General Zia's unelected military regime. One commentator noticed that under General Zia the leadership of Jama'at-i Islami

> passed into non-ideological hands and it became extremely thuggish with university branches becoming gun-toting fascist paramilitary organizations ... [enjoying] government patronage ... [it] moved from religious radicalism to become an arch-conservative religious legitimiser of a military dictatorship.[84]

The endless struggle in the way of God, jihad, while at times exhilarating, at other times could seem exhausting, joyless and emotionally arid. Three of the group admit now to enjoying the more emotional world of the *qawwali* and two are back in a Barelwi tradition. Also, any youth movement without paid workers – by the late 1970s the last of the three South Asian personnel seconded to this work had left – leaves a huge burden on its young leaders, who eventually leave for university and start working.

It remains to be seen whether the Young Muslims UK can avoid some of these pitfalls. It formally came into being in Bradford in the autumn of 1984, the successor to the defunct IYM. It has been fortunate to enjoy the services of a dedicated local GP, Dr Munir Ahmed, and of his wife, who organizes the meetings for the 'sisters'. This latter is an innovation, since attempts in the 1970s to get such a group off the ground failed. Young Muslims UK holds an annual camp for males and females. Over 1,000 attended the one in 1988 at Wolverhampton, with a packed programme from a Wednesday evening to Sunday afternoon.

Its new magazine, *Trends*, is attractively laid out, professionally produced and contains an excellent 'agony aunt' section, where youngsters can raise any issue which worries or perplexes them. The questions range from masturbation, the Islamic position on watching television, girl friends, Western clothes, religious freedom, women's rights, divorce, polygamy and contraception. With regard to contraception, Dr Jamal Badawi distances himself from Maulana Maududi's strictures against it and argues for situations where it is not *haram* (forbidden by Isalamic law), e.g. if man and wife are students and want to attend to their studies.[85] This example indicates that some questioning of Maulana Maududi's legacy is beginning to be possible.

In 1989 in Bradford Young Muslims UK had three male groups and two female groups, meeting in local community centres and at the UK Islamic Mission mosque, each of which attracted between 15 and 25 people. Their gatherings combine recreation with study. One local leader wryly remarked to me that the rhetoric of Islamic state notwithstanding, the main focus of the local groups was to keep Islam alive for youngsters as a living option, for which good reasons could be advanced. Also, the aim was to create an environment in which questions could be asked and aspects of received Indo-Pakistani culture, such as excessive self-display, expensive gifts and Hindu customs at weddings, could be challenged.

In Bradford in the late 1980s Young Muslims UK began to distance themselves from the UKIM mosque so as to develop a more independent public persona. Their library of books, pamphlets and videos was moved to another address, and many began to pray at the mosque in the city intended for college and university students. This was, in sectarian terms, a neutral place, and the language spoken was English, more congenial to many of the Young Muslims. One factor behind the move was the failure of Dr Munir Ahmed to feel at home in the UK Islamic Mission mosque. In 1986 Dr Munir Ahmed and a Pakistani Jama'at-i Islami friend had been given UK Islamic Mission membership and authority in the local mosque. In the event, the cultural and linguistic gap proved too great: many in the congregation were not ready for the address at Friday prayers to be in English; they resented the equality assumed by these educated young men with their elders, and they were not enamoured of the Western dress worn by them.

Perhaps it is not surprising that a sense of being a beleaguered minority under attack runs through Young Muslims UK publications. In 1986 Khurram Murad wrote an essay, which is part of their required reading, entitled, 'Muslim Youth in the West: towards a new educational strategy', in which he asked rhetorically, 'Should ... we accept to live as a grudgingly accepted minority sub-culture, always under siege, always struggling to retain the little niche it has been allowed to carve out for itself? That perhaps is the destiny to which most of us seem resigned.'[86] Khurram Murad's answer was to argue for the creation of a 'potent counter-culture'. To aim merely to survive was not enough, since 'a tiny cultural island in a vast alien sea, constantly under siege by high and mighty waves, can hardly hope to escape intrusion and encroachment.'[87]

The dilemma facing Young Muslims is that it is questionable whether the Jama'at-i Islami tradition has at present developed the intellectual resources for living creatively and with good conscience with minority status and relative powerlessness in a pluralist state. The central preoccupation of the Islamist movement worldwide has been to capture power and translate the Islamic ideology into practice. The emphases have been activist rather than reflective and intellectual. This ambivalence runs throughout Young Muslim literature: thus in a moving editorial in a 1991 issue of *Trends*, reviewing the tragedies which had overwhelmed the Islamic world, whether the Gulf crisis, the plight of the Kurds or the atrocities being committed in Kashmir, Mahmud al Rashid, the editor, remarked that, 'The Muslims today are full of anger and many have lost even the ability to dream of better times ahead. But worst of all some of us blame Islam for our troubles. And some even harbour a feeling that just being a Muslim is a curse – something to be hidden or played down.'[88]

Rashid returns to the example of the Prophet at Ta'if – the same episode which features so prominently in the Tablighi Jama'at compendium of traditions – where he was mocked and humiliated but did not lose hope. Yet in the same issue of *Trends* there is a full-blooded reiteration of the principles of the Islamist movement: 'we want ... in every region ... a government of Allah, and we should enforce the Shariah of Allah ... We are an organisation of Truth, Power and Freedom.'[89]

By 1991 many of its energetic leaders in Bradford had moved on and there was a lull in activities. Such continuity as the Young Muslims had enjoyed in the city was largely due to the devoted work of Dr Munir Ahmed, but by 1992 he was over 30 years old and the Young Muslims could not rely on him indefinitely to fulfil such a role. Until the movement acquires some paid workers, institutional continuity will remain precarious locally. Further, the dilemma for the ex-members, namely where they might feel at home when they graduate from the youth movement, has not been resolved. UK Islamic Mission is not apparently attrac-

Table 4.1 The Response of Different Islamic Traditions to the Needs of Young British Muslims

	Barelwi	*Deobandi*	*Jama'at-i Islami*
English materials			+
Local seminaries		+	
Youth work	+		+
Use of electronic media	+		+

tive for activists like Dr Ahmed. It remain to be seen whether an initiative launched in 1990 in Leicester will address this need. In June 1990 the Islamic Society of Britain was formally inaugurated by members of UKIM and ex-members of Young Muslims UK, including Mashuq Ally and Farooq Murad. This society seeks to embody 'a more creative and imaginative outlook ... [raising] the consciousness of Muslims about their Islamic contribution to British society'.[90]

Retrospect and Prospect

The three main traditions of Islamic expression reproduced in Bradford, the Barelwi, Deobandi/Tablighi Jama'at and Jama'at-i Islami, each exhibits strengths and weaknesses when measured against the checklist of four questions posed at the beginning of this chapter. This can be clearly expressed in tabular form (see Table 4.1). These questions sought to identify some of the challenges Islamic traditions faced if they were to connect with the linguistic and cultural world of Muslims born and educated in Bradford. These same issues will be considered more explicitly from the perspective of young Muslims themselves in Chapter 7.

What is evident is that all three Islamic traditions maintain strong links with their parent organizations in South Asia. In the case of the two Deobandi seminaries their curriculum and ethos unmistakably bear this South Asian impress. While Young Muslims UK are self-consciously Western in dress and unashamedly modern in their use of the electronic media, their Islamic ideology owes more to Pakistan than Britain. The Barelwi tradition, while hospitable to change, is largely frustrated in giving it institutional expression by shortage of funds and personal rivalries carried over from South Asia.

As yet there is no clear answer to two other important questions facing all three traditions. The first is the extent to which some questioning of the traditions will be tolerated, as their relevance for Muslims in the West is scrutinized. The next chapter will seek to shed some light on this. The second question is the extent to which sectarian differences can be managed, so enabling Muslims to co-operate in tackling the new issues they all face in Britain. Chapter 6 explores this issue.

5

The *'Ulama*: The Making and Influence of a British Muslim Leadership

No group of contemporary Muslims is less understood by non-Muslims than the *'ulama*, a generic category covering scholars and religious functionaries of Islam. Those familiar with Western religious history assume that they can de described simply as Muslim 'priests'. Others, aware of the considerable influence exercised by the Iranian religious leader, the Ayatollah Khomeini, invest them all with exaggerated influence. This is to ignore the very different role and status enjoyed by Shi'ite religious leaders in Iran compared to Sunni *'ulama* in South Asia.[1]

The Sunni *'ulama* do not enjoy a good press in South Asia. Islamists and modernists alike have sought to bypass them and their institutions, blaming them for projecting a fossilized image of Islam which does not connect with the concerns of the modern world. A Pakistani anthropologist, after 'lengthy and intimate discussions' with the *'ulama*, concluded that for them 'the outside world simply does not exist. The works of Marx or Weber are unknown'.[2] Members of the revivalist Tablighi Jama'at pay them formal respect but insist that every Muslim has a responsibilty for 'enjoining what is right and forbidding what is wrong' (sura 3:104) – the Qur'anic rationale for preaching, *tabligh* – and challenge the view that *'tabligh* is the sole and special responsibility of the "ulema"'.[3]

Muslims touched by sufism often dismiss them as pedants concerned with the mere externals of Islam, an unflattering assessment with a long history in South Asia. Thus Dara Shikoh, a seventeenth-century sufi and poet, and heir apparent of the Mughal Empire, could write, 'Paradise is there, where there is no *molla.*' In the true mystical spirit, he emphasized immediate experience as contrasted with blind imitation.[4]

One of the founders of the seminary in Deoband in 1867, Maulana Nanautawi, in trying to hold together a reformed sufism and traditional scholarly disciplines, lamented that 'among the Sufis I have the stain of *maulawiyyat*' – maulvi-itis.[5] In the new and challenging environment of Britain these accusations are repeated by a generation of educated and English-speaking Muslims. Shabbir Akhtar, a member of the Bradford Council for Mosques from 1988 to 1990, observed that, 'traditional Islam is in sorry decline; many in the educated classes are repelled by it. By refusing to address the problems that plague the modern mind ... Islam is gradually losing control ... over the daily life of secularised believers.'[6]

An Indian Barelwi imam, resident in Britain for some 15 years, recently provided an insider's perspective on his fellow imams active in Britain. He painted a bleak picture:

The majority ... lack a thorough knowledge of Islam. Their knowledge is limited to the sectarian parameters ... [they] do not know anything about the context in which they are resident. They can neither speak the English language nor are they acquainted with the socio-political context of the dominating British culture ... [the imam] is dogmatic or does not know how to reason.[7]

This chapter will review the functions of the Sunni *'ulama*; explore the economic and contractual insecurity with which many have to live; identify the difficulties for those trained in South Asia to feel at ease in the very different linguistic and cultural environment of Britain, even if they know English; consider the curriculum studied in the *dar al-'ulum*, both in South Asia and Bury; and, finally, ask why their activities in the supplementary schools remain a cause of concern for many Muslims. This will enable us to evaluate some of the accusations levelled against the *'ulama* and contribute to understanding their continuing role in the education and religious formation of local Muslims.

The World of the Imam and Mufti

The term *'ulama* is the plural of the Arabic noun, *'alim*, which means a learned man. The term is used today in a specialist sense, denoting scholars of religious knowledge who have completed an accredited course of study in an Islamic seminary, *dar al-'ulum*. The category of *'ulama* comprises a variety of religious practitioners, ranging from the imam – prayer leader in a mosque – to such specialists as the mufti, an expert in Islamic law, able to give an advisory decision, fatwa, on a range of questions put to him. An *'alim* will be variously referred to in South Asia and Bradford as a *mulla*, *maulvi*, *maulana* or *'allama*, in an ascending scale of respect.[8]

This section will rehearse the roles of six local *'ulama*, which illustrate the variety of tasks they fulfil and the extent to which some have a public role outside the mosque, an issue also addressed in Chapter 6, where their circumscribed role in the Bradford Council for Mosques is reviewed. The six men chosen include a father and son. This should enable us to compare the continuities and discontinuities in attitudes and perspectives of an *'alim* educated in Britain with an *'alim* educated in Pakistan. Two others are muftis, important figures who have remained largely invisible in studies on Muslim communities in Britain.

'Allama Nishtar, the imam of a large Barelwi mosque, already referred to in the previous chapter, is not only a certificated *'alim* but also has an MA in Arabic from the Punjab University, Pakistan. He has lived in Bradford for some 20 years, has a good command of English, has taught in local schools and colleges, is much respected in the community and enjoys a commanding position in a mosque, whose committee he selected. He has overall responsibilty for teaching about 150 children and he himself teaches a group of girls Arabic GCSE in the mosque through the medium of English.

To help him in his teaching responsibility he has a full-time assistant, a Mirpuri *'alim*, and four part-time teachers, one a local liaison teacher with an MA in Arabic from the Punjab University. 'Allama Nishtar has also fronted the efforts to raise money for a new purpose-built mosque, not far from that being built by Pir Maroof's association. The foundation stone was laid in November

1982. Some 12 years later it is almost complete, costing about £1 million and drawing extensively on the generosity and voluntary labour of many of his congregation.

He is a member of the Imams and Mosques Council of Great Britain – one of two umbrella organizations set up in London in 1984, largely reflecting the Barelwi/Wahhabi divide – and a local consultant for them in Islamic law.[9] Those who worship in the Bradford mosque comprise people from Mirpur, Gujar Khan and Chhachh, the majority of whom have little formal education. 'Allama Nishtar worries that most parents are content for their children to imbibe little more than the minimalist Islamic education to which they were exposed in Pakistan. This involves devoting a couple of years to learning to read the Qur'an in Arabic, without understanding it – completion of which is understood to carry religious merit, *sawab* – and knowledge of the formal prayers and their accompanying rituals.

While the Prophet's birthday is celebrated in the mosque, 'Allama Nishtar has little patience with the expense of organizing and advertising a public procession, which he feels is often little more than an exercise in self-display by local leaders. He prefers to spend the money on developing a good lending library of books in English, Urdu and Arabic. Within the sufi tradition himself, he likens religion to a banana: the externals of religion, Qur'anic study, Hadith and Islamic law are the 'outside', *zahir*, strong for protection; but sufism is the fruit 'inside', *batin*. Both are necessary. He is also alert to the need to help youngsters disentangle aspects of South Asian culture from Islam – e.g. he reassures them that there is nothing un-Islamic about Western dress, so long as the wearer conforms to Qur'anic canons of modesty.

In education, influence, status, public role outside the mosque and security, 'Allama Nishtar has few equals in Bradford. He owns his own house and has a compliant mosque committee. More typical of the city's *'ulama* with regard to influence and public visibility is a Gujarati *'alim*, Maulana 'Yusuf'. Although he has little English, he is well-trained, having completed a ten-year programme at a Deobandi *dar al-'ulum* in Gujarat, India. He serves a small house mosque, whose worshippers are from Chhachh in Pakistan. His register of pupils at the mosque school indicated that his 37 students all live in the surrounding four streets. The register is an innovation encouraged by the local authority's supplementary schools' officer, who had also left some books on Islam in English, for use by the children. The imam depends on the large Howard Street mosque for lists of prayer times and for use of their funeral facility. He lives in a small tied house owned by the mosque committee, and can usually expect about 50 worshippers on a Friday. He works alone in the mosque, lives a quiet, unobserved life, with no public role.

Imam Mahmud al Hasan is bilingual, having had all his formal education in state schools in Bradford, before going on to the Bury seminary at the age of 13. Imam Hasan, in the autumn of 1989, became the first Deobandi imam appointed in Bradford to graduate from a British *dar al-'ulum*. He identifies the functions of an imam as the following: to lead the five daily prayers; to teach the children in the supplementary school; to give the Friday address, *khutba* (in Arabic) and the accompanying sermon in Urdu; to preside over the rites of passage – at birth to whisper the call to prayer, *azaan*, into the child's ear, to solemnize the marriage contract, *nikah*, and to prepare the dead for burial; to prepare *ta'wiz*, amulets, for those fearful of the evil eye; to offer advice, within his competence, on the application of Islamic teaching and law, on a range of issues put to him.

It is worth expanding and illustrating such categories to identify changes in style, content and approach, between Imam Hasan and his father, Maulana Lutfur Rahman (who was referred to in the last chapter). His father, a Pathan trained in Pakistan and without a working knowledge of English, was imam in the mosque for 20 years, a trustee of the Bury *dar al-'ulum*, and president, for most of that time, of the Jami'at-i 'Ulama Britannia, the national umbrella organization for Deobandi *'ulama*. The Friday mosque address would see few differences between father and son: Imam Hasan's sermon comprises a 25-minute Qur'anic exposition in Urdu, without notes – he is working his way through the whole Qur'an, using in his preparation the multi-volume commentary by a famous Pakistani commentator, Maulana Shafi' (d. 1976), recommended for use at both Bury and Dewsbury.

The obvious differences become apparent in teaching children in the mosque. While both will use Mufti Kifayatullah's textbook, *Lessons in Islam*, Imam Hasan is able to make sure that each lesson is read in Urdu and English, and will pause to illustrate a point with reference to the children's world. Thus when listing the things not to do in a mosque, reading Batman cards and playing marbles are added! He can also recommend a new boardgame in English, entitled 'Steps to Paradise', which tests Islamic knowledge. The game includes a board with a colourful, imagined picture of paradise at its centre, dice and 150 Islamic question and answer cards, which contain some 600 questions and 150 Hadith quotations; instead of using paper money to acquire property as in the game Monopoly, the player builds up a bank of different coloured *sawab/*'religious merit' cards, which contain anything between five and 50,000 units. The aim of the game is to get enough correct answers to acquire sufficient religious merit to enter paradise. We have moved a long way from the environment and ethos of a traditional mosque, staffed by a South Asian imam, described by S.M. Darsh – an Egyptian who was imam of the prestigious Islamic Cultural Centre, in Regent's Park, London – as 'stern, long-bearded and intolerant of the most trivial breaches of the behavioural code'.[10]

Many in the mosque will come to both father and son with similar worries. Thus, taxi-drivers, aware of Islam's prohibition of alcohol, will ask whether it is sinful for them to take customers to pubs and clubs where alcohol is consumed. Imam Hasan's response is that it is allowed since they are no more personally responsible for what their clients do than the owner of a house is personally responsible for the adulterous behaviour of a tenant who rents his property. Imam Hasan is aware that on certain issues, such as whether or not contraception is allowed, men will approach him but not his father. This is largely a difference in outlook: his parents' generation were much more reticent about the whole area of sexuality than his, brought up in England.[11]

If father or son feel a question is outside their competence they can refer the issue to a mufti, a specialist in Islamic law. Bradford's Deobandi *'ulama* can refer to Mufti Sacha, a teacher at the Dewsbury seminary. The availability of muftis has always been a priority for the Deoband tradition, which institutionalized the provision and publication of advisory decisions, fatwas, in late-nineteenth-century India, as a way of disseminating their reformist understanding of Islam.[12] In a Muslim state a mufti was a court official, who delivered such fatwas for the guidance of the *qazi* or judge. In British India the Deobandi mufti began to give such fatwas directly to believers. This form of guidance 'in the innumerable details of life ... created a distinctive pattern of religious fidelity, whatever the vicissitudes of political life'.[13]

Mufti Sacha was joined in Britain in 1988 by his old teacher Mufti Kachholvi who, as seen in the last chapter, was appointed in that year to run the Institute of Islamic Jurisprudence UK in Bradford. Mufti Kachholvi is a full-time mufti, while Mufti Sacha combines this responsibility with his teaching at Dewsbury. Both are Gujaratis trained in India, and accredited *'ulama* who have specialized in Islamic law. In addition Mufti Kachholvi was designated a *khalifa*, a successor, of the famous Hadith scholar, Maulana Zakariya, author of the *Tablighi Nisab*, the authoritative and widely used textbook of the revivalist Tablighi Jama'at.

Both muftis keep copies of all their written fatwas. Since these provide a unique window into the day-to-day concerns of British Muslims it is worth exploring some of the continuities and discontinuities with the questions asked by Muslims in South Asia. In an advertisement, in English, Urdu and Gujarati, reporting the activities of the institute, printed two years after its opening, it was stated that Mufti Kachholvi had dealt with some 350 written questions and 150 enquiries over the phone. Individuals 'share their predicaments ... over many issues, ranging from simple queries on prayers, fasting, zakat, hajj ... to more complex ones on marriage, divorce, custody, inheritance, investments'. It pointed to the anxieties many Muslims felt at having to go through civil courts regarding divorce, custody, or inheritance. 'Many divorces pronounced by the courts are invalid in the eyes of shari'ah. It is unfortunate that many husbands abuse the system to their wife's detriment by not pronouncing the talaaq.'[14]

Some of the issues both muftis addressed were common to Britain and South Asia. Thus one enquiry concerned whether it was lawful to have pictures on a prayer mat – the answer given was that such did not render prayer invalid but, since decoration tended to distract the attention from God, it was better not to use illustrated prayer mats. Another questioner asked who should lead funeral prayers and whether their status was equivalent to *salat*, one of the five daily prayers – the answer was that the imam of the mosque was responsible for the prayers; if he was absent a relative of the deceased could decide who should lead them and, finally, such prayers did not carry the religious merit of *salat*.

Most enquiries dealt with Muslim family law, since the rulings of British courts could create problems. The abuse of *talaaq* – the pronouncement of the divorce formula by the husband – mentioned in the institute's report refers to the insistence that for a divorce to be lawful, according to traditional Hanafi jurisprudence, the man must pronounce *talaaq*. If her husband refused to do so, a woman could find herself in the anomalous position where she was divorced according to British law but not according to Islamic law, and thus could find it difficult to remarry within the Muslim community.

A detailed letter to Mufti Sacha by an accountant offers an unrivalled insight into the anxieties of a devout Muslim in a non-Muslim business environment. The accountant listed the following questions which suggest he was thinking of setting up his own firm, and wondered if the shift from employee to self-employed status would exacerbate or relieve his dilemmas:

1. In ... accountancy it is normal practice to prepare accounts for business of all types, which include ... off-licences, pubs, insurance consultants, building societ[ies] ... Is it permissible to prepare accounts for such: (a) as an employee? (b) as self-employed?

2. Clients often consult accountants to seek advice on obtaining bank/building society loans and mortgages to purchase or expand businesses or homes. Is it permissible to give advice to such clients: (i) as an employee? (ii) as self-employed?

3. Is it permissible to charge or pay 'goodwill' when selling or buying an accountancy practice (i.e. taking over the clients)?

Mufti Sacha replied that with reference to the first question, it was lawful, if an employee, but better not to prepare such accounts if self-employed. With regard to the second question it was allowed if one's job depended on it, otherwise it was better to avoid having to give such advice. Further, if the client was a Muslim it was incumbent on a Muslim accountant to remind him that loans/mortgages were *haram*, illegal with regard to Islamic law, since they involved interest. His answer to the third question was that 'goodwill' payments were not allowed but it was permissible instead to leave some goods in the building and charge for them whatever the accountant decided. This latter was an example of a *hilah*, or legal device, developed to circumvent the full rigours of the law.

On certain issues there was a difference of opinion between the two muftis. One of them felt that television and video were *haram*. This was consistent with Mufti Kifayatullah's teaching in *Lessons in Islam* that visiting the cinema and theatre was sinful.[15] The other felt that it depended on the content of the programme, with sport, documentaries and educational programmes allowed.

One issue which troubles many Muslims, in all traditions, is the issue of mortgage. Everyone agrees that it is *haram*, since it involves interest. However, there were a variety of views about whether it was ever permitted because of circumstances. One mufti argued that if there was no rented accommodation available and the alternative was going on the street then it was possible to contract a mortgage. The other felt that this latter could never happen in Britain, given the elaborate safety net of welfare provision, therefore it remained *haram*. The issue becomes particularly poignant for mosque committees since many worshippers are not happy about praying behind an imam who owns a house bought on a mortgage. In the 1970s, pre-recession, with few mosques and cheap housing many a congregation would dig deep into their resources and provide an interest-free loan for an imam. However, it was conceded by some Muslim leaders that with recession, the proliferation of mosques and house prices rocketing in the 1980s, some imams had recourse to mortgages, albeit with a bad conscience.

It is evident from this review that, within Bradford, the *'ulama* constitute an amorphous category, including a trained specialist, the mufti, a few who enjoy a public role outside the mosque, and those whose world is largely circumscribed by their duties within the mosque. Since the majority of settlers in Bradford – from whom the mosque committees are largely drawn – came from rural areas, they understandably preferred as imams people from their own district, who knew their locale and dialect, and who shared their view of the role of an imam and his responsibilities with regard to their children. They, after all, remain the employers of the imam. However, such appointments were not always possible. In 1989 of 19 'ulama employed by Deobandi mosques nine were Gujaratis, five serving a mixed congregation but four employed in four mosques controlled by and serving a Pathan/ Chhachh constituency. In the same year Pir Maroof's Barelwi organization also relied on eight Gujarati imams.[16]

Economic and Contractual Insecurity

A Muslim political scientist provides a useful window into the social status of 'ulama in Pakistan, where the term is used

> loosely ... and tends to include the entire religious establishment. At the base is the imam, who leads prayers in the village mosque ... He is usually semi-literate, and has some rudimentary knowledge of Islamic theology ... The village community regards him as a low-ranking functionary equal to the barber, washerman, cobbler, or carpenter and compensates him partly in kind ... He may be consulted in some matters, but he will not be admitted to a leadership role, unless ... he belongs to a higher caste, has independent income, and leads the prayers as a labor of love ... The imams, and especially [those] ... who deliver the Friday orations at the larger better-known mosques in cities, are more learned and command greater respect.[17]

It is evident that Bradford's 70 'ulama – used as a hold-all to include all mosque personnel – occupy positions right across this spectrum. The lowly huffaz (plural of hafiz), of whom there were 30 in 1989, in addition to learning the Qur'an by heart, often have little more than elementary knowledge of Islam, and their position is akin to the village imam. The remaining 39 'ulama in Bradford are more variegated in status: nine had university and college degrees from South Asia, in addition to their formal 'alim qualifications. The greatest difficulty most face is that they are not fluent in English. Indeed, only half a dozen have a good command of the language. A major disincentive to learning English is insecurity – economic and contractual.

Only three of the 'ulama in 1989 had formal contracts of employment. Many who came to Britain as visitors have to renew their visas annually, and are very much at the mercy of their mosque committee, since the latter have to confirm to the Home

Office that the 'alim is still wanted. Those who stay for five years enjoy rights of domicile and, if they have acquired a particular reputation as a good speaker, Qur'an reciter, or have learned English, gain a measure of autonomy, since other mosques may want to employ them. Many of the 'ulama are clearly dissatisfied with this state of affairs, since it also means they have to be very careful about criticizing committee policy or seeking to implement changes. Since they are mosque committee employees very few sit on those committees. It is hardly surprising that Dr Zaki Badawi, the chairman of the national Imams and Mosques Council of Great Britain has 'proposed a model contract for imams and instituted a pension scheme … [since they] should be secure'. He sees this as a necessary corrective to the 'contempt' Muslims have developed for their imams.[18]

The economic situation of the majority of the 'ulama is also precarious. In 1989 an 'alim who was paid more than £80 per week was the exception, and many had to live on less. Of course, some accommodation was provided, but this could vary between a room in the mosque, a tied house or, if the imam was very fortunate, a house bought with an interest-free loan. There are various reasons why the 'ulama are badly paid. One factor is that the general economic situation of the Muslim communities in the city is parlous, due to the dramatic recession affecting the very industries for which they were recruited.

Another reason that there is little money for the wages of an imam is that many mosque committees are still burdened with large expenses over and above the costs incurred in buying a building to be used as a mosque. Many of these buildings were bought before planning permission was sought for converting them into mosques. Mosque committees, then, often found themselves required to make expensive alterations to satisfy stringent building controls and fire precautions. It needs to be remembered that as late as 1992 only one mosque was purpose-built, although three more were under construction; for the rest, two are in converted cinemas, three in old church buildings, nine in industrial premises/mills and over 20 in houses. Because the community is still relatively new to Britain, resources have not been accumulated to provide religious endowments, auqaf, for the maintenance of such buildings and provision of salaries.

This means that the wage for the imam has to come from the weekly contributions of the congregation and the sums charged for teaching children. The latter is seldom more than £1 a week per child, and even this may have to be reduced where families have large numbers of young children. One or two of the larger mosques have additional sources of income, such as rented property, car parking space and large rooms, which can be let out for social functions such as weddings. However, these remain the exception.

There is also little central or local government funding available for centres devoted to religious purposes. £100,000 from the Department of the Environment was provided in 1983 for essential repair work to supplementary schools in the city, which included non-Muslim premises; similarly, in 1988 the local authority made another £100,000 available to help them satisfy new stringent fire precautions. From the early 1980s three mosques in the city enjoyed Community Programme funding for teaching community languages on their premises. For the rest, the mosques had to compete with other groups for such funding as was available for voluntary groups in the city.

In 1988/9 Bradford's Urban Programme funding of £3 million pounds included a component of 30 per cent for ethnic minority projects. Among the recipients were a few mosques: six successfully made bids for funding in the category of environmental improvement, for either buildings or environs. But such amounts were generally no more than £10,000. One other mosque qualified for £19,000 under the social-needs category, to provide adequate heating provision in a disused mill for a day centre for elderly Asians.[19] Very little of the fabled petrodollar wealth of the Arab countries finds its way into Bradford's mosques either. The fact that the city is still awaiting the completion of a large central, purpose-built mosque, 30 years after the first house-mosque was established, gives the lie to rumours of such funding.

Another important factor which militates against the payment to 'ulama of a realistic wage is the experience and expectations many of the elders brought with them from their villages in South Asia. There the imam would be paid partly in kind, and through ex gratia payments: these would be made during the rites of passage, over which the imam presided; during the month of fasting, when an imam with a skill in Qur'anic recitation would be expected to recite the entire Qur'an; other 'ulama who enjoyed a reputation as reciters of devotional hymns would be involved in the cycle of sufi festivals which punctuate the Barelwi year; some would be involved in khatm i qur'an, completing the entire Qur'an, to invoke God's blessing, intervention and protection at times of 'illness, risk or danger'.[20] Such additional payments, however welcome, do not amount to a regular wage. Indeed, among some 'ulama there is a reluctance to accept such monies for fear of compromising, by commercial considerations, right intention, niyat, a precondition for acceptable worship and devotion.

Inadequate remuneration could prove one of the most powerful disincentives to able British Muslims choosing to become 'ulama. In 1989 only one 'alim in the city could tap into foreign funding, a graduate of Medina University, supported by a Saudi Arabian religious foundation. Pir Maroof and the UK Islamic Mission have both failed to sustain viable dar al-'ulum, in part for this reason. Three of the most able local 'ulama, all with good English, have already left local mosques; two of them have gained postgraduate certificates in education and have joined the state education system. The third is pursuing the same route. The three represent the main traditions of Islamic expression in the city, the Deobandi, the Barelwi and the Jama'at-i Islami. Even the English-speaking graduates from Bury and Dewsbury, so important for the future staffing of the city's Deobandi mosques, may follow suit. One of the two employed in Bradford's mosques has begun to establish a local business. He may continue to teach in the mosque on a part-time basis, but he can no longer afford to be their imam. British Muslims, trained in dar al-'ulum in this country, necessarily have different expectations from South Asian elders about what counts as a realistic wage.

Occidentalism and the Challenge of Living in Two Cultures

It is not always easy to live in two linguistic and cultural worlds. As was evident from the previous chapter Dr Munir Ahmed, an educated British Muslim, was unable to assume authority within the UK Islamic Mission mosque. This was partly because of these difficulties, exacerbated by trying to operate across an oral and literate cultural divide, complicated by class differences.

If Dr Ahmed found this movement difficult within a shared Islamic context it is worth exploring the pitfalls that attend attempts to move from a South Asian Muslim environment into a British educational and professional world. Mention has already been made of three *'ulama*, all educated in South Asia, who have left the full-time employment of their Bradford mosques to pursue teaching qualifications. Such a move requires a certain boldness, since it involves engaging with another linguistic and cultural world that is not considered morally and religiously neutral but rather subversive of Islamic religion and culture.

Mohammad Raza, an imam himself, in seeking to explain what he sees as a renewed sectarianism among British Muslims, locates it within a reaction to the secular context.

> If [a Muslim] goes to a restaurant, he cannot eat meat because it is not *Halal* ... If his girls are going to a mixed school, he fears that his daughter will become pregnant. If she attends any classes on sex education, he fears the teacher will teach her how to have sex. He fears sending his children to educational institutions because they may indoctrinate them with secular values. He does not want his children to watch television because explicit love scenes are sometimes shown ... Such Muslims may seem to have become paranoid about Western culture, society and civilization.[21]

This response, dubbed 'occidentalism' by the celebrated Pakistani anthropologist Akbar Ahmed, can in part be understood by the anxieties which Raza and others attach to the word 'secular'.[22] Most of the *'ulama* I consulted in Bradford gloss the term by two Urdu words, *ladini* and *ghairmazhabi*.[23] Both mean non-religious and carry the association of irreligious/anti-religious. The President of the Bradford Council for Mosques in 1991 and 1992, Liaqat Hussain, himself a Barelwi, pointed out that the religious opposition to the Pakistan People's Party was rooted in the perception that it was socialist, secular and therefore irreligious. 'The Muslim Manifesto – a strategy for survival', published by the Muslim Institute in 1990, can speak of 'the demands of rampant, immoral secularism ... [within] a post-Christian, largely pagan, society'.[24] Here, within Islamist discourse, the 'secular' is similarly derided.[25]

The 'secular' is almost universally descried in contemporary Islamic writings, by modernists, Islamists and traditionalists alike. The same author who laments the emergence of 'occidentalism' in Muslim attitudes to Western society insists, in the same work, that '"secular" and "Muslim" are by definition incompatible words ... There can be no Muslim without God'. Thus the secular is being interpreted as equivalent to atheism.[26]

A few dissenting voices do exist, and two are particularly instructive. Maulana Azmi, an Indian *'alim* who used to work in Bradford, reflecting out of his Indian experience, considers that the widely shared perception that secular necessarily implies irreligion is simply wrong. In India, he contends, a secular state can offer security to Muslims since it is compatible with acknowledging that religion is important, but that in a religiously plural environment the state does not allow believers in one religious tradition to enjoy a privileged status. All are citizens with equal rights. Indeed, in India, Muslims are allowed to conform to their own Muslim family law.

The second dissenting voice is D.H. Khaled, who was an associate professor at the Islamic Research Institute, and lecturer in Pakistan Studies at the University of Islamabad, Pakistan, during the 1970s. Khaled observed that,

> the Urdu translation of secularism as *la-dini* has wrought havoc in India and Pakistan ... [since vested interests] have succeeded in attributing to secularism not only a western origin but also an essentially Christian character ... By doing so they have given secularism the stigma of a foreign ideology, whereas in reality it is ... a sociological process and ... a method of religious reform.[27]

Progressive writers in Pakistan today seek to avoid this trap by transliterating the English word into Urdu and then offering a contrary interpretation of it. A book of essays by Syed Sibte Hasan, *Navid-i Fiqr*, Invitation to Thought, written in 1982, included an essay entitled 'secularism'. The book was reviewed in the Pakistan press and one reviewer noted approvingly that,

> the most essential aspect of the analysis is the contention that secularism has no antireligious connotations as our fundamentalists are fond of arguing. It merely means aspects of life which have to do with the world as opposed to those which are called spiritual.[28]

Imam 'Rashid', one of two Bradford *'ulama* to negotiate successfully the transfer from the South Asian to the British educational system, and gain a postgraduate certificate in education from a local polytechnic, is innocent of such semantic subtleties. It is to his credit that he persisted with his studies in an environment routinely labelled and understood by fellow imams as 'secular'/irreligious. So far very few from an *'alim* background have completed such courses. Three other *'ulama*, who attended a preliminary course put on by a local college to help them manage the transfer, dropped out. Imam 'Rashid' enjoyed certain advantages over other *'ulama*, in that his educational background was broader than most; as well as being a Barelwi *'alim* he had gained an MA in Islamic Studies from the Punjab University in Pakistan. His MA, unlike many *'alim* courses, included the study of Islamic history, other religions, Islam and science, as well as study of the Qur'an, Hadith and *fiqh*, Islamic jurisprudence.

Much of the method, ethos and content of his educational course was unfamiliar and involved different levels of difficulty and anxiety. To rehearse the difficulties an exceptionally well qualified *'alim* from South Asia experienced in negotiating two educational systems, located within distinct social, cultural and linguistic worlds, is revealing. It highlights the huge task facing South Asian *'ulama* in Britain who want to connect with the experiences and concerns of the increasing numbers of British Muslims who are graduates of institutions of higher education in this country.

Imam 'Rashid' found the main difficulty with which he had to contend was his imperfect grasp of English. The medium of instruction for an *'alim* in Pakistan would be Urdu. He would also be expected to develop a good knowledge of Arabic and a working knowledge of Persian. For studies at a Pakistani university some knowledge of English was expected but not a mastery of the language. Thus to succeed in the British educational system most South Asian students would be at a disadvantage unless they had previously attended one of the few good English-medium schools patronized by the elite.

Imam 'Rashid' also found the methods of study unfamiliar. In Pakistan the focus of study, whether in a *dar al-'ulum* or in many state universities and colleges, was mastery of certain textbooks.

In Britain, by contrast, he was expected to be at ease with the world of projects and written assignments. The questioning approach to education was also new: in a mosque the imam's opinion was almost sacrosanct and the student was not expected to question it; an attitude of deference to authority which has transferred to many teachers in higher education in Pakistan. Further, according to 'Rashid', the assumption was that the imam 'knows everything and is expected to answer any query immediately. For him to say that he does not know, or that he needs to consult a book, is taken as a sign of incompetence!' This is very much the expectation of those operating from within an oral rather than a literate culture – the majority of the elders in Bradford's mosques.

As regards the subject areas with which he was expected to be acquainted, in preparation for teaching in Britain, he had most difficulties with music, art, dance, PE and sex education. A South Asian Islamic culture with its gender specific dress codes, intended to preserve modesty, its preference for single-sex institutions after girls reach puberty, its reticence about uncovering the human body in public and discussion of sexuality in mixed company, all run counter to assumptions and practices taken for granted in the British educational system. Seen within the context of British educational practice, modelling human figures out of clay can seem a very innocent activity, but for Imam 'Rashid' it was tantamount to idolatry, since it usurped the place of the creator. Explicit illustrations of the human body and mixed sex education were also the cause of anxiety. What is remarkable is that 'Rashid' stayed the course.

Other difficulties were practical as he sought first to understand and then negotiate appropriate responses to the conventions of a very different social arena. As an imam, he wore a definable 'uniform', easily recognizable within a South Asian Muslim environment: the traditional *shalwar qamiz*, *achkan*, top coat and hat. Outside a Muslim context this same traditional dress could invite unwelcome attention, even racist taunts. However, to change into a Western suit could open him to criticism from members of his congregation that he had changed his identity and become Westernized. The irony, as he himself noted, was that many of his congregation themselves wore Western clothes.

Social gatherings with fellow students were attended by anxieties: would there be alcohol, would halal meat be available, how would he cope with a knife and fork? A Muslim is expected to eat with his right hand, while a fork is usually held in the left hand. Imam 'Rashid', like many Muslims, would cut the food with their knife in their right hand and eat it also with this hand by shifting his fork from left to right. Such skills can soon be acquired, but initially a measure of unfamiliarity contributed to increased psychological tension.

Although his course comprised men and women there was only one other male on it. He admits that had he been the only male he might not have persevered. Other problems were created by the difficulty of participating in the Friday congregational prayers. There was a limited time between lectures and assignments during which the student was supposed to eat lunch and go to the library. One final area of sensitivity was that as an *'alim* he enjoyed a respected position within his community. On teaching practice this was not understood and he was expected to do tasks which were either demeaning or with which he was unfamiliar, whether tying children's laces or washing dishes. He was able to laugh at this, in retrospect, since he realized no insult was intended.

Imam 'Rashid' recognized that staff, when they became aware of his disquiet, were supportive and helpful. However, he often felt isolated and reluctant to share his anxieties for fear of being misunderstood or considered difficult. His experience illuminates the many pitfalls an educated imam encounters when moving from a Muslim majority culture, like Pakistan, into the very different social and cultural world of a British college or university. In the next section, which reviews the sort of curriculum an *'alim* might study in an Islamic seminary in South Asia and in Britain, the experience of an English-educated *'alim* will be explored and will offer a useful counterpoint to those of 'Rashid'.

Curriculum and Change in the *dar al-'ulum*

Lucknow in India, in the eighteenth century, was home to the Firangi Mahal dynasty of Islamic scholars, who generated a syllabus of study – *dars-i nizami* – which was to prove hugely influential amongst the Muslim elites. This syllabus enhanced the importance of the rational disciplines of logic and philosophy alongside the traditional subjects of Qur'an and Hadith. Such study was congenial to those who would become the lawyers, judges and administrators of the Mughal empire.

> The study of advanced books of logic, philosophy and dialectic sharp-ened the rational faculties and ... brought to the business of govern-ment men with better trained minds and better formed judgement ... the emphasis on the development of reasoning skills meant an em-phasis on the understanding rather than merely rote learning ... It could help ... to develop opposition to dogmatic and extreme religion ... [and] bring the continued possibility of a truly understanding interaction with other traditions ... whether Shia or Hindu.[29]

The prestige of this scholastic tradition was such that 'it came to be investigated at al-Azhar ... and in the nineteenth century its books were used to try to revive the rational sciences in Cairo.'[30] However, in South Asia in the nineteenth century this tradition of rational sciences was increasingly eroded in favour of a renewed emphasis on the traditional subjects of Qur'an and Hadith. There are various reasons for this development. The centres of patron-age of Firangi Mahal – the Mughal courts – disapppeared. The Mughal service elites had to develop a competence in Western knowledge if they were to find employment under the British. As seen in Chapter 2, the Muhammedan Anglo-Indian College in Aligarh and the Deoband seminary were the institutions Muslims created for surviving without political power. Aligarh took West-ern knowledge seriously but this was not integrated with Islamic studies. Deoband stressed the importance of the Qur'an and Hadith, but had little interest in Western disciplines or the rational tradition within Islamic scholarship.

The need for changes in the methodology and curriculum of Islamic seminaries in South Asia in the twentieth century has become urgent.[31] Modernizing governments in Pakistan, eager to introduce legal changes, have established Islamic research centres to bypass their perceived obscurantism.[32] Alongside such attempts to develop a corpus of modernist scholarship, South Asian govern-ments have also sought to introduce changes in the curriculum of the Islamic seminaries. Such attempts have enjoyed only limited success. It is necessary to understand the reasons why change is desired, as well as the resistance to it from the *'ulama* in South Asia. Only then will we understand the intellectual world of Bury and Dewsbury and the challenges such *dar al-'ulum* face in Britain if they are to develop a curriculum relevant to a new environment.

The imperative for change can be illustrated from the famous work *The Reconstruction of Religious Thought in Islam* (1934) by Muhammad Iqbal (d. 1938), the South Asian poet and philosopher. Iqbal illustrated the need for reform and the dead hand of *fiqh*, Islamic jurisprudence, with a striking example:

> In the Punjab, as everybody knows, there have been cases in which Muslim women wishing to get rid of undesirable husbands have been driven to apostasy ... Does the working of the rule relating to apostasy, as laid down in the Hedaya, tend to protect the interests of the Faith in this country?[33]

Iqbal's point was that in the widely used twelfth-century compilation of Islamic case-law *Hidaya* (guidance), by Marghinani, who died in 1196, divorce was considered the unilateral prerogative of the husband. In such a situation apostasy alone provided a way out of an impossible marriage for a woman, since this same text declares that in such cases 'a separation takes place without divorce'.[34] This example is of more than academic interest since the *Hidaya* remains one of the key texts on Islamic law studied in both Bury and Dewsbury seminaries.

Iqbal's answer to this dilemma was to have recourse to the principle of *ijtihad*, independent reasoning, to 're-interpret the foundational legal principles in the light of ... [contemporary] experience and the altered conditions of modern life'.[35] This, of course, raised further difficult issues, namely who was competent to exercise such *ijtihad*, if the need for it was granted; also, how important was the study of Islamic history in contextualizing such venerable works as *Hidaya* – a preliminary to legal reform – and how was the community to arrive at consensus, *ijma'*, on such contested issues?[36]

These issues of authority, competence and how to arrive at consensus have continued to bedevil Pakistani politics. For traditional jurists *ijtihad* is not a faculty to be applied to any and every issue but only to those questions on which no consensus has been reached. The Deobandi Maulana Mufti Mohammad Shafi, the leading mufti in Pakistan, argued that the category of irrevocable consensus was rooted in the Qur'an and the Hadith.[37]

It is clear why the Pakistani scholar Fazlur Rahman could insist that the debate between modernism and traditionalism could only move beyond sterile name-calling if the 'basic questions of method and hermeneutics were ... squarely addressed'.[38] Too often issues were simply resolved by the political expedient of packing committees. Thus in 1956 a Pakistani Commission on Marriage and Family Laws called for reforms in marriage, divorce and inheritance, and most contentiously sought to limit the possibility of polygamy. The commission of seven members included only one *'alim*, who vehemently dissented from its recommendations. Similarly, the Council of Islamic Ideology, set up in 1960 as an advisory body for the Pakistani government, always included a substantial majority of members outside the ranks of the *'ulama*, until the pendulum swung the other way in the 1980s.[39]

While there has been no meeting of minds between traditionalism and modernism on issues of methodology – *ijtihad*, and how to arrive at consensus, *ijma'*, in the area of legal change – federal governments in Pakistan have sought, with only a little more success, to introduce changes in the curriculum that the *'ulama* study in *dar al-'ulum*. In 1962 the first of a number of government reports, intended to enable the *'ulama* to take a 'full part as citizens' by widening their outlook and 'to increase their mental horizon', recommended the inclusion of such subjects as mathematics, English, social sciences and modern Arabic, while cutting back on logic, philosophy and certain books of Islamic law.[40]

In 1979 another national committee published its deliberations, the Halepota report, named after its chairman. This time various incentives were offered to the *dar al-'ulum* to introduce changes in curriculum. Equivalence between their certificates and a BA awarded in state universities and colleges was proposed, thereby enabling *'ulama* to teach Islamic studies and Islamic ideology in such institutions. English was made compulsory for those wanting to teach other subjects. It was envisaged that a third of the time-table would be devoted to modern subjects, now including Islamic history and comparative religion, while the books for such subjects would be prescribed by the Department of Education, thereby bridging the gap between state and religious institutions. Money from centralized collection of *zakat*, itself a controversial innovation, was also to be made available to *dar al-'ulum* prepared to co-operate. The Deobandis, particularly, resisted this process of centralization and bureaucratic control and launched 'a nation-wide campaign against it, calling the Government 'secular' (*la-dini*; lit. without religion)'.[41]

A scholar who has studied this process considers the government has had little real success in seeking to integrate the curriculum of the state educational system with that of the *dar al-'ulum*. At primary level such integration did not occur, except for a willingness by some mosques and *dar al-'ulum* to use state-provided textbooks for Urdu and arithmetic. All refused to include 'Pakistan studies', intended by the government as a vehicle of national integration, since they were not interested in promoting nationalism. Little more than lip service was paid to the inclusion of other subjects. The resistance of the *'ulama* to the introduction of new subjects was, in part, rooted in the fact that they themselves were simply not trained to teach such subjects.[42] Some in-service training for *'ulama* was offered by an 'Ulema Academy', set up in 1961 in Lahore, but inevitably its impact was limited to the few who participated in its courses.[43]

If such attempts must be judged a failure in a Muslim majority state like Pakistan it is hardly surprising that a non-Muslim government in India has never tried. A Muslim minority is understandably sensitive to any interference by the state in its educational institutes or Muslim family law. The furore which attended the Shah Bano judgement in 1985 indicates the strength of feeling on such issues.[44]

It will now be clear that *'ulama* in Bradford who are trained in South Asia, unless they have additional qualifications from universities and colleges, are unlikely to be able to engage with the intellectual and cultural world of Britain. Dr I.H. Qureshi (d. 1981), a chancellor of Karachi University and himself a distinguished educationalist, writing of the situation in Pakistan, pessimistically concluded that,

> [the leaders of traditional education] have neglected modern knowledge to an extent that there is no scope left for a dialogue be-

tween those who have received a modern education and the graduates of the seminaries ... The seminaries are doing useful ... work in
the preservation of the classical learning and providing ill-paid, ill-
educated and ill-informed imams of the mosques [sic]. It is quite
obvious that such education cannot help the growth of religious
consciousness.[45]

The Deobandi seminaries in Bury and Dewsbury face a huge
task if they are to avoid many of these same dilemmas. The
curriculum of the Bury *dar al-'ulum*, established in 1975, will be
the focus of the present discussion. It preceded that of Dewsbury
(1982) and has developed links with Azhar in Cairo and Medina
University in Saudi Arabia, where many of its students go after
completing their six-year programme of study. Dewsbury is in
some respects a derivative of Bury, sharing much of its syllabus
but closed to the wider academic world, Muslim and non-Muslim
alike; its students spend a final year in Pakistan or India and
their studies are unapologetically subordinate to the practice of
revivalist preaching. Indeed, Hafiz Patel, in charge of Dewsbury,
is not himself an *'alim*, but the national organizer of the revivalist
movement, Tablighi Jama'at in Britain.

In 1989, the six-year syllabus at Bury started with the basics of
the Arabic language – grammar (*sarf*), and syntax (*nahw*) – taught
with Urdu textbooks; elementary works in Arabic on literature
and language; the life of the Prophet, his companions and the
history of early Islam, taught in Urdu. In the second year more
difficult books in Arabic on grammar and syntax are introduced,
along with a textbook on composition in Arabic and translation
exercises from Arabic into Urdu. Arabic literature and language
are given priority. History drops out and *fiqh*, Islamic jurisprudence, is introduced, through selections from a Hanafi text.
Qur'anic recitation, *tajwid*, also makes its first appearance. The
third year includes the same stress on Arabic with the addition
of Arabic rhetoric, and for the first time Qur'anic commentary,
tafsir, with half the Qur'an translated from Arabic into Urdu. A
beginning is made on the study of the principles of Islamic jurisprudence. The life of the Prophet, selections from Hadith and
tajwid complete the year's study.

The fourth year includes classical Arabic literature and Arabic
rhetoric, and the second half of the Qur'an is translated from

Arabic into Urdu. An elementary work of logic is introduced as
an aid to understanding the Qur'an. The principles of Islamic
jurisprudence are further explored; Hadith and *tajwid* complete
this year's study. In the fifth year there is study of an Arabic
textbook mapping the changes in language from classical to
modern Arabic; a Hanafi textbook on the terminology and the
principles of Hadith selection; a short Arabic commentary of the
Qur'an by Suyuti (d. 1505), written in co-operation with his
teacher, known as *Tafsir al-Jalalayn*; Tibrizi's famous compilation
of Hadith, *Mishkat al-Masabih*, 'niche of the lamps' (sura 24:35);
Marghinani's *Hidaya*; a text of apologetic theology, *kalam*, on
articles of belief, *al-'aqa'id*, by Nasafi (d. 1143); and *tajwid*. The
final year is devoted entirely to reading in Arabic and translating
into Urdu all the six collections of Hadith, along with Imam
Malik's *Muwatta*.

This syllabus clearly reflects the scripturalist and reformist
Deobandi emphasis on the traditional sciences of Qur'an and
Hadith as against the rational sciences of logic and philosophy of
the Firangi Mahal *dars-i nizami* syllabus developed in Lucknow in
the eighteenth century. There is, nonetheless, some continued
dependence on *dars-i nizami* in such works as Suyuti's short
Qur'anic commentary, Tibrizi's compilation of Hadith, Nasafi's
textbook on *kalam*, apologetic theology, and the *Hidaya*. The distinguished Indian Arabist and historian Maulana Shibli Nu'mani
(d. 1916) criticized the *dars-i nizami* syllabus for the importance
given to the slight works by Suyuti and Nasafi, which he felt had
hardly begun to do justice to the rich treasury of Muslim scholarship in the areas of *tafsir* and *kalam*.[46] The same criticism can be
levelled at Bury's curriculum.

The potential of history as a valuable tool for a contextual
appreciation of the strengths and weaknesses of key Islamic texts
– not least the twelfth-century *Hidaya* – has yet to be explored at
Bury. Its emphasis on Hadith, with some 20 per cent of the time-
table devoted to it, means that outside the first year's cursory
study of early Islamic history, there is no other study of Islamic
history, nor any exposure to the works of great Muslim thinkers
such as al Ghazali in the twelfth century, Ibn Khaldun in the
fourteenth century or indeed the eighteenth-century Indian
scholar, Shah Wali Allah (one of the few South Asian scholars

whose work in Arabic is studied at Azhar in Cairo).[47] Only in the private school, catering for boys between 13 and 16 years old, are English and modern subjects studied at all. Since so little Islamic history or Islamic philosophy is studied, it is difficult to envisage the graduates of such a centre developing the confidence to study British philosophy, history and literature, still less politics, economics, and more recent disciplines such as the social sciences and psychology.

It would, however, be wrong to assume that Bury is impervious to change or that it would be impossible for anyone to move from such an educational context to a Western university. Imam 'Akhtar' is a young *'alim*, who has successfully traversed three educational, linguistic and cultural worlds: a graduate from Bury in 1988, he received a BA in Islamic studies from Azhar in 1990 and an MA from the Department of Middle Eastern Studies of Manchester University in 1992.

'Akhtar' considers that Bury has benefited from its links with Azhar, which already has had some impact on curriculum and teaching methods. He instanced the inclusion of the book by the twentieth-century Indian scholar Abul Hasan Ali Nadwi on developments within the Arabic language, from the classical to the modern age, and in 1990 the famous *tafsir* by Baidawi (d. 1286) was introduced to complement the shorter work of Suyuti.[48] With regard to method, one major innovation has been borrowed from Azhar: the inclusion of a 10,000- and 15,000-word thesis at the end of the fifth and sixth years. Such a thesis can be written in Arabic, English or Urdu and involves some minimal research.

The principal of Bury had also encouraged a few students to go on to study Islamics, law and Arabic at British universities. 'Akhtar' was confident that, in time, this would have a further impact on Bury in both the content of the curriculum and methods of study. He acknowledged, however, that Bury was a long way from having its courses in Islamics and Arabic accredited by British universities. They had been advised that if they introduced some 'A' level studies their students could, at least, transfer to a British university more easily than at present.

'Akhtar' conceded that his move to Egypt had not been easy. Bury has an arrangement with Azhar, whereby their students can miss the first two years of the BA in Islamic Studies, which are

of a general nature, and proceed directly to either specialist studies
in Hadith, *fiqh* or *tafsir* for the final two years. 'Akhtar' opted for
Hadith. What he found difficult was the medium of instruction,
Arabic, since Bury focuses on classical rather than modern
Arabic. Also, Bury is a relatively self-contained all-male boarding
school, and to negotiate the move into the chaotic, cosmopolitan
city of Cairo, was far from easy. The teaching methods, however,
were traditional and familiar.

The comments by 'Akhtar' on the transition to Manchester
University are revealing. His course involved him in four subject
areas, classical Arabic, modern Arabic, Islamic thought in its
formative period in the first four centuries and the history of the
Ottoman Empire. Here the difficulties were largely with English,
and an unfamiliarity with the methods of teaching and the general ethos of a Western university. He had not studied English for
ten years since completing 'O' levels. Thus, like Imam 'Rashid',
he found this difficult, not least because of his lack of acquaintance with the technical vocabulary in his area of study. There
was also a heavy dependence on essay writing which had not
been the case at Bury or Azhar.

The ethos of a Western university was very different from what
he was used to, not least the presence of male and female
students: Bury and Azhar were concerned to initiate the male
student into the accumulated wisdom of a religious tradition,
personalized in the life and teaching of a respected teacher. In
Manchester, he felt, disciplined study was concerned with the
intellect rather than character formation. A favourite phrase was
'hypothetically speaking', which for 'Akhtar' meant that study
could degenerate into intellectual games. One final difference was
that there was more emphasis on secondary literature and less on
close textual study of primary texts, as compared to Bury and
Azhar.

What was surprising was that 'Akhtar' had not encountered the
works of modernist Islamic scholarship in Egypt. He had, for
example, not studied any of the works of the greatest of Azhar's
reformers, Muhammad Abduh (d. 1905). He had gained a cursory
knowledge of Western scholarship in his study of Islamic thought
at Manchester. However, he appeared innocent of the concerns
and anxieties of modernist Muslims. Thus he expressed no diffi-

culty with the section in *Hidaya* which, in the context of prescribing rules of evidence, insists that in most cases 'the evidence required is of two men or of one man and two women, whether the case relates to property ... marriage, divorce, agency, executorship.'[49] The formula 'one man equals two women' has been extrapolated from a Qur'anic verse touching on witnesses to a financial transaction, where the reasons are stated: 'if one of them [women] should make a mistake, the other could remind her'.[50]

The traditionalist, nourished by such esteemed works as *Hidaya*, considers,

> the law that two female witnesses equal one male is eternal and a social change that enabled a woman to get used to financial transactions would be un-Islamic. The modernist ... would say ... when women become conversant with such matters ... their evidence can equal that of a man.[51]

This whole debate, a storm centre in Pakistan in the 1980s and one of the factors behind the emergence there of a women's movement, has simply passed 'Akhtar' by, and he exhibited no understanding of why such teaching might be considered problematic to some of his Muslim contemporaries.[52]

Various Muslim institutions in Britain have reflected on the *desiderata* for an Islamic curriculum in Britain, whether the 'Muslim Parliament' in its educational white paper published in 1992, or the Muslim College in London in its provisional prospectus. All agree on the need to teach in English and to add history and philosophy – Islamic and Western – to the traditional curriculum of Qur'an, Hadith and *fiqh*. If the Muslim College is right to insist that for Islam to 'survive and prosper in modern Europe it must learn the techniques and frames of reference of modern European culture' then it is clear that Bury has a long way to go.[53] The Barelwi tradition seems more hospitable to such an engagement with modernity. In the Urdu prospectus for the Islamic Missionary College in Bradford, written in 1974, it was already pointing to the necessity for training *'ulama* in bilingual skills, and sought to offer a three-year programme including science, philosophy, administration and the comparative study of other religions and ideologies.[54] Sadly, this initiative foundered because of funding problems and personal rivalries.

Supplementary Schools: A Continuing Cause of Concern

More than ten years ago a researcher who studied a mosque and
its imam in Bradford – one of the best trained of the city's *'ulama*
– noted that in its Qur'an school the children, for the most part,
'work without direct instruction or supervision and the room can
become very noisy and chaotic'; 'the imam ... enforces a degree
of order by use of a short cane' and that 'imitation and repetition
are the chief methods of learning.'[55]

The Qur'an school/supplementary school, held after state
school, continues to be the focus of deep anxiety among many
Muslims. Reference was made in earlier in this chapter to the
changes in style of teaching, discipline and use of English books
introduced by *'ulama* trained at Bury or exposed to the British
educational system. To these can be added the handful of *huffaz*
educated in Britain and English-speaking who now do some
teaching in the supplementary schools. Such welcome changes
should not obscure the fact that such teachers remain a minority.
Further, classes are still often impossibly large – sometimes as
many as 70 children in one room – with an age spread ranging
from 5 to 16.

In the autumn of 1983 a 'supplementary schools' officer' was
appointed by the local education authority, to begin to bridge the
gap between teaching methods in supplementary schools and state
schools, and to provide in-service training for mosque teachers in
the area of language teaching. In 1990 a distinguished Muslim
educationalist from Bradford, in a paper delivered at a national
conference in the city, repeated almost word for word comments
made by the supplementary schools' officer in his 1986 report:

> There are grave doubts expressed by almost everyone about the na-
> ture of supplementary provision, style of teaching, methods of instruc-
> tion, disciplinary procedures ... it may be said that they meet the
> needs of ritualistic self-identity ... but one doubts whether the major-
> ity ... come anywhere near meeting the spiritual and actual [needs]
> ... of our children.[56]

The style of teaching remains highly authoritarian, the cane is
still in evidence and its continued use was supported by the
Bradford Council for Mosques, despite a ban on corporal punish-

ment in state schools.[57] The leader of Bradford's Young Muslims, Dr Munir Ahmed, in seeking to identify the reasons why so many young Muslims were adopting what he dubbed a 'pop-cum-bhangra' lifestyle, far away from Islamic norms, noted that 'at the first opportunity [the boys] rebelled against a religion, which has sometimes been literally beaten into them.'[58]

The favoured textbooks, whether for community languages or Islam, remain those written in South Asia. The supplementary schools' officer, in conversation in 1990, acknowledged that despite the good intentions of the local authority there were few takers for in-service courses and little demand for the English books the local authority was willing to supply. Once again the lack of confidence in English remains a huge disincentive to use such books. In 1991/2 neither the UK Islamic Mission nor the Ahl-i Hadith mosque in Bradford had an imam competent in English. Therefore the excellent teaching syllabus in English which both traditions have produced remains unused.

An additional discontinuity between state and mosque school is that the latter offers little space for questioning. The ethos of *dar al-'ulum* and mosque alike is to absorb and reproduce the teaching of the *'alim*. This is echoed in the practice of Pakistan's primary schools, where,

> the major emphasis in school tests was the accurate memorization and reproduction of the lessons in textbooks [and] the main determinants of what the teachers teach ... is a kind of dreary tradition of 'survival teaching' handed down from one hard-pressed, undertrained teacher to another ... [a] tradition, rigid, formal and unimaginative in the extreme.[59]

It seems that Muslim parents have begun to lose confidence in many of the imams. A Muslim educational researcher, who studied a Bradford middle school in 1985/6 with a 90 per cent Muslim intake, found that all wanted Islamic religious education in the syllabus. At the same time,

> they were almost unanimous in their ... opinion that [the] imam should not be appointed in schools to teach religion but ... qualified Muslim teachers ... The parents have said that these imams inculcate

the germs of anti-western education ... and their young children soon
get trapped in their magical and ... fantasy world.[60]

It is clear, in the words of Imam 'Akhtar', the young *'alim* who
successfully negotiated three educational, linguistic and cultural
worlds, that 'the imam is not a role model for young people'.
Many parents also entertain doubts about the imam's competence
to connect with the world of their children. Even where an able
student like 'Akhtar' becomes an *'alim*, it is an open question
whether mosque committees will be able or willing to offer him
the salary and job security he deserves. There is a real danger
that there will be a haemorrhaging of the most able into the state
educational system.

Beyond Sectarianism: The Role of the Council for Mosques

'Settlement by tiptoe' was the striking phrase used in a 1981 Bradford Council report to characterize the history of migration into the inner city over the previous 20 years: a dual society had emerged, whose members looked outward to mainstream British society for jobs, schools and services, but who still looked inward in their desire to preserve their traditional culture, religion and language. While the city had been free of the racial and inter-communal unrest which had marked other cities in that year, the authors of the report worried that,

> we have no direct knowledge of Asian needs and requirements, and we have no automatic way of knowing the issues they feel important ... [we need] some new channel of communication between the Council and the communities – something to compensate for the lack of political representation.[1]

Ten years later a national newspaper discussing the opening of the controversial 'Muslim Parliament' in London cited with evident approval the remarks of the president of the Bradford Council for Mosques, for whom this new initiative was 'a cruel joke for the Muslim community', threatening both to raise unrealistic expectations and fix in the public mind 'the image of every Muslim being a warlike separatist, ready to fight jihads at every opportunity'. Mihir Bose, who wrote the piece, contrasted the unelected 'Muslim Parliament' with the Bradford Council for Mosques, 'an elected body ... probably the most representative voice of Islam in the land'.[2]

This chapter explores the significance, locally and nationally, of the Bradford Council for Mosques, formally constituted in September 1981. The Council for Mosques was an institution whose time had come. Bradford Council had found that 'new channel of communication' it had sought – at least for Muslims – and other public bodies welcomed the creation of an organization which they could consult on a range of issues. Many Muslims in the city supported its creation as an advocate and pressure group for their concerns.

This chapter divides naturally into three sections which, cumulatively, will enable an assessment of the large claims made for the Council for Mosques' significance by Mihir Bose. The first section reviews the Council's early history and some of its activities from its creation until the publication of *The Satanic Verses* in September 1988. During this period the Council for Mosques was essentially a local body with a modest remit to address issues of concern, especially in the area of education. However, it was to gain in confidence and to develop its campaign skills as it became embroiled in a number of public controversies. The second section unravels some of the important issues interwoven in the *Satanic Verses* affair. This convulsion in inter-communal relations catapulted the Council for Mosques onto the national stage; its personnel were active both in seeking to translate anger and outrage at the novel into institutional unity at a national level, and to begin a debate on a range of issues exercising Muslims in Britain.

The final section moves forward to the Gulf crisis and its aftermath. The Gulf crisis exposed the difficulty the Bradford Council for Mosques encountered in seeking to manage and reconcile the multiple identities and loyalties of local Muslims, whether to Britain, to countries in South Asia, or to the *umma*, the worldwide Muslim community. The Gulf war also saw Muslim politicians in Bradford involving themselves in public debate and disagreement with the Council for Mosques. Muslim professionals and businessmen, too, were organizing themselves into self-consciously Muslim groupings and taking initiatives independent of the Council. An attempt is made to map relationships between the Council for Mosques and these two other centres of influence amongst local Muslims and thus clarify the issue of the loci of authority in the Muslim communities.

The Council for Mosques: A Vehicle for Local Unity

The six founding members of the Bradford Council for Mosques represented all traditions of Islam present in the city.[3] Three were local businessmen – the most successful was Sher Azam, whose name was to become almost synonymous with the Council for Mosques in the late 1980s, at the height of the Rushdie affair.[4] Sher Azam was president of the Council for almost half of its first decade, which speaks both of the importance of the Deobandi presence in the city – he had been president or vice-president of the Howard Street mosque for the previous six years – and the trust and respect he commanded across the different traditions. Pir Maroof, another of the founding fathers, was never an elected officer of the Council but his Barelwi organization, Jami'at-i Tabligh al-Islam, always provided the president or one of its two general-secretaries throughout this period, except during its first year.

The first president of the Council for Mosques was Umar Warraich, a public health inspector. He was the only president who did not belong to either of the large Barelwi or Deobandi groupings in the city and his presidency testifies to his role as the prime mover behind this initiative. Mr Warraich identified three interrelated concerns which led him to propose the creation of such a Council: Muslims required a common platform from which to negotiate with the local authority in the vexed arena of educational provision, the focus of widely shared anxieties; a Council for Mosques could manage and reduce sectarianism and create a forum for members of different mosques to meet; finally, such an organization would be in a strong position to elicit financial help from local and central government.

It is no accident that, with the exception of Pir Maroof, none of the prime movers behind the Council were 'ulama. Indeed, the Council has never had an 'alim as president. The role of the 'ulama within the Council was severely circumscribed from its inception. The Council was, in part, intended to relate to public bodies in the city, and most 'ulama possessed neither the language, skills, nor experience to fulfil such a task. Further, the Council was intended to minimize sectarian differences, another reason for limiting their active involvement. Umar Warraich and others of the founding fathers, however, were used to co-operating in a variety of local political and social arenas with men with different sectarian, regional and caste loyalties (as documented in Chapter 3). As employees of mosque committees the 'ulama were effectively excluded from the Council by its constitution, which declared ineligible for membership anyone who 'held a paid position in the Council or with any member organization'. They served a consultancy role when required.

The Council for Mosques' constitution was framed to maximize co-operation. Thus, the Council was committed to non-interference in the internal affairs of its member organizations and could only support the views of one of its members when these were not at variance with those held by other constituent bodies. The only group excluded from the Council was the Ahmadiyya sect.[5] The constitution declared that one of its objectives was 'to promote understanding, unity and Islamic Brotherhood'. In this regard it has been more successful than a similar initiative in Birmingham which fragmented into rival mosque councils. The president and general-secretary had to belong to different organizations. This constitutional coda has meant that in Bradford whenever the president belonged to the Barelwi group – invariably Jami'at-i Tabligh al-Islam – the general-secretary was a Deobandi and vice versa, thus preventing any rupture between the two most numerous groupings in the city.

Mr Warraich's hopes for the Council for Mosques were to prove realistic. The city council supported the Council for Mosques with a Community Programme grant of £13,000, enabling it to purchase a large semi-detached house to serve as its headquarters. From 1983 until the autumn of 1988, when the ground rules for Manpower Services Commission (MSC) projects were redefined, the Council for Mosques was the centre for an ambitious MSC scheme providing at its height some 50 workers servicing a range of projects: two centres for the elderly, a variety of advice workers, male and female, for the various mosques and Islamic centres, and a service for women in hospitals and clinics.

The success of the Council for Mosques in the 1980s in persuading the local education authority to be responsive in the curriculum and ethos of local schools to their religious and cultural traditions turned on two main factors. One was reviewed in Chapter 3, the education authority's willingness to respond to the special needs of minorities under the new educational banner of 'multiculturalism'. The second factor was the political support ethnic minorities could muster locally. This was facilitated by the overlapping membership and co-operation between Muslim councillors and Muslims active in the Council for Mosques and the Community Relations Council (CRC). When an issue fell clearly within an anti-racist framework the Council for Mosques was able to capitalize on tactical alliances with other minority groups involved in the CRC, and mobilize political support through Muslim councillors; from 1981 there was cross-party political support for a twelve-point race relations plan.

It is worth stressing the significance of the CRC as an organization where Muslim councillors and Muslims active in the Council for Mosques could meet. The CRC has functioned as a nursery for Muslim politicians, where the necessary skills, confidence and contacts were developed. Five Muslim councillors were active in the CRC in the 1980s.[6] The cross-cutting membership is clearly seen with Councillor Ajeeb, who was the first South Asian chairman of the CRC from 1976 to 1983 and held other positions in the organization throughout the 1980s. He was elected a councillor in 1979 and for two years was senior supervisor of the MSC project located at the Council for Mosques, a position from which he resigned when he became the first 'Asian' Lord Mayor in 1985. In 1984, a crucial year which saw the resolution of the halal meat crisis and the beginning of the Honeyford affair, the CRC executive included two councillors – Ajeeb and Hameed – as well as the president of the Council for Mosques, Sher Azam, and C.M. Khan, the president for the following two years.[7] Thus the CRC was the main forum where officers of the Council for Mosques and Muslim councillors met and where support for Muslim concerns in the wider community could be tested.

Three major educational controversies in the early 1980s highlight both the influence of the Council for Mosques and its limits. In 1982 Bradford education authority had issued guidelines to schools – *Education for a Multi-cultural Society: Provisions for Pupils of Ethnic Minority Communities* – intended to accommodate Muslim cultural and religious needs 'within one educational system and within the framework of a common school curriculum'. As part of this package of measures the authority stated that it was 'considering the provision of Halal meat in schools and ... actively investigating ways in which this can be done'.[8] The wild card in the pack was the Muslim Parents Association (MPA), which in January 1983 submitted a request to convert five schools with a largely Muslim intake into Muslim voluntary-aided schools (two first schools, two middle schools and one upper school). The education authority clearly wanted to maximize concessions to Muslims so as to preserve the integrity of the local education system by undercutting support for the MPA.

On 17 July 1983, the Council for Mosques and members of the education authority met. The Council for Mosques was frank that there was no consensus on the MPA proposals since Muslims in Bradford comprised 'different ethnic, national and sectarian strands'. However, they had rejected, for practical reasons, by a margin of thirteen to eight, with four abstentions, the particular MPA proposal. They were not convinced that 'this organisation would be able to run and administer (let alone finance) the five schools'. There was a sting in the tail for the education authority: the Council stressed that they had *not* taken a decision on the principle of separate Muslim schools, and that it would become increasingly hard to convince its members that 'what was good for Catholics was not good for Muslims unless the Authority did all in its power to honour its new found commitment to multicultural education in both spirit and letter.'[9]

The Council for Mosques, by rejecting the MPA proposal – a spectre which continues to haunt the education authority – won the gratitude of the authority. In return the LEA retained 'its two single sex upper schools instead of amalgamating them into a co-educational comprehensive'.[10] Also the authority did not delay in providing halal meat to 1,400 Muslim children in September 1983. The intention was to extend the service across the metropolitan area and within two years to provide such meals to all of the authority's 15,000 Muslim pupils.

Far from being the end of the matter, the publicity surrounding the provision of halal food triggered an angry campaign led by animal rights activists, who objected to the fact that the prescribed method of slaughter precluded the pre-stunning of animals. In December an editorial in the local press, entitled 'Prejudice', worried that 'behind the veil of respectability offered by the animal rights people, racists have relished the chance to criticise Muslims in our community.'[11] One animal rights campaigner refused to pay her rates and courted imprisonment. In February 1984 the Bradford Council conceded to requests for a debate on halal meat in full council.

The Muslim community was angered by this decision, which seemed to threaten their recently won right, as tax-payers, to have school meals which their children could eat. The Council for Mosques began to mobilize. It circulated an appeal, in Urdu, 'Historic Decision on Halal Meat', to Muslim parents asking them to boycott school on 6 March 1983 – the day on which Bradford Council would debate the issue – and, with their children, to demonstrate outside City Hall. A large majority of Muslim parents heeded this appeal, with an estimated 10,000 children taken out of school and many participating in the demonstration.

The Council for Mosques could rely on a broad-based alliance of groups to support them. The Community Relations Council was incensed that a racist backlash threatened to reverse a decision to meet the 'special needs' of a minority community. Muslim councillors spoke eloquently in the crucial debate on 6 March in the Town Hall. Councillor Iftikhar Qureshi (SDP) warned the city council that if 'it went back on its decision it would be regarded as unworthy and biased by the Muslim community'.[12] In the event the Bradford Council voted by 59 votes to 15 to retain halal meat. The local press dubbed the furore 'the issue of the year'.[13] A public boycott of schools and thousands of Muslims demonstrating outside City Hall guaranteed that the national media, too, were beginning to take an interest in the city's Muslim presence.

No sooner had the halal debate been resolved than another controversy erupted. This time it turned on the articles by Ray Honeyford, the head of Drummond Road Middle School. Although first published in an article in the *Times Educational Supplement* under the heading 'Multi-racial myths' in 1982, it was only in early March 1984 that his opinions entered the public domain, when his article in the January edition of a small circulation, right-wing journal, *The Salisbury Review*, entitled 'Education and Race – an Alternative View', was summarized in the *Yorkshire Post*.[14]

Press coverage of his opinions triggered a conflict which was not to be resolved until December 1985 when he agreed to take early retirement and accept a cash settlement of £71,000. Between these two dates an astonishing saga unfolded: a Drummond Parents' Action Committee (DPAC) came into being, pressing for the head's dismissal; an alternative school was set up in the local Pakistan Community Centre; Ray Honeyford was first dismissed and then his reinstatement was upheld by the High Court; an adjournment debate in the House of Commons was granted to a local Conservative MP, Marcus Fox; a boycott of the city's schools by Muslim pupils proved abortive; the Prime Minister, Mrs Thatcher, invited the head to attend a discussion of educationalists; and finally the Appeal Court overturned the High Court decision and thus allowed the local authority to resolve the affair.

The Council for Mosques was involved although, unlike the halal issue, they neither initiated nor fronted the campaign, which was done by the DPAC. The Council for Mosques had been alerted to the article in the *Salisbury Review* by Mr Naqvi, one of the founder members of the Council and a future chairman of the DPAC.[15]

Marcus Fox, in the adjournment debate in the House of Commons, sought to identify the issues and groups behind the protests against Mr Honeyford. According to the MP the consequences of the affair,

> go beyond the issue of race relations or ... education. They strike at the very root of our democracy ... the freedom of speech ... [Mr Honeyford] dared to suggest that in a classroom dominated by coloured children white children suffer educationally ... Who are Mr Honeyford's detractors? ... they are all on the Left of British politics. The Marxists and the Trots are here in full force ... [in collusion with those who] recently formed an alternative school ... some people in the area wanted a separate Moslim school in the first place. Therefore it was not difficult to get a bandwagon rolling.[16]

Marcus Fox, in articulating what became the 'Authorized Version' of the Honeyford affair, ignored the possibility that a headteacher, in a school comprising some 90 per cent children

from a Pakistani Muslim backgound, needed to show some professional reticence in publicly criticizing both aspects of their parents' home country and features of Islam.[17] He also managed to
pass over in silence the ethics of a situation in which a head
chose to criticize his education authority's policies on multicultural
education, or the wisdom of doing so in a periodical committed
to repatriation of ethnic minorities.

One irony of the affair was that Ray Honeyford was by no
means unsympathetic to many Muslim attitudes; the writer Hanif
Kureishi, in an essay on Bradford, was able to identify several
overlapping concerns between the headteacher and C.M. Khan,
the president of the Council for Mosques during much of the
crisis.[18] However, such commonalities were obscured by Honeyford's intemperate asides and innumerable *non sequiturs* in both
the *Times Educational Supplement* article and that in the *Salisbury
Review*. Pragmatic concessions to Muslim sensibilities such as
allowing girls to wear tracksuits in PE were variously described as
capitulating to 'Moslem extremists' and 'religious fanaticism' by
those intent on subverting sexual equality by a 'purdah mental-
ity'. The term 'fundamentalist Moslem', as imprecise as it is sin-
ister in connotation, was bandied about. Halal methods of killing
animals were presented as 'indifference to animal care' in conflict
with 'one of the school's values – love of dumb creatures and
respect for their welfare'.[19]

In addition, he compounded his folly by rehearsing stereotypes
about West Indians and Indians and thus ensured the Community
Relations Council's support for the DPAC campaign to remove
him from the school.[20] Since in 1984 the CRC included on its
executive committee two Muslim Councillors and two members
of the Council for Mosques the campaign against the headteacher
was assured of wide support.

The Council for Mosques was involved throughout the campaign, often as a moderating voice, increasingly worried at the
escalation of tension. On 21 June 1985 there was a demonstration
numbering some 420 marchers.

There were eleven speakers: six Pakistanis, two Bangladeshis, one
Hindu, one Sikh and one white ... Mr C.M. Khan (President of the
Council for Mosques) was effective to the extent that he curbed the

would-be rabble-rousers. Despite their efforts, and the high percentage of Angry Young ... Men in the audience, everyone dispersed quietly.[21]

With Honeyford's return to the school in September 1985 picketing intensified, children were given stickers to wear in their class-rooms on which was written 'Honeyford Out' and 'Ray-CIST', and leaflets produced insisting that the headteacher had 'insulted your religion,' and your culture'.[22] On 15 October the DPAC declared a Day of Action and the Council for Mosques issued a leaflet in Urdu urging Muslim parents to boycott the city's schools on that day in protest against the head who had 'displayed defamatory opinions against Asian and African parents' – a clause indicating that the Council never presented the issue as simply one involving Muslims.

If the Council for Mosques was hoping for a boycott as successful as that against the threat to halal meat in 1984, it was disappointed. This time only one child in four was withdrawn.[23] After this débâcle the Council for Mosques decided to support a cooling off period. Sher Azam explained to the CRC that after consulting with the parents and assessing the situation in the city as a whole they realized that they could 'not fight a campaign when the majority of the population was not on their side'.[24]

The Council for Mosques was understandably anxious. One mosque had withdrawn in 1985 objecting to the politicization of the Council under the presidency of C.M. Khan, a member of the Labour Party – the first and last president who was a member of any political party. Umar Warraich, a founder member of the Council, had tried to set up an alternative mosque council in 1985, the Council of Masajid and Islamic Centres. This initiative, which included little more than the UK Islamic Mission mosque and the Dawat al-Islam mosque, was to prove abortive but it did indicate disquiet with the direction the Council for Mosques was taking under C.M. Khan. Anxiety was evidenced by the poor response to the Council's request to Muslim parents to withdraw their children from school on 15 October in support of the DPAC Day of Action.

The Council for Mosques' reputation and standing had been diminished by its involvement in the Honeyford affair, both within the Muslim community and in the city at large. The headteacher's opinions on three important inter-related issues – racism, free speech and accountability, the nature and limits of multi-culturalism – were never exposed to open debate but merely shouted down. Both right and left of the political spectrum were responsible for this: the right narrowed the issue down to one of freedom of speech, while the left presented the issue as one of racism. Neither perspective allowed for any real debate on such issues as: 'how to resolve the tensions between the preservation of the distinct cultural identity of minority communities on the one hand and the encouragement of social integration on the other.'[25]

In a campaign that the Council for Mosques did not even control locally and which soon moved out of the local into the national political arena, Muslims found themselves tarred with the excesses committed by opponents of Ray Honeyford. The affair was misconstrued as simply a 'Muslim' issue with negative terminology – fundamentalism, extremism and fanaticism – and disturbing images of 'Muslims' fixed in the public mind; pictures of angry parents and children baying for the head's blood outside the gates of the school became the staple fare of national tele-vision. Marcus Fox's 'Authorized Version' of the affair even presented Muslims, with others, as a threat to democracy for their supposed attack on freedom of speech – an accusation antici-pating those which would be made against Muslims in the Rushdie affair. The often moderate and pragmatic stance of the Council for Mosques' leadership remained invisible. Thus the resolution of the issue in December 1985 with the headteacher's early retirement and financial settlement was a pyrrhic victory for the Council.

The Council for Mosques' Response to *The Satanic Verses*

On 28 May 1985 a civic service was held for the new Lord Mayor, Councillor Ajeeb. Since he was the first Muslim to hold this office the service was held in a mosque – the central mosque of Jami'at-i Tabligh al-Islam in Southfield Square. Civic dignitaries attended the service, which included selections from the Barelwi devotional poem *Salaam*, translated into English. The verses chosen included the following in praise of the Prophet:

Blessed be my strength in misery,
My hope and wealth in poverty.

Blessed be that rose of nature,
Glorious symbol of Creator.

Blessed be the look affectionate
Caring, kind and compassionate.

Blessed be that magnanimous mind,
Which sought God's mercy for mankind.

Blessed be his mission of Islam
Replacing violence by peace and calm.

Blessed be the Prophet's family members,
Who are all like heavenly flowers.[26]

Much has been written about the *Satanic Verses* affair. In order to understand the sense of outrage which galvanized the Muslim communities in Bradford when news of the 'contents' of the novel began to circulate, two factors have to be kept in mind. First, although the book was published in Britain, news of its 'contents' and the shape of the indictment against it were formulated and mediated to Bradford's Muslims by their co-religionists in India.[27] In that country marked by troubled and deteriorating inter-communal relations it is hardly surprising that the distinguished Sikh writer Khushwant Singh, an editorial adviser to Penguin Books in India, on reading a novel in which 'the Prophet had been made to be a small-time imposter' advised against publication.[28] Second, the city's Muslims shared with their South Asian co-religionists a deep devotion to the Prophet. It is hard to exaggerate the veneration of the Prophet which informs Islamic piety and practice in South Asia in all traditions, but especially amongst the Barelwis, as evidenced in the *Salaam*.[29]

Any work which can be construed as insulting the Prophet can be guaranteed to unite the most diverse groupings of Muslims in South Asia and throughout the South Asian Muslim diaspora. Forty years ago the historian Wilfred Cantwell Smith, writing on Islam in South Asia, noted that,

Muslims will allow attacks on Allah; there are atheists and atheistic publications, and rationalistic societies; but to disparage Muhammad will provoke from even the most 'liberal' sections of the community a fanaticism of blazing vehemence.[30]

In 1924 a Hindu in Lahore published a work in Urdu with the deliberately provocative title, *Rangila Rasul* (The Pleasure-Loving Prophet), portraying the Prophet as a libertine. This book so enaged Muslim sensibilities that its author was murdered by two Muslims. They themselves were considered martyrs when they were sentenced to death and executed by the British.[31] The British, to forestall a repeat of this episode, introduced Article 295A to the Indian penal code, making it an offence to 'insult or outrage the religious feelings of any class'.[32] The sentiments underlying such an enactment have been given a sharpened focus recently in Pakistan. In July 1986 the National Assembly of Pakistan adopted the Criminal Law (Amendment) Bill which,

> provides that whoever by words, either spoken or written, or by visible representation or by any imputation, innuendo or insinuation, directly or indirectly, defiles the sacred name of the Holy Prophet ... shall be punished with death or imprisonment.[33]

The Satanic Verses, seen through South Asian Muslim eyes, could hardly fail to trigger outrage. Bhikhu Parekh, deputy chair of the Commission for Racial Equality, in one of the most perceptive of the early articles on the book and the furore it was to generate, argued that journalists and 'high-minded literary critics' alike were unlikely to have understood the work fully, given its distinctly Bombay ambience, argot and allusions. Further,

> the chapters dealing with 'Mahound' (Muhammad) and his new religion are suffused with subtle allusions and insinuations likely to be lost or misunderstood by those not well-versed in the history of Islam ... Muhammad is called a 'smart bastard', a debauchee who after his wife's death, slept with so many women that his beard turned 'half-white' in a year ... [his] three revered colleagues ... are 'those goons – those fucking clowns' ... Like any great religious text, the Koran is full of rules and injunctions about forms of worship, helping the poor, concern for those in need, moral purity, self-discipline and surrender to the will of God. *The Satanic Verses* mockingly reduces it to a book 'spouting' rules about how to 'fart', 'fuck' and 'clean one's behind' ...

These remarks lack artistic justification ... they insult and provoke the devout: they challenge Muslim men to stand up and fight back if they have any self-respect and sense of honour.[34]

Parekh, a professor of political theory, a non-Muslim from a Hindu background, had taken the trouble to read the novel and to elicit comments from Muslims who had also read it. It was not simply those unschooled in the subtleties of magic realism who could find the novel offensive. There is no need here to comment on the novel as fiction, the vexed issue of authorial intent, nor to attempt some assessment of the mutual responsibility of Salman Rushdie and his readers, Muslim and non-Muslim alike, issues exhaustively treated by others. The value of Professor Parekh's comment is simply to underline the fact that the book's contents were inevitably explosive amongst Muslims from a South Asian background.

The Bradford Council for Mosques kept a documentary record of the letters they sent, the replies they received and the coverage given to their protests in the local and national media between October 1988 and the end of March 1989. From this record it was clear that their response to the publication of the novel in Britain on 26 September 1988 was initially shaped by expectations informed by a South Asian legal and cultural context, which gradually yielded to the painful realization that the British situation was markedly different. The Council's decision to burn a copy of the novel on 14 January 1989 – which ironically emphasized how little the Muslim elders understood of their new legal, political and cultural context – was part of an attempt to draw attention to their continued anguish and anger when confronted by incomprehension of politicians and media alike.

The first letters in their file are those in Urdu and English from the Deobandi organization in Blackburn, Hizb ul 'ulama, the Society of Muslim Scholars in the UK. This largely Gujarati association sent the Bradford Council for Mosques an account of the novel summarized by two editors of Urdu newspapers published in Delhi and in Surat, Gujarat – summaries of the novel drawn, in all probability, from interviews with Salman Rushdie in the Indian press – with the recommendation that Muslims should petition 'either Her Majesty the Queen, the Prime Minister or the Home Office Minister' to ban the book.

The president of the Council for Mosques, Sher Azam, then wrote to the Prime Minister on 12 November, repeating much of the contents of the Blackburn letter. He made no claim to have read the novel himself:

> informed about the novel ... The Muslims of Bradford and all over the world are shocked ... [since] the writer ... has attacked our beloved Prophet ... and his wives using dirty language which no ... Muslim can tolerate ... [Mr Azam then repeats the summary of the novel in the two Indian Muslim papers, e.g.] ... an Indian film star named GIBRIL FARISHTA ... is supposedly a reincarnation o the Prophet Mohammad ... MAKKAH is called 'EVIL CITY'. The author ... also mentions, The Devil's synonym Mohoud [sic] which means ... MOHAMMAD.

Mr Azam took heart that the Indian government had already banned the novel and appealed to the Prime Minister to follow their example. He focused on the 'distress' the work had caused Muslims. There were no threats to the author and, unlike the Blackburn letter, he did not refer to Mr Rushdie as an apostate, *murtadd*, a serious accusation in Islamic law.[35]

This was the first of a series of letters the Council sent to the publishers, local MPs and councillors, the UN, and Bradford's chief executive. They urged Bradford's local authority to refuse to provide the book to libraries, schools and other educational institutions. The response from the book's publishers was predictable: Viking insisted that as 'a serious publisher' they were committed to 'freedom of expression'; they disavowed any intention to offend by publishing the novel; they quoted Salman Rushdie's comment that the offending sections of the work occur 'in a dream, the fictional dream of an individual movie star and one who is losing his mind, at that'; and finally pointed out that the work had been acclaimed in certain sections of the Indian press, had been shortlisted for the 1988 Booker Prize and had just won the fiction category of the Whitbread Award.

The responses of two of the local MPs are instructive. Pat Wall reminded the Council for Mosques of his advocacy for Muslims when victims of racism, but reminded them that the government had recently made a fool of themselves in trying to ban *Spycatcher*, which proved counterproductive and 'resulted in a colossal increase in the sales internationally'. Another MP who proved sympathetic to Muslim sensibilities was Max Madden. His constituency included a large proportion of Muslims, from whom he was able to gauge directly the depth of anger and outrage, still invisible to the majority of the local community. He suggested to the publishers that they might insert a statement by Muslims as to why they found the work offensive and urged a television debate between the author and his Muslim critics. In his letter to the publishers he drew attention to 'the extraordinary anomaly in modern multi-faith Britain' of a blasphemy law which only protected the established Christian faith.

It was the Council for Mosques' misfortune that they invariably misread the situation in Britain. Their initial letters fuelled the suspicion that they wanted to ban a novel by a distinguished author on the basis of little more than hearsay. Only later did they co-opt on to the Council, as an individual member, Shabbir Akhtar, a Cambridge graduate in philosophy, who was able forcibly to *argue* a Muslim case in the national media and in his book, *Be Careful with Muhammad!* The Council's appeal to the Bishop of Bradford for 'justice' and a 'change in the law of blasphemy' was only made after the book-burning episode at a regional rally organized by the Council on 14 January 1989 had alienated would-be sympathizers.[36] In an editorial in the *Yorkshire Post*, under the heading 'Satanic Fires', Muslims were excoriated as 'intellectual hooligans' manipulated by demagogues into burning a book most had not read, and they were likened to the Nazis.[37]

For the national media Bradford had become the epicentre of the shock waves convulsing the Muslim communities across Britain. Ayatollah Khomeini's intervention a month later was to prove disastrous for the Muslim campaign in Bradford and in Britain. Two members of the Bradford Council for Mosques' executive exacerbated the situation by allegedly supporting the fatwa, the legal decision sentencing to death the author and publishers responsible. A public outcry ensued, and the West Yorkshire Police passed on these comments to the Crown Prosecution Service. The local press reported that 'the world's press converges on Bradford' as the Council for Mosques held an emergency meeting distancing themselves from these comments. A spokesman for the Council for Mosques insisted that the two had been misquoted and that 'we do not support the Ayatollah ... he is not our leader ... we are living in England ... and do not take directives from him.'[38]

The Council for Mosques was now centre-stage but no more in control of presentation of the issues than it had been in the Honeyford affair. A process of demonization of Muslims already begun in this earlier episode now accelerated.[39] Sometimes local Muslims themselves colluded in this process. Dr Shabbir Akhtar penned a defence of 'religious fundamentalism' in a national daily, arguing that 'any faith which compromises its internal temper of militant wrath is destined for the dustbin of history.'[40] Since the article introduced him as a member of Bradford Council for Mosques the impression was left that the Council was full of passionate 'fundamentalists'. His later book on the Rushdie affair showed that he, too, had learned from this episode: militant wrath was now qualified by the adjective 'constructive'![41]

As with the Honeyford saga, media images of angry demonstrations and inflammatory placards projected and fixed in the public imagination a fearsome and negative picture of Muslims and served to alienate rather than enlist support. In June 1989, a rally organized by the Council erupted into sporadic violence engineered by a small group of Muslim youngsters. This appeared on the front page of the local press with a colour picture of an effigy of Salman Rushdie 'daubed with red paint and slogans such as "Kill the Pig"'.[42] The Bradford Council for Mosques was to suspend public demonstrations locally, when violence flared again at what had been a peaceful Muslim youth rally. The Council concluded that 'open-air rallies were too vulnerable to provocateurs and others looking for trouble'.[43] By then the damage had been done, not least by the media's 'remorseless tendency to trivialise, or where feelings are running high, to polarise'.[44]

It became clear to the Council for Mosques that on this issue the Muslim communities were increasingly isolated with few allies, with the exception of the MP Max Madden and the Anglican bishop.[45] The Community Relations Council was caught in a dilemma: Salman Rushdie was respected for his views on anti-racism and his written and video materials were widely used. Moreover *The Satanic Verses* included much material congenial to the left and accessible to an anti-racist constituency. Therefore, the CRC decided to 'adopt no position on the book ... [since] the specific issues relating to the concerns of the Muslim community ... are of a religious nature ... the best people to represent [their] concerns ... are the properly constituted religious organisations in the city.'[46] This was somewhat disingenuous since the CRC had supported Muslims earlier on the provision of halal meat, an avowedly religious issue, specific to that community. However, the report pertinently observed that recent events had,

> increased the awareness of all of us about the significance of religious demands in meeting the specific needs of ethnic minority communities. Perhaps we have been too ready to fit all issues into an equal opportunities framework at the expense of those needs which are of a specifically religious nature.[47]

The National and International Dimensions of the Campaign

It was clear to the Council for Mosques that concerted national action was required both to direct the anger the book generated into constructive channels and to bring pressure to bear on the government. The difficulty was to create a national body which could transcend the Barelwi/Wahhabi split. Here the Bradford Council for Mosques had a vital role to play, in that it included both groupings and was supported by two personalities who enjoyed a national following in both traditions, Pir Maroof and Sher Azam.

Sher Azam's role in lending credibility to any such national initiative was crucial. He was president of a respected local Council for Mosques which had several significant gains to its credit, and whose campaign experience had been honed in lengthy local campaigns. Moreover, he was already known outside Bradford through his involvement with the the Council of Mosques UK and Eire. This organization, created in 1984, was sponsored by the Muslim World League, based in Mecca, and chaired by the director of the London branch of that organization. Its policy was to have a British Muslim as vice-chairman, and Sher Azam held that position from 1986 to 1988.

Thus, when in October 1988 the UK Action Committee on Islamic Affairs, UKACIA, was formed in London to oppose the book, its convenor was a Saudi diplomat, Mughram Al Ghamdi, director of Regent's Park mosque, and Sher Azam was one of its twelve-strong steering committee. The presence of Mr Azam and Mr Maan of the Islamic Council of Scotland, who both belonged to groupings comprising various sects, meant that there were always some Barelwis affiliated to UKACIA, including Pir Maroof's World Islamic Mission. The UKACIA was a useful mechanism for bringing pressure to bear on the government, through Muslim ambassadors in London and lobbying the Organization of the Islamic Conference (OIC).

Sher Azam was one of a UKACIA delegation attending the OIC meeting held on 13–16 of March 1989 in Riyadh, Saudi Arabia. Its lobbying met with qualified success when the OIC adopted a declaration against blasphemy which, while not endorsing the Iranian fatwa, urged member states 'to ban the book ... to prevent the entry of its author in all Islamic countries and [to call] upon publishing houses to immediately withdraw the book from circulation and ... to boycott any publishing house that does not comply.'[48]

The UKACIA newsletter in July 1989 offered a realistic assessment of the difficulties confronting their campaign, reminding its readers that the Muslim community in Britain was:

> not a homogenous community ... not yet a united community ... an inexperienced community ... [with] a lot to learn. Compared to other communities it has as yet no effective clout in the seats of power, in the media or in economic circles ... [However, for the first time] people whose work was localized or limited to members of their own particular school of thought have now got to know, meet and appreciate others ... Muslims as a result of this campaign are beginning to learn more about the political ... and legal processes of the country ... it is heartening to note the support ... from some MPS, leading members of the Church, the Jewish and other religious communities.[49]

The UKACIA was not the only group seeking to mobilize Muslim anger. On 1 April 1989, Kalim Siddiqui, director of the pro-Iranian Muslim Institute in London, in his presidential address to a conference convened to consider the implications of the

Rushdie affair, suggested 'symbolic breaking of the law' might be necessary. This suggestion was quickly repudiated by the UKACIA. However, many British Muslims were growing restive with the UKACIA's apparent lack of success, and Barelwis, particularly, were inclined to put it down to a want of resolve and commitment to defend the Prophet's honour on the part of the Saudis and their surrogate organizations.

An individual member of the Bradford Council for Mosques voiced such impatience. He noted that many Muslims 'applauded Khomeini as a hero' since he had 'stood up for the honour of the Prophet' in contrast to 'the deafening silence' from the Arab heartlands. The vigour of the Saudi response to the prospective showing in Britain of the film, *Death of a Princess* – deemed an insult to the Saudi royal family – which triggered a withdrawal of ambassador and a hint of economic sanctions, was contrasted to their 'unduly soft appoach' when confronted with an insult to the Prophet. This was put down to their being Wahhabi and thus having 'no adequate appreciation of the greatness of Muhammad'.[50]

It is to the credit of the Bradford Council for Mosques, under Sher Azam's presidency, that they deftly negotiated these difficult crosscurrents without fragmenting. They continued to explore all avenues to influence public opinion, taking local initiatives and co-operating with the UKACIA when the situation required a national response. In April 1989 they sent questionnaires to all MPs to gauge the level of support for their campaign. Only 50 replied, but an analysis of these made it clear that in all the furore, 'Muslims have never really presented their case clearly, for example, to explain that they have no fear of intellectual ... criticisms ... [but] what is untenable is a slur on the integrity of the Prophet.'[51]

When the Minister of State at the Home Office, John Patten, set out the government's thinking on the issues raised by the Rushdie affair in an open letter to 'influential British Muslims' on 4 July 1989, the Council for Mosques chose to be part of a considered national response written under the aegis of the UKACIA. Mr Patten argued that the government had been 'guided by two principles: the freedom of speech, thought and expression; and the notion of the rule of law'. The only principle the government and law could 'realistically protect' was that 'individuals should be free to choose their own faith and to worship without interference, in an atmosphere of mutual respect and toleration'. The UKACIA rejoinder pressed for amendments to the law of blasphemy to include within its purview non-Christian works clearly antipathetic to 'mutual respect'.[52]

On 17 July 1989 the Bradford Council for Mosques launched a ten-point charter during a public demonstration. The charter included lobbying local and national politicians, making future electoral support conditional upon a positive response and the establishment of a Muslim think-tank to combat anti-Muslim propaganda in the media. They continued to participate in and to organize regional meetings. Together with the UKACIA they organized a five-day vigil held on 8–12 January 1990 outside the headquarters of Viking Penguin in London.

Although Muslims did not succeed in banning the book, the Bradford Council for Mosques' campaign, as it unfolded, indicated that certain lessons had been learned. Nothing shows this more clearly than the shift from book-burning to vigil as a way of winning a more sympathetic hearing for their grievances. The Council also organized a national conference of Muslims in Bradford on 29 April 1990. Under the title of 'Fair Laws for All' they sought to 'begin a nationwide debate on the future of Muslims in this country', and structured the day to include input on Muslim aspirations and anxieties in the areas of education, social and economic life, political participation and the responsiblities of mosques and *'ulama*. Realizing how isolated Muslims had become, the conference invited the Bishop of Bradford, and leaders of the Hindu and Sikh communities in the city, as well as local politicians. According to Sher Azam the conference was an attempt to begin a new phase in the campaign to enlist the support of key institutions by convincing them 'through discussion of the rights of our cause'.[53]

What was impressive about the conference was the range of speakers enlisted, locally and nationally. These included Yusuf Islam, a leading British Muslim convert; Maulana Rabbani, the president of the Jami'at-i 'Ulama Britannia, the umbrella organization for Deobandi *'ulama*; Pir Wahhab Siddiqui, a distinguished Barelwi from Coventry; Asif Hussain, a sociologist and the director of the Muslim Community Studies Institute in Leicester; and Akram Khan Cheema, a Bradford educationalist, who was the chairman of the education sub-committee of the Council of Mosques, UK and Eire. It is hard to imagine any other Muslim organization in the country enjoying the trust of all the sects and able to host such a gathering of professionals and religious leaders alike.

The emphasis of the conference was on the need for a constructive engagement with the nation's institutions; political, social and educational. Muslim concerns were articulated in an idiom accessible to the non-Muslim majority: Akram Khan Cheema coined the helpful slogan of 'special but not separate' to encapsulate Muslim demands on the educational system. There was a readiness to be self-critical. Yusuf Islam upbraided the *'ulama* for being slow to engage with contemporary issues, whether genetic engineering, abortion or ecology. Such a conference was a tribute to the realism of the Bradford Council for Mosques and a refusal to allow Muslims to withdraw into sullen resentment.

After the Gulf Crisis: Who Speaks for Muslims?

Throughout *The Satanic Verses* affair the Council for Mosques was aware of the need to work out a pattern of relationships with other Muslim groups nationally, and transnational organizations within the *umma*, which did not suggest that their agenda was being dictated by Muslims outside Britain. This difficulty was compounded by a local community with limited resources: if many mosques had problems in paying their *'ulama* a living wage it was not surprising that national initiatives often depended on foreign funding and could involve Muslims in rivalries between different Muslim powers. The *umma* was after all an 'imagined community' which, with the end of the Caliphate in 1924, had no recognizable centre, political or symbolic.[54]

One aspect of the Rushdie affair, often invisible to non-Muslims, was a growing impatience with the seeming lack of zeal exhibited by Saudi Arabia in using its influence to bring pressure to bear on the British government. Such antagonism was fuelled by sectarian differences between South Asian Barelwis and Saudi

Arabian Wahhabis, and exacerbated by the bitter experiences of many South Asian Muslim guestworkers in the Arab Gulf States. In the 1980s there were some two million Pakistanis working there. Many had little sympathy for their employers, who were considered to have squandered the oil wealth, a trust from God, and amongst whom 'courtesy to strangers ... [had been] lost in the transition from camel to cadillac'.[55]

Anti-Saudi sentiment amongst Muslims from a South Asian background was much more public during the Gulf crisis. Many Muslims outside the Barelwi tradition were aghast that the Saudis could invite American and European forces onto Saudi territory – albeit under a UN mandate – for defence and, if necessary, for an offensive to liberate one Muslim country, Kuwait, from the aggression of another. To add salt to Muslim wounds there were some 2,000 Jewish personnel among the huge American presence, with Jewish rabbis to minister to them, and reports of 'the first mass observance of the Jewish festival of Purim on Saudi Arabian soil for more than 800 years' – in contravention of Saudi law.[56]

While Saudi Arabia was home of the most revered centres of Islamic devotion and pilgrimage, Iraq too contained many sites sacred to Shi'a and Sunni alike: the shrine at Karbala, the site of the martyrdom of Hussain, the grandson of the Prophet, was one of the great pilgrimage centres of the Muslim world. Many Barelwis from South Asia visited the shrines of holy men in Iraq, particularly that of Abdul Qadir Jilani, buried in Baghdad, the founder of the trans-national Qadiri order. Pir Maroof of Bradford traced his spiritual ancestry back to the Prophet via Jilani, whose shrine he regularly visited. It was little wonder that the possibility of a war in proximity to such sites evoked fear and anger.

The majority of the public was, of course, unaware of such Muslim sensitivities. Iraq was perceived to be the aggressor, and with other UN forces British troops were preparing for the possibility of war. This situation required great wisdom on the part of British Muslims if their public pronouncements were not to be heard as partisan and unpatriotic. Between August 1990, when American and British troops began to enter Saudi Arabia, and 14 January 1991 – the UN deadline for Iraqi withdrawal from Kuwait

– the Bradford Council for Mosques was central in mobilizing Muslim opinion in Britain to voice their concerns about developments in the Gulf. This time Barelwi perspectives and personnel were more in evidence and, as events unfolded, criticism of Iraq became so muted as to suggest a pro-Iraqi stance. When this happened Muslim councillors in Bradford, better able to assess the dangers of such a stance in the middle of a war with Iraq, publicly distanced themselves from the Council.

On 12 August 1990 the Bradford Council for Mosques supported a declaration produced by Muslim organizations that had met at the Islamic Cultural Centre in London to discuss the developing crisis in the Gulf. The declaration pressed for the recall of British forces – indeed, all non-Muslim forces from Muslim territories in the Gulf – and insisted that,

> current national borders ... are artificial divisions. The nation of Islam (ummah) is one ... [and] national borders cannot be more sacred than the security of Muslim blood and land. The build up of non-Muslim military forces in the vicinity of Islam's most holy shrines ... is not acceptable ... Any government in Muslim lands co-operating with the non-Muslim armies cannot demand the support of Muslims worldwide ... [and] the present imbalance of wealth and resources among various peoples within the Ummah [should be remedied].[57]

The declaration deplored 'the name of Islam being used for national interests or the desire [sic] of one or other Muslim ruler if they do not themselves obey Islamic law'. This comment, alone in the declaration, could be interpreted as a veiled criticism of Iraq, whose invasion of Kuwait was otherwise passed over in silence. Such a declaration was a useful indication of Muslim suspicion of nationalism, seen as a creation of the West to fragment the *umma*, but it hardly seemed to engage with, still less to address, the realities of Iraqi aggression, the trigger of the immediate crisis.

Increasingly Barelwi members of the Bradford Council for Mosques were prepared, over the next few months, to take unilateral anti-Saudi initiatives. While six Muslims, including the president of the Council, Sher Azam, and Yusuf Islam, visited the Iraqi embassy in London on 16 August calling for the withdrawal of Iraqi troops from Kuwait and access to a Muslim peace-keeping force, Liaqat Hussain, the Barelwi general-secretary of the Council for Mosques, a few days later led some 200 Bradford Muslims, as part of a large national demonstration outside the Saudi embassy in London, protesting against the presence of Western troops in the country. Mr Hussain declared such Saudi behaviour to be 'an act of treason against Islam'.[58]

On 1 September 1990 Muslims met in Bradford and a statement signed by Sher Azam was sent to the Queen and members of the government. The statement criticized the government's 'provocative' act in dispatching British forces to the Gulf. This was interpreted as part of a Western conspiracy 'to eliminate the threat of a Third World Muslim Power developing economic and technological capability equal to that already possessed by the West and its close allies such as Israel'.[59] The meeting also mandated a group of seven to visit Iraq and Saudi Arabia on a fact-finding tour. The group included two members of the Council for Mosques: Sher Azam and Liaqat Hussain, the assistant of Pir Maroof.[60] In January Pir Maroof, the founder of Jami'at-i Tabligh al-Islam, was the only Bradford delegate of eight British Muslims invited to a three-day conference in Iraq of Muslims from all over the world. On his return, Pir Maroof had convinced himself that the Iraqi president had learned the folly of his ways in the war with Iran. 'Now he knows that Islam must come first...'[61]

The resolutions of a national Muslim conference at Bradford on 20 January, a few days after the war had begun, while consistent with earlier Muslim pronouncements, came as a shock to non-Muslims in its one-sidedness: the resolutions insisted that 'the USA led aggression against Iraq' must stop and these forces withdraw from Muslim territories; the Saudi ruling family was condemned for allowing non-Muslim forces access to the Islamic heartlands and declared unfit to be the custodian of Mecca and Medina; therefore, it was every Muslim's duty to 'restore [their] custody to rightful hands ... and work towards the restoration of the Khilafat [Caliphate]'.[62] It was clear that there was a debate within the ranks of local Muslims attending the meeting: Sher Azam was 'barracked when he proposed more moderate resolutions condemning the Iraqis as well ... and calling for simultaneous withdrawal of ... [Iraq's] troops from Kuwait and

Western forces.'[63] However, he was no longer president of the Council for Mosques; Liaqat Hussain now held this position.

Such conference resolutions, understandably, drew much adverse comment from the local and national media. More inflammatory comment from the Council for Mosques was to follow. On 13 February (after a tragic episode when Baghdad civilians were incinerated in an attack on what was wrongly identified as a military target) the Council for Mosques issued a press release headed 'Baghdad Massacre'. It amounted to an astonishing and intemperate attack on the British government, whom it held responsible for the massacre. It declared that 'these deaths must ... be avenged in accordance with Islamic law ... The House of Islam is at war with all those who attack its interest including those so called Muslims who are ... fellow conspirators with the forces of western imperialism.'[64]

Local Muslim politicians – well placed to assess the damage such statements were doing to community relations and public perceptions of Muslims – for the first time since the *Satanic Verses* affair quickly stepped in and publicly criticized this statement. Councillor Ajeeb pointed out that outrage at civilian casualties was not confined to Muslims, cautioned against 'talk about vengeance', insisted that 'politics and economics' – not religion – was the cause of the war and reminded Muslims that 'we are at war with Iraq'.[65]

Muhammed Riaz, a Tory candidate for a local ward, challenged the perception that the Gulf crisis was a holy war by pointing to the innumerable Muslim powers fighting under a UN mandate against Iraq and the fact that (Arab) Christians, not least in Iraq, were on both sides. He pointedly remarked that 'the views, actions and emotional statement' by any individual or Muslim organization does not do justice to the city's 60,000 Muslims since no individual nor organization has ever been 'given the mandate by ... the Muslims of Bradford to act as their representative or spokesman'.[66]

In 1981 there had been only three Muslim councillors. This under-representation of Muslims had influenced the local authority's willingness to support the Council for Mosques as a channel of communication with Muslims in the city. Ten years later the situation was quite different. After the May elections in 1991 there were nine, and in the following year eleven Muslim councillors, all Labour, the ruling group since 1990. Indeed, by 1992 Councillor Ajeeb was deputy leader of the Labour group and Muslim councillors began to enjoy influence commensurate with their numbers.[67] Since they were elected to wards where a large percentage of voters were Muslims, these councillors could properly claim they had as much right as the Council for Mosques to reflect on the Gulf situation and publicly voice opinions as Muslims, however uncongenial to some members of that Council.

Muslim Businessmen and Professionals Find Their Voice

While Muslim councillors had become a significant centre of influence in the city, able and willing to contest the opinion of the Council for Mosques on certain issues, they were not alone. Muslim businessmen were growing in confidence and generating initiatives which signalled that they too were going to be increasingly important participants in debates in the city touching Muslims. Two developments were particularly important in this context: the establishment of Bradford City Radio and the creation of an Eid Committee.

Bradford City Radio, BCR, was set up in 1989 to serve the ethnic minority communities. It included investment by Muslim businessmen, its chief executive was a Muslim and it employed some Muslim staff. Its chief executive saw the value of BCR as rendering public the many debates within the Muslim communities, and providing a forum for Muslim women, who publicly had remained largely invisible. BCR did not shy away from controversy. In August 1990 they invited Councillor Hussain and a local businessman, Zafar Khan, both Muslims, to take part in a phone-in to discuss the 'Muslim Manifesto', a draft document drawn up by the Muslim Institute in London, which proposed the creation of a 'Muslim Parliament'. Between 60 and 70 per cent of those who phoned were against the manifesto.

The programme generated a public controversy conducted in the local press between the Muslim councillor who had participated in it and a future member of the 'Muslim Parliament', M. Siddique, with the latter complaining that the programme 'distorted' and 'mocked' the manifesto.[68] Mr Siddique was also the leader of a local Barelwi youth group, named the Muslim Youth Movement – one of a number formed in the wake of the Rushdie affair. Councillor Hussain responded by criticizing Mr Siddique for damaging race relations locally with his 'bizarre, confusing and often conflicting views on Muslim affairs'. While the the phone-in gave an opportunity to canvas a wide spectrum of local opinion 'the Muslim Youth Movement', he claimed, represented 'only a handful of people'.[69] In January 1991 BCR broadcast a two-hour English-speaking phone-in with Salman Rushdie, despite some local opposition and threats, again from 'the Muslim Youth Movement'.[70] BCR also released details of their local radio poll which 'suggested that 90 per cent of Muslims were against the fatwa'.[71]

The Eid Committee came into being in the spring of 1991. It comprised nine local businessmen and professionals, mostly young men, born or educated in Britain, belonging to different sects. Most of their parents had migrated from rural or urban Pakistan. Their spokesman, Aurangzeb Iqbal, was a successful lawyer, a member of a local Barelwi mosque and an accomplished poet in English. Their first event was a two-day, weekend celebration of the festival (*eid*) which completes the month of fasting. Their aim was to involve people from the non-Muslim community; therefore, they had invited schools and colleges and 'arrangements had been made to bus in residents of old people's homes.'[72]

This was to be the first of a series of events for which they were responsible. The Eid Committee organized a large charity dinner for Muslims and non-Muslims alike after the Bangladesh cyclone disaster, which raised over £12,000. They held an Eid Mela, a community fête, in July to celebrate the end of the month of pilgrimage. In all, the committee has sought to break down barriers between communities as well as develop good links with city dignitaries. Such self-conscious philanthropic work reflects a new confidence among the Muslim professional and business elite, aware of the need to project positive images of the Muslim community to counteract the proliferating negative ones generated after the *Satanic Verses* affair and the Gulf crisis.

In 1992 the same Mr Iqbal negotiated the licence for a pioneer radio station to broadcast during the whole month of fasting from

6 March to 6 April, Radio Fast FM. This community radio was to provide religious programmes throughout the month. It was Radio Fast FM, not the Council for Mosques, which hosted a debate among *'ulama* of various sects in the city as to why they were unable to agree on dates for the month: in 1992 Muslims found themselves starting and ending the month on three different days. This caused hardship in families, chaos and embarrassment in factories, businesses and schools.[73]

These remarks are not intended to suggest that Muslim councillors, businessmen and members of the Council for Mosques inhabit separate and competing worlds. It was made clear in Chapter 3 that Muslims have multiple identities, linguistic, cultural, sectarian and political, with members of different sects and from diverse regions, for example, belonging to the same South Asian political parties. Similarly, businessmen featured prominently among the founders of the Council for Mosques and there was an overlap in membership between councillors, the Community Relations Council, the Council for Mosques and the business community.

In the early 1990s Muslims in Bradford have become very much part of the political, administrative, economic and cultural life of the city. An example of co-operation between the Council for Mosques, local authority and councillors was the permission granted to the Council for Mosques by the directorate of Housing and Environment in September 1991 for eight mosques to use loudspeakers for three *azaan* – the call to prayer – on a trial basis of three months. Significantly permission was given for only three of the five daily prayers: *fajr*, the dawn prayer before sunrise, and *'isha*, the night prayer, were excluded to minimize the possibility of public complaint. In December the authority, having monitored the noise levels and environmental impact, gave the Council for Mosques permission to continue broadcasting the three *azaan* and extended this permission to include a further seven mosques. In all, this decision reflected a healthy pragmatism by all those party to the agreement.

Nonetheless, it is clear that it has also become more difficult to identify one unambiguous source of authority in the Muslim community. For a time it seemed that the Council for Mosques fulfilled that function. However, it needs to be remembered that as early as 1983 the Council itself, in rejecting the proposals of the Muslim Parents Association, frankly admitted the debate and diversity within its own ranks, inevitable in a body reflecting 'different ethnic, national and sectarian strands'. The debate and disquiet within sectors of the Council surfaced again during the Honeyford affair, when one mosque withdrew and, for a while, an alternative council emerged. The impressive solidarity exhibited during the *Satanic Verses* affair has probably served to obscure the debate and disagreement amongst Muslims inside and outside the Council on a range of other issues.

Throughout the 1980s when it enjoyed success, whether over the issue of halal meat in schools or educational changes responsive to their concerns, the Council for Mosques had always worked closely with Muslim politicians and the Community Relations Council. However questionable some of the Council's decisions during the *Satanic Verses* affair, it showed itself able to learn quickly from its mistakes. It was inevitable that once the number of Muslim councillors multiplied they would increasingly be consulted by the local authority and public bodies. Similarly, with the growing confidence of Muslim businessmen it was not surprising that they, too, would search out a public role for themselves. In the 1990s it is evident that there are now these three centres of influence, each capable of initiating or participating in Muslim debates and activities.

This is not to belittle the Council's achievement. Its importance in lending credibility to national Muslim organizations was an acknowledgement of its ability to transcend sectarianism, its grassroots support and the respect with which its leaders, especially Pir Maroof and Sher Azam, were held in Barelwi and Deobandi circles outside Bradford. Mihir Bose's assessment of the Bradford Council for Mosques, with which this chapter began – 'an elected body ... probably the most representative voice of Islam in the land' – was not without some substance. However, in the 1990s there were other elected and non-elected Muslim bodies in the city ready to challenge the view that the Council was mandated to act as the representatives or spokesmen of Bradford's Muslims.

Looking Forward: Muslim Communities in the 1990s

On 25 August 1991 the UK Islamic Mission held its annual conference in Bradford. The morning session was a seminar exploring 'Muslim Rights in Britain', to which distinguished local Muslims were invited. The seminar, chaired by Councillor Ajeeb, was conducted in English and was a sober rehearsal of the agenda and anxieties of British Muslims. The conference was held in the wake of a worrying industrial tribunal decision which confirmed that a (Rotherham) employer was not guilty of unlawful direct discrimination under the terms of the Race Relations Act by refusing to employ Muslims.[1]

Dr Wasti, a Bangladeshi speaker, and a vice-president of UK Islamic Mission, presented his shopping list of Muslim demands, which included: new legislation to prevent discrimination against Muslims in employment, housing and education; legislation to prevent the defamation of Islam; accommodation of Muslim family law; and the provision of voluntary-aided Muslim schools. Another speaker, Dr Mustafa, urged a patient engagement with British institutions and participation in issues of contemporary concern, such as the environment. Mashuq Ally, who was involved as a Muslim consultant in the industrial tribunal, reminded the conference of some unpalatable stereotypes of British Muslims, which underpinned the Rotherham employer's refusal to employ them – terrorists, analogous to the IRA, and racist in their own practices. He urged his listeners to challenge such stereotypes by their involvement in the wider society.

Mr Riaz, a local Muslim and Conservative parliamentary candidate for a Bradford constituency, likened seminar participants to 'frogs in a well', scarcely aware of the world out-side, still less of how to relate to its structures. He urged Muslims to vote for the five Muslim parliamentary candidates selected in constituencies across the country by mainstream parties and not to worry about which party they represented. The priority, he insisted, was to transcend their differences – regional, linguistic and sectarian – and capitalize on their numbers in key marginal constituencies to return some Muslim MPs to Westminster.

The seminar's stress on pragmatism, increased participation in the institutional life of the nation, especially politics, and a willing-ness to engage in self-criticism were seen as the key to winning a sympathetic hearing for Muslim concerns. These emphases seem congenial to increasing numbers of Bradford's Muslims. When Bradford schools came bottom of the national league table testing seven-year-olds in English, science and maths in December 1991, Muslim leaders agreed to use the mosque schools, which many young Muslim children attend after state school to learn the Qur'an and Urdu, for additional English tuition. The local authority would provide training for the teachers in the schools and provide books and equipment. Sher Azam, for the Council for Mosques, welcomed the initiative as 'build[ing] on the strengths of our system'.[2]

Similarly, Bradford's Muslims voted for the mainstream politi-cal parties at the time of the general election in 1992 rather than the British Islamic Party.[3] South Asian and local issues continued to exercise the majority of the eleven Muslim councillors in 1992. In that year unemployment was hitting minority communities twice as hard as the white community, and in the inner-city University ward, with the highest concentration of Muslims, 'almost half of the young people [were] without jobs'.[4]

Muslim councillors and the Bradford Council for Mosques have many gains to their credit in the 1980s, as documented in the previous chapter, but realize that certain issues are not amenable to local solutions since they require legislative change. To this end both groups are pressing to have a voice nationally, whether in Parliament or in explicitly Islamic organizations. What is clear is that any organization which seeks to reflect the diversity of Muslim groupings in Britain today and enjoy grassroot support among different sects cannot afford to ignore the Bradford

Council for Mosques. If the 'Muslim Parliament' fails it may well be because it opted to select individuals itself and thus bypassed established organizations.

The UK Islamic Mission seminar included one angry voice dissenting from its general plea for a patient engagement with British institutions, locally and nationally. Dr Munir Ahmed, the Bradford president of Young Muslims UK, fulminated against the preoccupation with 'little rights as a minority'; he poured scorn on the panacea proposed of 'a few Muslims by name in Parliament'. Dr Ahmed pointedly reminded the seminar that the Prophet did not labour in Mecca for 13 years for minority rights but rather to rid society of idolatry and to achieve success in this world and the hereafter. Muslims were in Britain, the land of *kufr* (disbelief), not to ask for 'petty little things' but to offer the greatest gift, Islam and the Qur'an, a light for all to 'save ourselves and the whole of humanity from the fire'. He bewailed the lack of unity in the community, seduced into competition for state grants, and insisted that God would look after the rights of the community once they behaved like real Muslims. Dr Ahmed sought to recall the seminar to the challenge implicit in Islam: guidance for all, a religion of the Book intended 'to prevail over all other ways of life'.

This passionate desire for *da'wa*, to invite others to Islam, and his impatience with the compromises inevitable in any shared life in a democracy point up an abiding dilemma faced by Muslims in a minority situation. The dilemma was articulated by Wilfred Cantwell Smith three decades ago in his seminal work, *Islam in Modern History*. Writing about Muslims in the secular Republic of India he noted that, 'The question of political power and social organization, so central to Islam, has in the past always been considered in yes-or-no terms. Muslims have either had political power or they have not. *Never before have they shared it with others.*'[5]

To share power with others, whether locally or nationally, means that Bradford's Muslims would be working within political parties whose priorities, ethos and culture owe nothing to Islam. The Rushdie affair and the Gulf crisis showed that British political parties were not particularly hospitable to Muslim sensibilities and concerns. Yet within a democracy – if the option of a separate Muslim party is discounted – there is no alternative. In such an environment community identity rather than personal piety counts: numbers translate into votes. This was the logic of Mr Riaz's position at the seminar. For Dr Ahmed, within an Islamist perspective, mere community belonging and customary practices are not enough. They can obscure true Islam and be a barrier to *da'wa*.

Certainly 'customary practice' is being increasingly exposed to careful scrutiny by young British-educated Muslims, male and female, inside and outside the Islamist perspective. This was the burden of a conference held in Bradford in April 1990 to discuss 'The future of Muslim youth in Britain'. The conference was organized by the Muslim Youth Movement, a Barelwi youth group. 'It was the first time that youths of both sexes addressed the conference on a national level, in the presence of their elders.'[6] The conference was characterized by anger at the community's powerlessness in the face of *The Satanic Verses* and unusual candour about the difficulties facing Muslim youth.

A journalist who covered the meeting captured its tone and content well:

It is a confusing time to be young, Muslim and British. Responding to the Rushdie affair, Muslim cries for unity, and the renewal of an Islamic identity have exposed disunity and the fractured intellectual tradition of a religion transported from several different countries. Several of the younger delegates said the Muslim leadership in Britain was bankrupt of ideas. It is the difficulties of living a religious life in a secular society which should be addressed ... [instead] elders insist on fighting the battle of Pakistan in Bradford ... Dr Sheila Qureshi, an industrial chemist, [remarked that youngsters] 'learn the Koran in Arabic, which they don't understand. There is a communication gap between the elders and the young ... The Koran says we are caretakers of the world. We should be involved in Green politics. We are not taking part in our host country enough.'[7]

While many parents attended the conference the *'ulama* were conspicuous by their absence from the platform. Two reasons can be advanced for their non-attendance: the conference was in English, with which most of the *'ulama* are not at ease, and many, especially in the Deobandi tradition, would not participate in a gathering that included women. The president of the Council for Mosques, who did attend, conceded that the youth were right to criticize the elders, who had not done enough, especially the *'ulama*: 'We need to be sure that the *'ulama*, who come from a long way away, are equipped.' Asaf Hussain, a sociologist and writer, pleaded for strategic thinking, careful study of the Qur'an, and warned against de-politicizing Islam. The headteacher of the private Muslim Girls Community School in Bradford was scathing in her indictment of her own community. She criticized a minimalist Islam, which considered regularity in prayer and learning Arabic enough, with 'no intellectual attempt to engage with issues'; 'mothers are the best school yet they are not allowed to read the Book' (e.g. not welcome to study the Qur'an in most mosques); she angrily asked, 'How can I seek knowledge when the doors are closed by Muslim men. We need the language and skills of this country (not slogans and emotionalism).'

This chapter will explore four important issues raised at these two conferences. First, what efforts are being made to connect with the world of young British-educated Muslims in their late teens and twenties so that Islam does not simply remain but one component in an inherited culture, of declining significance and relevance? Second, the 1990s are likely to see more Muslim women in work and in public life; can their concerns and aspirations be accommodated within an Islamic discourse? Third, what resources are being generated from within the Islamic intellectual tradition in *English* to address issues of concern to British Muslims, an increasing number of whom are not fluent in South Asian languages? Finally, how do Muslims locally assess the prospects for *da'wa*, an important issue if Islam is to be seen as authentically British rather than a South Asian import?

A Muslim or an Islamic Identity for the Young?

At the height of the Gulf crisis in a Bradford upper school with a largely Muslim intake it was evident that most youngsters were pro-Iraq. Yet, in this same school, throughout the crisis, no more than two or three prayed in the area set aside for prayer. This episode illustrates the distinction between Muslim and Islamic identity. The youngsters felt that, as with the demonization of

Islam in the wake of the Rushdie affair, their Muslim communal identity was once again under attack from negative media coverage. This perception, however, did not translate into prayer.

How to translate a residual Muslim identity into a self-consciously Islamic identity is the challenge facing Islamic thinkers and leaders in the 1990s. The issues are complex: how much of traditional South Asian religiosity is accessible, relevant and transferable to youngsters in Bradford? Who has the confidence of young Muslims and can thus be the agent of this process of religious transmission?

Writing of young Muslims in neighbouring Keighley, an anthropologist identified one group largely missing from this process in Britain,

> In Pakistan and Bangladesh, many facets of religious nurture are in the hands of grandparents who see the children daily; here, relatively young parents often lack the religious knowledge which such grandparents, who are not present in this country, would normally impart. Thus the great interest ... in establishing and supporting madrassahs.[8]

An earlier chapter documented the role of the supplementary schools and concluded that most 'ulama were not role models for youngsters. Few had enough English to connect with their world of experience or understood the questioning ethos of schools. Muhammad Azam, a young professional in Bradford, spent five years in Saudi Arabia learning Arabic and then completed a degree course in modern Arabic and Middle Eastern Studies at Durham University, and is thus possessed of an excellent knowledge of Islam, traditional mosque culture – a member of a Deobandi mosque in the city – and the British educational system. Mr Azam offered a bleak analysis of the situation facing many young Muslims, who inhabit three cultural arenas: the school, with its individualistic and critical ethos; the authoritarian mosque, which teaches a minimalist Islamic curriculum; and the home, where after mosque school the young are exposed to South Asian videos, with their beguiling fantasy world of music, drama and dance.[9] He itemized three desiderata for the mosques: the two hours youngsters spend there should be enjoyable, inviting affection rather than fear; the subjects should link with those taught in the state school; and there should be opportunities for recreation.

Relations between older adolescents and parents are seldom easy, but within Muslim communities in Bradford this uneasy relationship is exacerbated by a growing linguistic gap. The Muslim researcher who studied a Bradford middle school in 1985/ 6, with a 90 per cent Muslim intake, observed that already,

> Most of the times, parents were at a loss to understand their children because they have given up speaking in their mother tongue, practising their religion and were becoming disrespectful and arrogant to their parents ... their children soon begin to adopt English standards and ideas. They start to question not only traditional customs but also religious ideas which seem strangely alien to life in a Western materialistic society.[10]

These are adolescents who have finished at the mosque schools and for whom most mosques have no other facilities. Many parents and religious leaders are perplexed and confused. This was very clear in a report written in 1989 by Muslim youth workers and local residents, urging local authority support for a newly formed youth association. The report indicated that Muslim elders were intimidated by the youngsters milling around one particular area and usually responded by urging them 'to visit the local mosque'; the youngsters had little opportunity 'for personal development by way of participation in a social or youth club' since for the elders 'recreational activities (outside school and mosque) are ... seen as little more than a hindrance (to secular and religious study)'. Once again this lack of mutual support and understanding was attributed to 'the breakdown of communication' between English-speaking youngsters who have 'problems with their parents' mother tongue'.[11]

Increasingly it was the upper schools and youth and community centres, set up in the 1980s – which catered for Muslim youth – where a social space was created for youngsters to develop and enjoy a distinctive youth culture.[12] Since the majority of mosques had neither the interest, space, resources nor trained personnel to develop youth provision, this increasingly became the preserve of trained youth and community workers, of whom in 1992 some 20 were Muslim. The community centres were sensitive to Muslim culture and would provide sessions for young men or young women only, but were not self-consciously Islamic organizations. Music is a central component of this youth culture and offers a useful case-study of the tensions between Muslim and Islamic identity.

Bradford has a growing number of 'Asian' bands, two of which have a national following. Naseeb – an Urdu word meaning destiny – was founded in 1988. This bhangra group appeared live on BBC television in February 1991 to promote their first album, *Break in the City*, and their music was promoted by the local ethnic minority radio station, Bradford City Radio. The other, Fun-da-mental, is more controversial. This band emerged in the summer of 1991 and was enthusiastically profiled in a popular music weekly, which declared that,

> their live performances are more like political rallies than gigs. Samples of Louis Farrakhan, Malcolm X and Enoch Powell's 'Rivers of Blood' speech and the fact that the group dress like PLO terrorists further fuel the excitement ... their tracks have, however, not been welcomed by their community elders and the group were recently banned from two Asian music TV shows. As well as being unhappy with their Islamic chanting and the extracts from the Koran ... the programme producers were livid at the fact that 'Righteous Preacher' openly supports the fatwa against Salman Rushdie.[13]

A recent release by the group was warmly praised in the English section of *Jang*, the Urdu daily produced in London:

> Lyrics praising Islamic scriptures, Asian culture and condemning the West's oppression of them are sung in a newly released cassette single called 'Peace, Love and War' ... So if you are confused about your roots and your identity, it might be worthwhile giving this enthusiastic group a try.[14]

In *Jang*, then, such music was being presented as a vehicle for consolidating identity and even a means of Islamic teaching. A young Muslim councillor in Bradford recently complained to Yorkshire Television about their launch of Asian films and the music programme, 'Bhangra Beat'. His complaint was not that films and music were subverting Islamic values but that such programmes were on too late and needed to be rescheduled 'to a more acceptable time, otherwise the viewers might find a trip to their local video libraries a conventional alternative'.[15]

The councillor's acceptance of bhangra music was not shared
by the Council for Mosques. In 1988 the Council publicly pro-
tested to the education authority when they discovered that some
upper schools were playing bhangra music and holding discos
during school lunch times. The president of the Council for
Mosques was not amused:

> What these children are doing is forbidden by Islam ... Muslims re-
> gard disco dancing as sexually suggestive and is therefore banned by
> the Islamic faith. Exposing the body of a male or female in such a
> way as to attract the opposite sex is forbidden ... by having discos
> during the day the schools are not leading the children to proper
> development and preparing them for the exams.[16]

The Council for Mosques, which had been careful to distance
itself from the fatwa against Salman Rushdie, could hardly be
expected to be happy with the existence of Fun-da-mental, a band
claiming both to use music to articulate Islamic sentiments in
general, and to defend the fatwa in particular. However, Islamic
youth groups have realized that a more nuanced view towards
music is likely to win them a hearing. Thus Young Muslims UK
have begun to produce their own music cassettes. One is entitled
Lost Identity, the other *The Hour*. However, they are worried by the
spread of bhangra music for the same reasons as the Council for
Mosques. They also feel that many parents mistakenly support
such music in the hope that it 'brings them back to their culture
... they think that their children must learn to mix-in with the
Western culture, while not forgetting their own.'[17]

Two recent initiatives by young Muslims in their twenties working in journalism and the media to entertain, educate and inform
young Muslims in Bradford are worthy of comment. The first is
a magazine, *Sultan*, launched in 1989, and the second Radio Fast
FM, which has been referred to in the previous chapter. The
managing editor of *Sultan*, Irna Khan, targeted young sixth-
formers, for whom there was little material addressing their
interests and questions.

While there were one or two short articles, adverts and poems
in Urdu, most of *Sultan* was written in English. Its first issue contained articles on careers for South Asian women and the religious and cultural constraints within which such choices were

made; a feature on a double Muslim wedding and another on the experiences of a Bradford Muslim visiting her parents' village in Pakistan; other topics included an interview with an Indian law student, an article on car maintenance, recipes, the top ten South Asian films and music reviews.

The magazine was intent on providing positive images of South Asian Muslim culture, thus building up the self-esteem of its readership. Nonetheless, it was not uncritical. A Muslim youth worker was interviewed on the topic of arranged marriage:

> In the past women have turned to him for help when pressure has been on them to get married. The way he sees arranged marriages is somewhat different to the view of the overall Asian male community. His support for arranged marriages is purely on Islamic grounds. This being that a woman cannot be forced into marriage, and that she has the right to refuse a chosen partner. Otherwise the marriage is void … Our society is so male dominated and women hardly have a voice, and this is wrong … 'If Islam was followed correctly and positively, women would have an equal place in society. So give women their rights!'[18]

It is significant that a Muslim youth worker, rather than an 'alim, was approached for his comments. He was assumed to be sympathetic to the issue and to have some smattering of knowledge, culled directly from Islamic literature, whereby he could appeal to Islam against the norms of a patriarchal culture, often confused with Islam. This modernist sentiment is echoed in an article profiling Benazir Bhutto, the first female Prime Minister of Pakistan, a possible role model for Muslim women. Benazir's criticisms of her predecessor, General Zia, are repeated with evident approval:

> From 1979, Zia tried to take away any form of democracy Pakistan had … by using Islam in a negative and degrading way. Zia was enforcing laws which were not in any way progressive, which degraded women and insulted the Muslim religion. True Islam is a progressive and pure faith … the dictator used [Islam] to prevent women being equal in Muslim society.[19]

The driving force behind Bradford's first Muslim radio station is Masood Sadiq, chairman of the Bradford branch of the

National Union of Journalists and a lecturer in media studies. Radio Fast FM was intended to flag up the achievements of local Muslims, reflect their interests and provide some space for programmes in English, including translations of the Qur'an, to cater for the increasing number of local Muslims whose first language is English and who have only a smattering of Punjabi and Urdu. In conversation he remarked that in providing English material on Islamic themes there was no one in the local community he could turn to, so he had to rely on audio tapes produced by Jamal Badawi, an Egyptian, who is a Professor of Management Studies and an *'alim* in Canada.

Masood Sadiq is also the resident media expert for *Q News*, an innovative national Muslim weekly produced in English, which began publication in March 1992. It includes a fortnightly column by Syed Darsh, an Egyptian, and ex-imam of the prestigious Regent's Park Mosque, who answers questions about issues troubling British Muslims. *Q News* is sponsoring a forum in early 1993 for Muslims under 21, provocatively entitled, 'Beyond beards, scarves and halal meat: Is there a British Muslim identity in the 21st century?' The promotional literature identifies some of the issues confronting the young, whether an inability to distinguish between culture, tradition and Islam, the lack of positive and relevant role models, inadequate preparation for coming to terms with domestic and public life in a challenging and ever-changing environment, or a lack of forums and facilities enabling the development of community relations, personal development and family enrichment.

It is clear that young professionals such as Masood Sadiq and Irna Khan with their command of the print and electronic media are prepared simply to by-pass local *'ulama* and religious leaders in their effort to provide relevant and accessible information in English for young Muslims. They are eclectic in the material they use and impatient of sectarianism.

Muslim Women: A Place in the Public Domain?

Research into the situation of 'first generation' South Asian migrant women in Bradford 20 years ago, noticed that, unlike Sikh or Hindu women, few Muslims worked outside the home.

This was for two reasons. Most, from rural and uneducated backgrounds, lacked the social and linguistic skills, or were prevented by the cultural and religious constraints of purdah, which rendered working outside the home unacceptable.[20]

In 1992 two Muslim women gained public recognition in Bradford; one was elected as the first woman chair of the Racial Equality Council, the other became the first woman councillor from any of the city's ethnic minorities. They represent but the most dramatic expression of an increasing number of Muslim women working in the public, private and voluntary sectors of the city. Four factors, cumulatively, explain this change: restrictive immigration procedures, education of girls, recession and sex equality policies.

A Muslim education development officer, 'Yasmin', who works in a local upper school with many Muslim girls, explained how, paradoxically, the multiplication of difficulties in getting a husband from South Asia had worked to the advantage of some Muslim girls.[21] If a woman had money in the bank, a house in her name and a full-time job her chances of getting a fiancé into Britain increased markedly. These factors helped 'Yasmin' to encourage many parents to allow their daughters to stay on in the sixth-form and acquire a larger range of marketable skills and qualifications. Further, with recession beginning to hit the ethnic minority communities disproportionately hard, more parents were beginning to allow their daughters to work and thereby supplement the family income. Finally, the local authority was expanding the opportunities for single-sex job-training in the multiplying community centres.[22]

Some of these factors pushing Muslim women into the workplace also benefited women from South Asia who had come to Bradford to marry. 'Saira' came from Mirpur to marry when she was 19 years old. She already enjoyed education up to 'matriculation' level in Pakistan – the equivalent to GCSE in Britain. In Bradford after her marriage she continued her studies and passed GCSEs in English and 'A' level Urdu. When her two children were at school she had started working as an interpreter with the local health authority. She admits that she and her husband had to confront opposition to her working from her extended family, not least because it was in a mixed environment. Once again economic necessity prevailed. 'Saira' considers herself fortunate. She enjoys the stimulus of the job and values the freedom driving a car gives her. Anthropological studies of the South Asian Muslim communities in Oxford and Manchester suggest that such changes in the educaton and work culture of traditionally patriarchal communities is increasingly common.[23]

As with the dynamics of migration to Britain, rooted in economic rather than religious imperatives, the religious leaders have again been overtaken by the logic of developments over which they have little control. This time recession and changing immigration procedures are seeing more Muslim women in further education and in the workplace.[24] This poses uncomfortable questions for the custodians of the Islamic tradition, the *'ulama*. Most Muslim women are educated in a Western tradition which makes few concessions to Islam, and increasing numbers are working outside the home, exposed to non-related males and thereby transgressing gender norms.

As seen in Chapter 4, the different Islamic traditions have reacted variously to this challenge. The Deobandis have two private fee-paying schools for girls; seeking, thereby, to preserve purdah. The revivalist Tablighi Jama'at increasingly provides separate meetings for women. Barelwis such as 'Allama Nishtar seem more willing to educate girls and allow some to continue on to further education – a Barelwi youth movement, the Muslim Youth Movement, allowed males and females to share one platform in addressing their conference on the problems facing young Muslims. The Jama'at-i Islami youth wing, Young Muslims UK, caters separately for young women and girls, although both males and females attend their annual camps. However only four mosques, at the end of 1992, provided any facilities for women to attend Friday prayers. In all, the formal provision for women is extremely patchy. The exasperated comment of the headteacher of the private Muslim Girls' Community School voiced at the youth conference also raises questions about the relevance of what little is provided.

Some recent research has begun to contribute an answer by helpfully mapping the main pattern of relationship between Islam and ethnicity in the experience and multiple identities of young Muslim women. The research focused on a group between 14 and 18 years old, attending an all-girls state school in Bradford. Three of the four correlations they identified seem particularly significant. One group of five were 'well-versed in and comfortable with' South Asian Muslim culture. 'They enjoyed weddings and festivals, family visits, Hindi and Urdu films, and preferred the fashions of *shalwar qamiz*. They expressed considerable interest in ... *pirs* (holy men) and *taviz* (amulets), and were dutiful in their fasting ... and prayer with other family members.' A second group of six were 'devout and [yet] ... critical of the traditional culture and nominal religiosity often adhered to by their parents ... All were well-versed in scripture, in the details of religious practice, or both.' A final group of three were neither Islamically oriented nor at ease with traditional South Asian culture. 'None had been religiously nurtured, and all had little experience of Qur'an classes, family fasting and prayer. They saw themselves as rebellious, and had experimented ... with relationships, nightlife and smoking.'[25]

The researchers wisely saw the young women as bearers of multiple and changing identities. What was important was the recognition that it was possible for a young woman to be bilingual, enjoy some of the benefits of English cultural life, and yet remain fundamentally at ease within a Barelwi tradition – the world of *pirs* and *ta'wiz* – thereby endorsing much of the unselfconscious religiosity of their parents. The research also suggested that someone who operated most readily in English is likely to be attracted to Young Muslims UK or the progressive and secularist stance of activists in the Women against Fundamentalism movement. Whatever the intrinsic attraction of such religious and ideological options more research is required to establish possible correlations between them and language: a *prima facie* case can be made for assuming that where a person is fluent in English but not in Punjabi or Urdu the Barelwi or Deobandi traditions are likely to be less accessible and the traditional religious practices of their parents problematized. For such people religious belonging has to be more self-conscious.

The research can be queried at one point. It was assumed rather than demonstrated that the main catalyst for challenging aspects of traditional South Asian Islam was the Islamist tendency of Young Muslims UK. This was also the position taken by

Yasmin Ali in an otherwise stimulating essay on Muslim women in the North of England.[26] In reality, anyone exposed to the writings of Benazir Bhutto or Imran Khan, role models for many South Asian Muslims, runs up against a modernist sentiment, which also invites a reappraisal of aspects of traditional South Asian Islam and culture.[27] This is clearly the ethos of the Bradford magazine *Sultan*. It is also the declared emphasis of the women's movement in Pakistan, which has deliberately sought to 'expose the difference between *maulvis* and Islam as a first step, and between progressive and conservative Islam as a second'. This prevents the movement being dismissed as culturally in-authentic and 'Westernized'.[28]

What is clear is that aspects of belief and practice are now being contested *within* all the Islamic traditions. The Muslim teacher who can insist that 'by teaching about Islam we are giv-ing [Muslim girls] the tools with which to challenge and fight for their rights' is neither Islamist nor modernist but the head of the Muslim Girls Community School in Bradford.[29] This school serves a largely Deobandi constituency, including 'some of the most vulnerable and least wealthy families. The majority of parents would send their daughters "back home" so as not to be forced by law to attend a non-Muslim school.'[30]

Nighat Mirza, the headmistress, a science graduate, presents herself as a role model for parents and girls. Initially sceptical of the need for such a separate school, she sees it as part of her role to coax reluctant parents into trusting their daughters more and giving them more freedom, including allowing them to go on to further education. 'I keep telling the parents: "I'm a Muslim woman. I have a career, I have a family." I have to persuade them that it's all right ... without threatening them.'[31]

British-educated Muslim women, unlike many of their parents, who had little if any formal education, have direct access to the sources of the Islamic tradition in English. This can lead to searching questions. A Barelwi magazine, which circulates locally, devoted one and a half pages to answering this question from a female reader: 'How can men and women be equal in Islam, if the evidence of two women is treated as equal to that of one man in the Islamic court?'[32] Such a question, today, is just as likely to be prompted by reading literature from Pakistan, where this remains a burning issue for Muslim women, as by any direct acquaintance with Western feminism.[33]

Women attracted to Young Muslims UK and its Islamist perspective are no more enamoured of all aspects of that movement than those within the Barelwi or Deobandi tradition. A recent double page spread in *Trends*, written by a woman, was provocatively entitled 'A Woman's Place in Power'. Nilofer Alaud-Din quoted the Hadith used by Pakistani *'ulama* to challenge Benazir Bhutto's legitimacy as Prime Minister – 'The nation which puts the woman at the helm of its affairs will never attain to well-being' – and then discounted this 'infamous' tradition as 'weak'.[34] She expressed dismay at 'such un-Islamic chauvinism' and rebuked members of Jama'at-i Islami for their frequent recourse to 'sarcastic and derogatory' comments about Mrs Bhutto's claims to power. She concluded that the only relevant question the Islamist movement was entitled to address to a leader, male or female, was whether or not that leader supported Islamic reforms.[35]

This article generated angry and spirited responses. Yasmin and Laila Rajab-Ali, in the next issue, challenged the writer's contention that the Hadith, which appeared in *Bukhari*, the most revered compilation, was weak. Further, Yasmin insisted that the scholarly consensus that a woman cannot rule a country is 'reinforced by the fact that a woman cannot lead the prayer in a mosque and that two female witnesses are equal to one male witness in a trial'. Laila also pointed out that for a female head of state to attend meetings with men would itself be un-Islamic and recalled prophetic traditions recorded in *Bukhari* and *Muslim* that stated that a woman must be accompanied on journeys lasting more than a day and night by a male companion whom she cannot marry, a *mahram*. For the Rajab-Alis such teaching seemed cumulatively to discount the possibility of women ruling.[36]

It would be misleading to suggest that Muslim women spend most of their time agonizing over the status of women in Islam. Many like 'Saira', the health authority interpreter, are grateful for the increased freedom they enjoy, compared to their parents' generation, and regret the pockets of obscurantism in the community such as a preoccupation with *dopattas*, making sure women do not cut their hair and caste marriage. She had resolved to teach her children about Islam herself rather than expose them to the rote-learning regimen of many of the mosques. Increasingly, women like 'Saira', or the journalist Irna Khan, are happy to keep their distance from the *'ulama*, and content to learn about Islam from books.

Renewing the Islamic Intellectual Tradition: The Task Ahead

British Muslims are heirs to a fragmented Islamic tradition, with most of the *'ulama* and university graduates inhabiting separate intellectual worlds, with little meeting, still less creative interaction, between them. A distinguished Pakistani scholar, familiar with both intellectual environments, concluded his study of Islamic education and its response to modernity, with the observation that,

> the state of Muslim scholarship is, generally speaking, so poor that it is at times disheartening ... in the Middle East the level of intellectual life in the Islamic field is pitiable. In the subcontinent, where better quality is perhaps available, a sober historical scholarship that would anchor it meaningfully and reliably is lacking.[37]

The situation in Britain is further exacerbated by linguistic diversity. The *'ulama* educated here are still trained through the medium of Urdu and within a distinct South Asian cultural tradition that makes few concessions to their new location. British Muslims, by contrast, are increasingly more at ease in English than Urdu. Commercial considerations have forced even Urdu newspapers printed in England to introduce some measure of bilingualism. Thus the Urdu daily *Jang* began to publish a weekly supplement in English at the end of 1991; a year later *Awaz* began to appear in a bilingual daily edition. In 1989 an English monthly digest, *The Muslim News*, was first published, followed in 1992 by the polished and professional weekly, *Q News*. All of these dailies and periodicals circulate in Bradford.

The few Muslims who write in English, self-consciously addressing Islamic themes, usually lack a knowledge of Arabic, and thus would not be taken seriously by the *'ulama*.[38] They, in their turn, berate the *'ulama* and traditional Islam for being confined to a 'ghetto'.[39] The task confronting Muslims in developing the Islamic tradition in English is thus considerable. It is by no means clear which institutions are equipped for such a task. It is difficult to envisage the *'ulama* and their centres of learning as equal to such an undertaking.

Reviewing Islamic centres in Britain and the West, Akbar Ahmed noted that,

> they are centred around one man of learning and dedication. In spite of a general ideological and intellectual sympathy for each other they remain somewhat isolated from one another. There are, therefore, no schools or theoretical frames which are being developed; nor are young intellectuals, working under learned scholars, being groomed for scholarship. It is still too much of a hit or miss method.[40]

In a later work, Ahmed worried that such centres, financed by Saudis or Iranians, 'assume a surrogate position for the larger political confrontation in the Muslim world'.[41] This raises the suspicion that such centres are not primarily concerned with developing Islamically grounded responses to the problems a Muslim minority faces in Britain.

Shabbir Akhtar has recently delineated with great clarity desiderata for an Islamic engagement with the Western intellectual tradition. 'In an age more hospitable to rational philosophy than to dogmatic theology' he considers it imperative to develop 'a critical koranic scholarship' and 'a natural theology, responsive to the intellectual pressures and assumptions of a sceptical age, which could be used to remove some kinds of conscientious doubts about the truth of religious claims' – such a natural theology is necessary since Akhtar allows for the phenomenon of a principled rejection of Islam based on reason, morality and knowledge. Such an acknowledgement is alien to the Qur'an which by itself is 'clearly deficient for the purpose of developing any adequate theory of modern rejection'. For Akhtar such intellectual tasks are urgent, with the Qur'an 'palpably becoming a dead relic from a dead past ... fast becoming an irrelevance to our daily lives, to the mental travail of ordinary existence'.[42]

The burden of modernity is that in a context of secularity, and religious and ideological diversity, unselfconscious religiosity is no longer a credible option and unreflective piety a liability. Akhtar acknowledges that 'fate and destiny have been largely replaced by choice and decision as central categories of thought in the contemporary world'. Even fear of a Day of Judgment can no longer be relied on to sustain belief: 'the distant terrors of Hell are ... insufficient even to motivate deeply religious people'. It is not surprising that Akhtar is not impressed by rejectionist or isolationist responses to all things Western and reminds Muslims that, '"the West" is no longer some amorphous realm, some abstract foe, out there ... Muslims are *in* the West'. He concludes by excoriating the conceit entertained by many Muslims that 'contempt for our current situation of secularity and religious pluralism is an adequate substitute for an intellectual reckoning with it.'[43]

Shabbir Akhtar's plea to Muslims to develop an Islamic thought and praxis responsive to the social, institutional and intellectual realities as they exist in Britain today, provides a context in which self-consciously Islamic endeavour must be assessed.[44] The rest of this section will briefly review a selection of readily accessible Islamic literature and opinion in English, addressing three issues of contemporary concern: religious freedom, the relationship between science and Islam, and the status of women in Islam.

In the midst of the Rushdie debate the Minister of State at the Home Office, John Patten, had outlined the government's thinking on a range of issues generated by the novel and Muslim responses to it. His open letter to 'influential British Muslims' referred to earlier included the remark that the one principle the government could realistically protect was that 'individuals should be free to choose their own faith'.[45] Liaqat Hussain, the president of the Bradford Council for Mosques in 1991 and 1992, voiced a traditional Islamic perspective on such a freedom in an interview: 'There is no such thing as freedom in religion. You have to tame yourself to a discipline. We want our children to be good Muslims, whereas this society wants children to be independent in their thinking.'[46]

Freedom to accept or reject religion is clearly a living issue in a pluralist environment. One questioner in *Trends* pointedly asked:

I am seriously thinking of leaving Islam, but someone told me that I can't. I think this is silly and such statements only make me dislike Islam more. So can you tell me why he would say it and what are the consequences for a person who wants to leave Islam for a different religion ... or ideology?[47]

The answer given to this, and to the similar question framed in slightly different terms in a later issue, was that,

If a person wants to renounce Islam, he can, but it is a punishable sin in Islamic society. It is like treason. Islam is not just a religion but a system for organising human life. It is an ideology and Muslims are soldiers who carry forward this truth and are struggling to remove falsehood from the earth ... no army can operate successfully by allowing treason ... But, the punishment of death, is applicable in an Islamic society.[48]

In Britain, it was conceded, one was free to leave since 'Islam is not established. If it was, then you would not like to leave.'[49]

Trends operates from within an Islamist framework originally developed in majority Muslim contexts (Egypt and Pakistan) and these answers indicate how little thought Islamists have given to the question of living with integrity as a minority, the situation today facing a quarter of the world's Muslims. Religious freedom for the individual, as enjoyed in the West, is not seen as a positive good but rather an unfortunate necessity to be borne.[50]

The response of Shabbir Akhtar to such a question is markedly different. He sees the situation of Muslims as a minority in the West not simply as a situation to be deplored but as providing a new context in which Muslims are enabled to rediscover Qur'anic teaching overlaid by tradition. Thus he argues that God wills a voluntary response to Him, rooted in 'reflection and morally responsible choice'; therefore, 'heresy and apostasy are morally more acceptable than any hypocritical attachment to orthodox opinion out of fear of public sanctions'. He seeks to ground such a stance in two Qur'anic verses – 'There should be no compulsion in religion' (2:256) and 'To you your religion, to me mine' (109:6) – which together could begin to undergird 'a specifically Islamic manifesto on freedom of conscience and conviction'.[51] In this regard, Akhtar has a precedent in the work of the distinguished Pakistani scholar, the late Fazlur Rahman, for

whom the source of the Islamic law of apostasy was 'not the Qur'an but the logic of the Islamic Imperium'.[52]

The history of the relationship between science and religion in the West has been controversial and complex. A recent monograph documents 'the diversity, the subtlety, and ingenuity of the methods employed, both by apologists for science and for religion, as they have wrestled with fundamental questions concerning their relationship with nature and with God'. This same study warns that 'when the history of science is hijacked for apologetic purposes (whether by religious thinkers or secularists) it is often marred by a cultural chauvinism.'[53] Cultural chauvinism is an apt phrase to describe *The Bible, The Qur'an and Science*, by Maurice Bucaille, a work hugely influential among Muslims, first written in French in 1976 and translated subsequently into English and Arabic.[54] The work purports to do three things: review the teachings of the Bible and the Qur'an on natural phenomena, evaluate such material in terms of 'the cast-iron facts of modern science' – the Qur'an is judged to have passed this test, the Bible to have failed – and argue that science can illuminate Qur'anic verses which 'until now have remained enigmatic'.[55]

This work has spawned a new generation of 'Islam and science' monographs, described by one Muslim writer as 'Bucaillism', whereby enthusiasts claim to have discerned in the Qur'an everything from the theory of relativity and quantum mechanics to the big bang.[56] Ziauddin Sardar judges such works 'dangerous', since the Qur'an is misconstrued if understood as a textbook of science rather than 'a book of guidance'. The Qur'an becomes hostage to developments in science – few philosophers or historians of science would speak so unambiguously today of 'cast-iron facts of modern science'. Finally, such a stance undercuts any Islamic scrutiny of the scientific imagination. Sardar explains the popularity of such works as psychological and apologetic: 'It reinforces their faith in the Qur'an and Islam ... and confirms their belief in the superiority and universal validity of Western science.'[57]

Bucaille remains very popular, despite such strictures. The anti-Christian controversialist Ahmad Deedat, a Gujarati resident in South Africa, utilizes Bucaille's work and distributes his writings through his organization, the Islamic Propagation Centre International, with its British headquarters in Birmingham. Deedat is in a long tradition of Christian–Muslim polemic, which can be traced back to a series of debates staged between Karl Pfander, a Christian missionary, and Maulana Rahmat Kairanawi in Agra, north India, in 1854.[58] Indeed, Deedat claims to have been inspired by the latter's book, *Izhar al Haq*, the Demonstration of Truth.[59] His organization sells this nineteenth-century work of religious polemic in an English translation.

Deedat has a considerable following in Britain. He packed the Albert Hall in 1985 and his almost annual visits to Britain invariably include Bradford on their itineraries. His last tour in the autumn of 1989 saw him entering the lists against Mr Rushdie with a scabrous little pamphlet in which he convinced himself that once the British public woke up to the fact that *The Satanic Verses* also lampooned the Queen, the Prime Minister and white women it would be immediately banned.[60] His popularity can be gauged by the fact that his 1989 performance in Bradford was packed out, attracting more than 2,000 people.[61] At this meeting he distributed free a lecture by Bucaille, *The Qur'an and Modern Science*. Deedat has recently published a booklet, *Al Qur'an, the Miracle of Miracles*, which included a chapter on 'science and the Qur'anic revelations', where Bucaillism runs riot.[62]

What is surprising is that such a figure, whose work is by turns tendentious and abusive, was the recipient in 1986 of the Feisal Award, a prestigious and lucrative prize given by Saudi Arabia for services to Islam. Such a prize has inevitably lent a certain lustre to a writer and polemicist who contributes nothing to a serious Islamic engagement with modern science or non-Islamic religious traditions.

The issue of the status and function of Muslim women is assuming a greater salience in Islamic literature. Nadeem Ahmed, a young Muslim sociologist, writing in a widely-circulated educational newsletter, can take for granted that mosques are 'usually ridden with pensioners and infants … [and] are almost wholly male institutions. No wonder so many British born Muslim women/girls grow up detesting Islam.'[63] The Indian *'alim* Mohammad Raza, in his monograph on Islam in Britain, devotes an entire chapter to 'Muslim women and freedom'. Raza considers that 'the veneer of Islamic culture is spread thinly' over a South Asian patriarchal order to lend it legitimacy. He is anxious that if women are not enabled to distinguish between patriarchal customs and Islam 'the social distance and estrangement of Muslim women from the community will increase'. He is, nonetheless, confident that Muslim women who study the Qur'an and Sunna 'as primary and secondary sources' will be equipped to challenge such repressive customs.[64]

Shabbir Akhtar is also convinced that the time has come for Muslim women themselves 'to interpret the sacred text and question the traditional male bias that has patronised their oppression for so long ... [nonetheless] some divine imperatives may seem, to a modern secularised conscience, demanding and harsh.'[65] Many Islamic authors writing in English agree that an 'oppressive patriarchy' obtains within Muslim culture. There is less clarity on its cause. Akbar Ahmed considers colonialism the main villain.[66] Undoubtedly this exacerbated the situation but seclusion and exclusion of women from the public domain pre-dated Western imperialism. Indeed, there is evidence to suggest both were articulated very early within Islam, with the freedoms enjoyed in commercial and political life by Khadija and A'isha, wives of the prophet, soon negated by the codification of Islamic law.[67]

It is clear that apologetic is no substitute for research on the Qur'an, Sunna, the early history of Islam and the development of Islamic law. Until this is done any re-interpretation of Islam will remain insecurely grounded in the face of the massive weight of traditional scholarship and Islamic law. However uncongenial to the apologetic imagination, it might be less ahistorical to argue that 'patriarchal norms' are written into the Qur'an and Sunna, as traditionally understood, and that a huge task awaits those bold enough to challenge such venerable readings, enshrined in Islamic law.

The influential manual on Islamic norms for women, *Bihishti Zewar*, Heavenly Ornaments, by Maulana Thanawi, a work translated from Urdu into English, continues to be very popular in Muslim bookshops in Bradford and widely used in Deobandi mosques. This work, written by the most respected Deobandi *'alim* of his generation, takes for granted that what would now be dubbed 'patriarchal norms' are underwritten by the Qur'an, Sunna and Islamic law. The work makes explicit that women

should be secluded from all but close male relatives, should pray
at home rather than in a mosque, cannot initiate divorce proceedings, and when acting as witnesses to a wedding two women
are required to substitute for one of the two men required.[68] The
book includes two hadith from the most prestigious collections of
Bukhari and *Muslim*, which presuppose that women were created
'ontologically inferior, subordinate and crooked'.[69]

Riffat Hassan, a Pakistani academic, has studied these traditions about the creation of woman. They are absent from, and,
she contends, contradictory of, the Qur'anic data. Most, she
argues, are borrowed from the Genesis account with 'Muslim
biases ... added to the adopted text' to render their connotations
the more damaging to women.[70] The first hadith is worded thus:

> Treat women nicely, for a woman is created from a rib, and the curved
> portion of the rib is its upper portion, so if you would try to straighten
> it, it will break, but if you leave it as it is, it will remain crooked. So
> treat women nicely.[71]

The second adds the detail that Eve – Hawwa in the Islamic
tradition – was created from the 'left' rib of Adam.[72]

Dr Hassan notices that the Genesis account nowhere specifies
that it was the 'left' rib, nor explicitly mentions its 'crookedness'
or 'curvature'. In Arab and South Asian Muslim culture, the
'right' is auspicious and the 'left' its opposite. She concludes that
traditional Hadith criticism, which focused on a study of the
reliablity of the transmitters and the chain of transmission to
establish their authenticity and reliability – *isnad* criticism – needs
to be supplemented by criticism of their content, *matn*, to ascertain whether such are in conformity with Qur'anic teachings.

Such a task is as urgent as it is controversial. Hadith remain
the second source of revelation, after the Qur'an, within the
developed Islamic corpus, and undergirds Islamic law. The angry
response in *Trends* to an article criticizing a hadith in *Bukhari*,
used to challenge the legitimacy of women rulers, indicates the
psychological and emotional investment many Muslims have in
defending the reliability, even sanctity, of these venerable traditions. Fazlur Rahman was convinced that such critical study
would 'not only remove a big mental block but should promote
fresh thinking about Islam'.[73] Until this debate is widely joined

by Islamic scholars, conversant with the primary sources in Arabic, and able to develop a methodology to assess such traditions, any re-appraisal of the role and status of women will be vulnerable to accusations of infidelity and succumbing to Western fashion.

It is not surprising that scholars such as Shabbir Akhtar and Akbar Ahmed are silent on these issues. Since neither are Arabists they are not equipped to undertake such a sensitive issue as the critical sifting of the Hadith. Until it occurs apologetic must do service for serious scholarship, with *'ulama* and British Muslims engaged, at best, in shadow boxing. Where exchange takes place it is usually perfunctory and polemical. The losers are British Muslims, who, unless they have studied Islamics at university, are unlikely even to be aware of the scholarly labours of someone of the stature of the late Fazlur Rahman, the distinguished Pakistani scholar, who ended his academic life at Chicago University, where he produced a number of stimulating and accessible monographs and essays on the Qur'an, Islam and the Islamic intellectual tradition.[74] Rahman, in seeking to be faithful to the sources of the faith, while open to the academic disciplines and questioning of the modern world, remains a largely untapped resource for local Muslims.

Inviting Others to Islam: Promise and Predicament

'Shazia' is a young Muslim in a Bradford school. When young she identified 'Islam with Pakistaniness':

> My image of a Muslim before was Pakistani, *shalwar kamiz*, brown or whatever. I'd never considered anyone white being a Muslim, until I became involved with the organization [Young Muslims UK] and came into contact with different people ... [it)] keeps me going, seeing more people entering Islam and taking it seriously.[75]

New Muslims can thus serve to legitimize the faith, remind South Asians that Islam is a universal faith, loosen the link between ethnicity and religious identity, and, where they 'bring an inquisitive mind to their new religion ... may contribute to the continuous evolution of Islam helping to mould it to fit the conditions of contemporary European society'.[76]

The important question remains: who is to engage in *da'wa* – call/invitation to Islam – and *tabligh*, preaching? These two words, *da'wa* and *tabligh* are usually bracketed together in discussions by South Asian Muslims on how to commend Islam to non-Muslims in the West. Unlike Christianity, Islam – outside the Ismaili sect – had not formed distinct institutions or associations to engage in 'missionary' work. Such organizations only developed in the nineteenth century, in response to Christian missionary activities. While Christians, in justification of the missionary imperative within their tradition, point to 'the great commission' in St. Matthew's gospel (28:18–20) there is no similar verse in the Qur'an. However, Muslims often see *da'wa* and *tabligh* as implicit in the following Qur'anic verse:

> You are the best ummah [community] raised for the benefit of mankind. It is your duty to enjoin good and forbid evil because you believe in Allah (3:104).

This was one of the verses Maulana Ahmed cited in his presidential address to the UK Islamic Mission's twenty-fifth annual conference at Manchester in August 1988. The conference was devoted to the theme of 'Islamic Da'wah in Western Europe'. The addresses delivered at this conference, in addition to the booklet by Khurram Murad, a past director-general of the Islamic Foundation in Leicester, *Da'wah among non-Muslims in the West*, provide an honest review both of the difficulties such Muslims have in commending the imperatives of *daw'a* and *tabligh* to their co-religionists and non-Muslims in responding to it.

The reluctance of many Muslims to engage in *da'wa* is explained by a multiplicity of factors: a lack of co-ordination and internal feuding among the 450-plus Pakistani organizations in Britain absorbs all surplus time and energy; with the economic recession particularly hitting South Asian Muslims a preoccupation with making ends meet becomes paramount; lack of close ties with non-Muslim neighbours renders protestations of *da'wa* empty; an emphasis on preserving cultural, linguistic and ethnic identity suggests that to become a Muslim means becoming South Asian culturally, and reinforces the suspicion that Islam is alien to European culture; Islam's troubled relationship with the West often topples over into 'emotive diatribe, abusive polemic, against the West, the white man or the Hindu'; too often *da'wa* does not connect with the concerns and experiences of average British people; 'why should Islamic da'wah remain unconcerned with the questions of nuclear weapons, unemployment, old age... ?'[77]

Those in the Jama'at-i Islami tradition insist that *da'wa* is the responsibilty of all Muslims. Not so the Barelwi tradition. This is clear from the (Urdu) prospectus for the 'The Islamic Missionary College', set up in Bradford in 1974, by the Jami'at-i Tabligh al-Islam, the Association for Preaching Islam. The college was intended for *'ulama* who had completed their traditional course of studies but who did not have English or other languages. They were to be trained in a range of subjects, including science, philosophy and comparative religion, enabling them to preach to non-Muslims. Muslims who had graduated from British colleges and universities, while knowing English, were not deemed capable of *da'wa* and *tabligh* since their knowledge of Islam was judged inadequate.

If there was disagreement between different Muslim traditions as to who was responsible for *da'wa* and *tabligh*, there was also some confusion as to the implications of these terms. Tablighi Jama'at, the revivalist organization, networked to many of the Deobandi mosques in Bradford, has its European headquarters nearby in Dewsbury. While it encourages all Muslims to engage in preaching, the movement does not seek, by and large, to address non-Muslims.[78] *Tabligh* has been interiorized, confined to Muslims, and understood as 'a process of self-reformation and ... service to Allah ... to win [His] good pleasure'.[79] For this reason activists in Young Muslims UK are critical of it for its supposed failure to engage in an 'organized social, economic and political struggle to establish the Islamic way of life'.[80]

Organized activities apart, most become new Muslims through marriage or sufi groups. This is the judgement of Abdul Rashid Skinner, a local psychologist and founder member of the Association of British Muslims (ABM) in the late 1970s. Dr Skinner's judgement is corroborated by one of the few pieces of research into this group.[81] Daud Owen, the current president of ABM, explained the reason for the association and offered a typical profile of its members in a letter to the national press:

This association was set up originally to help converts to adjust to being Muslim Britons and the descendants of immigrants to adjust equally to being British Muslims ... The association represents the majority of converts, and a typical profile is middle class, professional, often public-school educated, monarchist, conservative, and involved with genuine mystic paths and masters.[82]

In conversation, Skinner concurred with Owen's comments but added that most of the 600 families who are networked through ABM belong to the Naqshbandi sufi order, a transnational, reformist order active in South Asia, Central Asia and the Arab world.[83] Dr Skinner, himself within the sufi tradition, in 1987 and 1988 unsuccessfully contested inner-city wards in Bradford on a Conservative/Muslim ticket, opposing South Asian Muslims, who represented Labour.

The need for such a support network as ABM is significant and indicates the difficulties many new Muslims have in feeling part of South Asian Muslim communities. To sustain an Islamic identity in public requires social support. Sociologists argue that, 'to have a conversion experience is nothing much. The real thing is to be able to keep on taking it seriously: to retain a sense of its plausibilty.'[84]

Dr Skinner admits that, with the exception of one local South Asian Naqshbandi sufi, South Asian expressions of sufism seem to owe too much to Hinduism to be accessible to him. He is able to sustain his Islamic identity through Friday worship in English at the local mosque, which serves an international student community, and his activities with ABM – he is now vice-president. He also attends regular meetings in London as a member of the Union of Muslim Organizations of the UK and Eire, one of a number of national bodies seeking to co-ordinate and speak for Britain's Muslim communities.[85]

If Abdul Rashid Skinner became a Muslim through sufism, Sufyan Gent did so, at a formal level, through marriage to an Iraqi. However, he only became an active Muslim on moving to Bradford in 1987. Unlike Skinner, Gent's spiritual odyssey owes nothing to sufism. Discovering the student mosque, he joined a Qur'anic study group, conducted in English. He found himself attracted to the austere and activist Wahhabi tradition, with its discipline and clear set of rules. By 1992 he was president of the small Bradford branch of the Islamic Society of Britain (ISB).

The ISB conducts its business in English, and attracts Muslims who see their future in Britain and want to present Islam as relevant to British society. Locally, it draws on the international student community, the few local English and Afro-Caribbean Muslims, and ex-members of Young Muslims UK. Such an English-speaking community is a vital support for Sufyan Gent, who like Skinner lives outside the inner cities where the majority of South Asian Muslims live.

Both men find it difficult to relate to aspects of South Asian religiosity and culture. Gent worries about a reactive identity exhibited by many young South Asian Muslims. He offered two illustrations: local graffiti, such as 'Islamic Jihad against whites' and the common application of the term *kafir*, non-believer, to white people. Since many British people are Christians, they are covered, he contends, by the Qur'anic category 'People of the Book', and should, therefore, not be spoken of as *kafir*, with its pejorative overtones.

Other Muslim commentators are beginning to worry about the divide between the *'ulama* and British Muslims, 'the growing and uncontrolled phenomenon of lay preachers ... emerging due to a vacuum in effective religious leadership'.[86] Their knowledge is often shallow, the Islam they propagate narrow and intolerant.[87] This intolerance was demonstrated in Bradford in March 1990 when a Muslim youth group responded angrily to a proposed visit to the city by Zaki Badawi. Since Dr Badawi's views on the Rushdie affair were uncongenial to them they distributed a pernicious hand-out in which they labelled him an 'enemy of Islam', declared his presence in Bradford a 'sin', and sought to dissuade him from coming. The same organization pointedly ignored the Council for Mosques' plea to halt street demonstrations in May 1990 after they had earlier been involved in a street fracas.[88]

It is evident that, for the moment, new Muslims have little impact locally. They may be respected for adding lustre and legitimacy to Islam but find themselves marginalized in Muslim deliberations. Indeed, it would be hard to imagine either Skinner or Gent at home in the Council for Mosques, whose business is generally conducted in Urdu. The poor showing of the British

Islamic Party, in part, can be attributed to the centrality Muslim converts played in it. They were strangers to *biradari* politics, the crucial networks for mobilizing Muslim votes. Similarly, impeccable Islamic credentials were not enough for Abdul Rashid Skinner to win the crucial Muslim vote in local elections.

Summary

It is evident that Muslims in Bradford are committed to participating in the mainstream of British political, institutional and intellectual life. A refreshing candour and self-criticism characterizes much of the debate within the communities, and Muslim women are increasingly participants. There are signs of a British Muslim culture developing with its own music, print and electronic media, and questioning ethos, whether debating the proper role of women, the relationship of South Asian Muslim culture to Islam, or the desire to contribute an Islamic perspective to contemporary debates such as the environment. As yet, much of what passes for Islamic writings in English, with a few exceptions, is apologetic or polemical work rather than serious scholarship. However, a new generation of professionals has emerged, more eclectic in its reading habits and, through its command of English, able to access a wider world of scholarship.

Many of these developments have simply bypassed the *'ulama*. The social control religious leaders can exercise is diminishing – not least over women, whether in school, community centre or the workplace. For young Muslims the significant other is more likely to be a Muslim youth worker than an *'alim*. It remains unclear whether more than a small proportion of the *'ulama* will be able to command the respect of British Muslims. Youngsters retain a Muslim community identity. Whether more than a small number will seek to adopt a self-consciously Islamic lifestyle in Britain remains an open question.

Conclusion

Bradford in the 1990s contains significant Muslim residential zones. Here Muslim communities feel secure amidst a relatively self-contained world of businesses and institutions, religious and cultural, which they have created to service their specific needs. The concentration of Muslim voters has also been translated into a sizeable number of local councillors. Muslims have demonstrated an increasing willingness to engage in the public life of the city, whether as councillors, magistrates, members of the Racial Equality Council, or professionals and businessmen involved in charitable activities.

As Muslims have developed an understanding of local government, as officers and councillors, they have learned to co-operate with the Council for Mosques to ensure that local services are responsive to their special needs. This is particularly evident in the field of education, where the local authority has sought to accommodate Muslim aspirations and allay their anxieties. While I have suggested that there are three overlapping centres of influence amongst local Muslims, namely the Council for Mosques, councillors and a professional and business community, on many issues their activities are mutually supportive. This is very clear in the steps taken to secure a future for the Urdu language, important both as a means of communication across the generations in families, a lingua franca for many Muslims from South Asia, and a storehouse of Islamic literature and Muslim culture. Thus many schools and local colleges provide the opportunity to study it up to examination level. It remains one of the languages of the local community radio station, supports a flourishing local audio and video cassette market and two Muslim book shops, is taught in many of the local mosque schools, and remains the *sine qua non* for admission to the two local Deobandi seminaries. Consensus on the importance of Urdu also transcends sectarian divisions.

The significance of Urdu points to the continuing vitality of links with South Asia. These are evident in the constant to-ing and fro-ing of politicians and religious leaders. Such links are institutionalized in various ways: political parties, especially those from Pakistan and Azad Kashmir, have offices in Bradford and other British cities; Bradford has a Pakistani consulate, and Manchester, Birmingham and Glasgow vice-consulates. All the main Islamic traditions active in the city (Barelwi, Deobandi and Jama'at-i Islami) retain strong links with their parent organizations in South Asia. Most mosques, outside the Deobandi tradition, continue to rely on *'ulama* from South Asia to staff their mosques. Many students at the two Deobandi seminaries in Dewsbury and Bury also spend time in India and Pakistan, either at a seminary or engaged in Tablighi Jama'at tours.

What is also evident is that the influence exercised by Gujaratis in the religious life of Bradford's Muslims is disproportionate to the small communities actually settled in the city. Gujarati Muslims largely staff and run both Deobandi seminaries, one of which is also hugely influential as the European headquarters of revivalist Tablighi Jama'at. They also manage the new private Muslim Girls' School, transferred from Kidderminster to Bradford in the autumn of 1992. Gujaratis feature prominently as *'ulama* in all sectarian traditions in the city. The regional organization for Gujarati *'ulama* in the Deobandi tradition, based in Blackburn, had a major role in alerting the Bradford Council for Mosques to the 'contents' of *The Satanic Verses*. Clearly the impact of the Gujarati *'ulama* in creating Islamic institutions – largely Deobandi – in the north of England, able to transmit the religious heritage to a new generation of British Muslims, is considerable. Once again a necessary precondition for such influence is Urdu as a common language for Islamic discourse in South Asia.

Leadership in the Muslim communities, whether as councillors, businessmen or in the Council for Mosques, generally turns on mastery of Urdu and English. Without this it would not be possible to win the confidence of elders in the Muslim communities – many of whom have little English – and at the same time be active in the majority community. What is evident is that many young Muslim councillors are equally at home in Labour politics and political and cultural associations rooted in South Asia. Where the new generation of Muslim politicians has been educated in Britain, this common education and shared competence in English also strengthens links transcending South Asian regional and linguistic solidarities.

It is also possible to argue that where religious leaders are bilingual and bi-cultural a creative encounter with British society is possible. To respond to the many bewildering challenges posed for the Islamic tradition as a minority in the West presupposes a rootedness in Islam – which for most 'ulama in Bradford means a Muslim tradition mediated through South Asian history, culture and languages – and an acquaintance with politics, law and culture in Britain today. Some of the activities in 'Allama Nishtar's Barelwi mosque indicate a pattern of patient engagement with wider society. He has built up an excellent library of Islamic books for use by students, many in English. He also teaches girls Arabic GCSE through the medium of English. A second example is the principal of the Bury seminary – which increasingly provides 'ulama for the city's Deobandi mosques – encouraging some of his students to go on to study Islamics, Arabic and law in British universities. He is aware of the need for some of the English-speaking 'ulama to be exposed to Western traditions of scholarship.

Both of these examples furnish instances of continuity and change within traditional Islam, as its custodians and interpreters seek to respond to the challenges of teaching British Muslims. However, the dilemma facing traditional Islam in both its Barelwi and Deobandi forms is that the majority of 'ulama are not bilingual, at least in the crucial sense of having a mastery of English, and with it an informed understanding of British culture. Therefore, they find it difficult to understand, still less engage with, the world and concerns of young British Muslims. Even in South Asia there is a widening gap in mutual comprehension between the products of tertiary education and the Islamic seminaries. This gap is exacerbated in Britain, where increasing numbers of British Muslims are only fluent in English. In Bradford, Islamists and modernists are generally not competent in Urdu, and thus hold aloof from any involvement with the

Council for Mosques, whose meetings are generally not conducted in English.

The implications of this disjunction in experience and cultural formation between many British Muslims and the *'ulama* are wide-ranging and worrying. Many Muslims sympathetic to Islamist or modernist views simply by-pass the *'ulama*. Their Islam is culled from pamphlets or such books as have been written or translated into English. It is, at best, a haphazard introduction to the riches of the Islamic tradition, lacking the disciplines and methodology of traditional scholarship. At worst, such works as are accessible are either polemical diatribes against the West or simplistic appeals to return to the sources of the Qur'an and Sunna and discount fifteen hundred years of history and disciplined reflection.[1] It is not surprising that some scholars active in the Islamist tradition are themselves signalling the dangers of such a cavalier attitude to history, which can topple over into extremism.[2]

It would be alarmist, however, to suggest that Bradford offers a home for radical Islamism. More pressing a worry for a lot of Muslim elders is that because Islam is inaccessible to many youngsters, beyond the minimalist diet to which most are exposed in mosque schools, Islam becomes simply one component in their cultural identity, a condition of community belonging, inescapable but of decreasing relevance to their daily lives. They may continue to keep the two main religious festivals, eschew pork and alcohol, enjoy the occasional *qawwali*, continue to marry within their *biradari* and identify with co-religionists across the world, whether in Kashmir, Palestine or Bosnia, but for the rest they will exhibit little real engagement with the tradition and keep their distance from its bearers.

The fact that increasing numbers of British Muslims are monolingual should not be dismissed as merely a liability. Mastery of English enables British Muslims from a variety of ethnic, regional and linguistic backgrounds to communicate and begin to work together. The Islamic Society of Britain, a new Jama'at-i Islami venture, conducts its meetings in English and self-consciously seeks to present Islam as increasingly rooted in this country, rather than a South Asian import. It offers the possibility of a creative exchange between British Muslims, whether by origin from South Asia or English-speaking Muslims from different parts of the world, including British converts. It will be interesting to see if this promise is realized in the next few years.

Initiatives such as *The Muslim News* and *Q News*, both professionally produced Muslim community papers with a national circulation, are themselves contributing to the emergence of a British Muslim identity. *Q News*, especially, appeals to young, educated Muslims, impatient of sectarianism, and is able through an international language, English, to access innovative and relevant Islamic scholarship. It also means that there is a growing market for Muslims in Britain writing in English. One encouragement in the last few years is the appearance in English of a number of books, scholarly and popular, which seek to address the challenges facing Muslims in Britain.[3]

There are other institutional developments which auger well for the emergence of a British Muslim identity. In 1991 a pioneer B.Ed. course began at Westhill College in Birmingham, incorporating Islam as its main subject, taught by Muslim scholars. The Centre for the Study of Islam and Christian–Muslim Relations, also in Birmingham, involving Christian and Muslim scholars, offers an increasing number of Muslim students accredited degree courses in Islam, as well as research programes. Engagement with the mainstream intellectual tradition is also evident in the fact that in the 1980s 'up to half the annual intake of undergraduates choosing to study Arabic at British Universities ... are British Muslims'.[4] It is reasonable to hope that from such a pool of Arabists some will go on to specialize in Islamic studies and thus provide a reservoir of British Islamic scholars able to operate across Islamic and Western traditions, and thus facilitate a creative dialogue. It is encouraging that a majority of British Muslims studying Arabic are from South Asian backgrounds.[5]

A critical issue facing Muslims in Britain is their ability to develop national organizations which reflect the diversity of sectarian, regional and linguistic backgrounds of the Muslim communities. There is now a plethora of bodies presuming to speak for all British Muslims. Leaders of the Bradford Council for Mosques have been active in many of these national initiatives, not least because the Council has been able to manage and transcend sectarian loyalties, a precondition for the emergence of successful national associations. Muslims in Bradford have learned to participate in, and influence, what sociologists call the local state. However, there is a growing recognition that on a range of issues Muslims need to be in Parliament and belonging to pressure groups if they are successfully to lobby for changes, whether in the legal or educational system.[6]

Another pressing issue for the Muslim communities will be the extent to which Islamic discourse can accommodate the aspirations of educated Muslim women, increasingly working in the public, private and voluntary sectors in the city. A recent collection of articles exploring the interface between women and religion included three contributions from Muslim women, two of which examined the lives of Muslim women in Bradford and the North of England. Both writers felt that there was an imperative need to challenge 'the hegemony of the [male] community leadership ... and to reinvigorate the secular and progressive traditions' within these communities.[7] What is encouraging is that the innovative Muslim weekly *Q News* will continue to provide a forum for Muslim women, since it is produced by a 'young, and mostly female staff'.[8]

It is evident in Bradford that the lively debate and diversity which characterizes Muslim communities in South Asia is continuing in Britain. Muslims in the city continue to have multiple identities – regional, 'caste', sectarian – continue to speak a variety of languages, and many continue to enjoy dual nationality. These communities have weathered the crises of *The Satanic Verses* and the Gulf war, when they were the object of public vilification and suspicion, without a withdrawal into sullen resentment. For this considerable credit needs to be given to the leadership of the Bradford Council for Mosques. The challenge facing Muslims in the 1990s is the extent to which there are the intellectual and imaginative resources within the Islamic tradition to engage with the religious, intellectual and cultural traditions of the West. Islamic traditions developed in South Asia contain a variety of perspectives honed in conflict with British hegemony, ranging from accommodation to isolation and defiance. The need now is for a critical and constructive exchange both within these traditions and with the majority society.

'Allama Nishtar's new purpose-built mosque is almost complete. With its striking golden dome it will beautify the Bradford skyline. It represents a huge investment of time, money and devotion, and signals clearly that Bradford is where Muslims see their future. It is a building of which they and the city can be proud. This mosque stands as a visible expression of developments within the Muslim communities. In a period of little over 30 years Muslims, from being hidden away on the margins of British life, have assumed an increasingly public profile. However, who will represent Islam to the wider society is unclear. Much will depend on how central government, the media and other national institutions respond to Muslims and whether they can feel secure and accepted.

Notes

Introduction

1. The work of this religious leader, Pir Maroof Hussain Shah, is profiled in Chapter 4. I have used the imprecise terms Muslim mystic and holy man in preference to the less familiar, but technically correct sufism.

2. Hanif Kureishi, 'Bradford', in *In Trouble Again*, Granta 20 (1986) pp 149–70.

3. Jorgen Nielsen, *Muslims in Western Europe* (Edinburgh, 1992) p 58.

4. A.H. Halsey, *Change in British Society* (Oxford, 1986) p 71.

5. See E.J.B. Rose and associates, *Colour & Citizenship, A Report on British Race Relations* (London, 1969).

6. Roy Jenkins, *Essays and Speeches* (London, 1967) p 267.

7. Fay Weldon, *Sacred Cows: A Portrait of Britain post-Rushdie, pre-Utopia* (London, 1989) pp 8 and 31.

8. *The Independent*, 4–3–89.

9. *Sunday Telegraph*, 3–2–91.

10. See Bhikhu Parekh, 'The Rushdie Affair and the British Press' in *The Salman Rushdie Controversy in Interrelgious Perspective* (Lampeter, 1990) pp 71–95.

11. For the material on Islamism I am indebted to Aziz Al-Azmeh, *Islams and Modernities* (London, 1993); and Gilles Kepel, *The Revenge of God, The Resurgence of Islam, Christianity, and Judaism in the Modern World* (Oxford, 1994).

12. Steven Vertovec, *Annotated Bibliography of Academic Publications regarding Islam and Muslims in the United Kingdom, 1985–1992*, Bibliographies in Ethnic Relations 11, Centre for Research in Ethnic Relations, University of Warwick (Coventry, 1993).

13. John Rex, *Ethnic Identity and Ethnic Mobilisation in Britain* (Coventry 1991) p 114.

14. Bhikhu Parekh, 'The Rushdie Affair: Research Agenda for Political Philosophy' in *Political Studies* xxxviii (1990) p 701.

15. M. Anwar, *The Myth of Return: Pakistanis in Britain* (London, 1979).

16. C. Peach, *Current Estimates of the Muslim Population of Great Britain* (forthcoming, University of Derby).

17. Albert Hourani, *Islam in European Thought* (Cambridge, 1991) p 4.

1. Britain's Muslim Communities

1. Bede, *A History of the English Church and People* (Harmondsworth, 1968) p 330.

2. R.W. Southern, *The Making of the Middle Ages* (London, 1953) pp 230–31.

3. M. Rodinson, *Europe and the Mystique of Islam* (London, 1988) p 33–7.

4. Cited in Albert Hourani, *Islam in European Thought* (Cambridge, 1991) p 11.

5. C. Adams, *Across Seven Seas and Thirteen Rivers* (London, 1987) p 18. The derivation of 'lascar' is probably the Arabic term *askari*, meaning soldier, which entered Anglo-Indian terminology through Persian and Urdu eqivalents.

6. F. Halliday, *Arabs in Exile, Yemeni Migrants in Urban Britain* (London, 1992).

7. P. Clark, *Marmaduke Pickthall, British Muslim* (London, 1986) p 39.

8. Chapter 4 looks at this movement and why it continues to be at the centre of controversy in Britain.

9. Clark, *Marmaduke Pickthall*, p 41.

10. R. Visram, *Ayahs, Lascars and Princes, Indians in Britain 1700–1947* (London, 1986) p 178.

11. S. Wolpert, *Jinnah of Pakistan* (Oxford, 1984) p 3.

12. Z. Badawi, *Islam in Britain* (London, 1981) p 23.

13. J. Nielsen, *Muslims in Europe* (Edinburgh, 1992) p 45.

14. The pitfalls in seeking to extrapolate from place of birth statistics to religious data are clearly identified in K. Knott and P. Noon, *Muslims, Sikhs and Hindus in the UK: Problems in the Estimation of Religious Statistics*, Religious Research Paper 7, Department of Sociology (University of Leeds, 1982).

15. C. Peach, *Current Estimates of the Muslim Population of Great Britain*, paper given to the seminar on Statistics and the UK Religious Communities at Derby University in May 1994 (the proceedings to be published by Derby University). I am grateful to Professor Peach for letting me have a copy of his paper.

16. Halliday, *Arabs in Exile*, p 2.

17. The figures are adapted from Nielsen, *Muslims in Europe*, p 42, with the additional figure for 1991 taken from the census.

18. These figures are given in M. Anwar, *Muslims in Britain: Census and other Statistical Sources*, Centre for the Study of Islam and Christian-Muslim Relations, CSIC Papers 9 (Birmingham, September 1993) pp 4–7. They are probably slight overestimates, since Anwar assumes that all Pakistanis and Bangladeshis are Muslim. Arguably 10 per cent of Bangladeshis are Hindu, while Christians and other non-Muslims account for some 4 per cent of Pakistanis. Indian statistics are even more problematic. Indian government census data suggest 10 per cent of the population are Muslim, while a 1982 Policy Studies Institute sample survey gave a figure of 16 per cent for Britain. Since the overall figure for Indians in the 1991 census is 841,000 much turns on which figure is accurate. The difference between the higher figure (134,000) and the the lower estimate is 50,000: approximately the number of Muslims in Bradford. Anwar opts for the higher figure.

19. Anwar, *Muslims in Britain* p 10.

20. R. Ballard and V.S. Kalra, *The Ethnic Dimensions of the 1991 Census: A Preliminary Report*, Manchester Census Group (Manchester, 1994) pp 14–16.

21. A. Shaw, *A Pakistani Community in Britain* (Oxford, 1988) p 9.

22. For caste rivalry see Shaw, *A Pakistani Community*, pp 26–7; and for Hindu–Muslim tension E. Kelly, 'Transcontinental families – Gujarat and

Lancashire: a comparative study', in C. Clarke, C. Peach and S. Vertovec (eds) *South Asians Overseas, Migration and Ethnicity* (Cambridge, 1990) pp 251–67. In South Asian Muslim society what is to count as *zat*/caste remains the centre of debate amongst social scientists. Writing of Muslims in Manchester an anthropolgist considers Punjabi Muslim *zats* resemble Hindu castes in being: '(1) hereditary; (2) ideally endogamous; (3) recruited from occupational categories and ethnic groups; (4) comprehensive and ranked hierarchically … [but] differ from Hindu castes in that (1) the Muslim *zat* system is not based, except at its extremes, on notions of ritual purity and pollution … [thus] commensality between members of all *zats* is permitted … (2) ritual services are not necessarily provided by a 'pure' caste but by lay specialists … (3) all Muslims are equal in matters of law, worship and religious conduct.' P. Werbner, *The Migration Process, Capital, Gifts and Offerings among British Pakistanis* (New York, 1990) p 85.

23. C. Peach, 'Estimating the growth of the Bangladeshi population of Great Britain', *New Community*, 16/4 (1990) p 483.

24. Adams, *Across Seven Seas*, p 52.

25. R. Singh, introduction to the pictorial history, *Here to Stay, Bradford's South Asian Communities* (Bradford Heritage Recording Unit, 1994) p 10.

26. Sadiq's case-study is given in Shaw, *A Pakistani Community*, pp 23–4.

27. Shaw, *A Pakistani Community*, pp 46–49.

28. R. Ballard, 'Migration and kinship: the differential effect of marriage rules on the processes of Punjabi migration to Britain', in Clarke, *South Asians Overseas*, p 238.

29. T. Jones, *Britain's Ethnic Minorities* (PSI, London, 1993) p 24.

30. Clarke, *South Asians Overseas*, p 167.

31. Halliday, *Arabs in Exile*, p x.

32. Kelly, 'Transcontinental families' pp 253 and 259.

33. Ballard, 'Migration and kinship' p 228.

34. Ballard, 'Migration and kinship', p 229.

35. *Biradari* literally means 'brotherhood', and has been usefully described in a recent anthropological study of Pakistani Muslims in Manchester as a 'localised intermarrying caste group'. Werbner, *The Migration Process*, p 46.

36. Werbner, *The Migration Process*, pp 149–50.

37. Jones, *Britain's Ethnic Minorities*, p 88.

38. The *British Muslims Monthly Survey* (BMMS) was started in January 1993 by the Centre for the Study of Islam and Christian-Muslim Relations in Birmingham. BMMS is important in that it draws on a multiplicity of sources, including the local press. The latter makes very clear the increased involvement of Muslims in public life across the country. This perspective is freqently lacking in the national press, which usually only considers Muslims as newsworthy when they can be presented as problem or victim.

39. Shaw, *A Pakistani Community*, p 146.

40. Shaw, *A Pakistani Community*, p 146.

41. J. Eade, 'Bangladeshi community organisation and leadership in Tower Hamlets, East London' in Clarke, *South Asians Overseas*, pp 327–8.

42. See R. Ballard's 'New Clothes for the Emperor? The Conceptual Nakedness of Britain's Race Relations Industry', *New Community*, 18, Spring 1992; and T. Modood, *Not Easy Being British: Colour, Culture and Citizenship*

(Runnymede Trust, 1992).

43. P. Werbner, 'Manchester Pakistanis: division and unity' in Clarke, *South Asians Oveseas*, p 335.

44. See Modood, *Not Easy Being British*. In one of the essays, 'Beyond Racial Dualism: the case of the Indian economic success' he cites some evidence to suggest that Muslims from a rural background in Gujarat in India may not share the same levels of economic success.

45. V. Robinson, 'Boom and gloom: the success and failure of South Asians in Britain' in Clarke, *South Asians Overseas*, p 270.

46. Robinson, 'Boom and gloom' p 291.

47. Ballard and Kalra, *The Ethnic Dimensions of the 1991 Census*, p 32.

48. Robinson, 'Boom and gloom', p 291.

49. T. Modood, *Racial Equality, Colour, Culture and Justice*, The Commission on Social Justice, Issue Paper 5, Institute for Public Policy Research (London, 1994) pp 2–3.

50. Halliday, *Arabs in Exile*, pp 59 and 107.

51. See D. Joly, *Making a Place for Islam in British Society: Muslims in Birmingham*, Research Papers in Ethnic Relations 4 (University of Warwick, Coventry 1987) p 8.

52. The role of this important Muslim leader is portrayed in Chapter 4. The term *pir* is Persian for elder and is an honorific title used for religious leaders active in the sufi tradition in South Asia – the Arabic equivalent, also used, is *shaikh*.

53. Y. Samad, 'Imagining a British Muslim Identification: context and strategy of umbrella organizations', in C. Peach and S. Vertovec (eds) *Muslims in Europe: Reproducing Religious and Ethnic Cultures* (London, forthcoming).

54. The Imams and Mosques Council of Great Britain was formed by Dr Zaki Badawi, an Egyptian scholar, who used to be the director of the prestigious Islamic Cultural Centre and mosque in Regent's Park, London. Dr Badawi, a graduate of both al Azhar in Egypt and London University, is one of the very few Muslim scholars active in Britain today who is equally at home in the world of traditional Islamic discourse and that of modern academic disciplines.

55. See The UK Action Committee on Islamic Affairs, *Need for Reform: Muslims and the Law in Multi-faith Britain* (London, 1993).

56. The phrase is taken from Aziz Al-Azmeh, *Islams and Modernities* (London, 1993) p 4. This passionate and polemical work at times seems to imply that there are no family resemblances shared by Muslims in different parts of the world, and no continuities surviving migration.

57. Hourani, *Islam in European Thought*, p 56.

2. Islam in South Asia

1. R. Nicholson, translation of al-Hujwiri's *Kashf al-Mahjub, the Oldest Persian Treatise on Sufism* (Lahore, 1976/1911) preface.

2. R.B. Williams, *Religions of Immigrants from India and Pakistan: New Threads in the American Tapestry* (Cambridge, 1988) p 280.

3. The Battle of Plassey in 1757 gave the British effective control of

Bengal; by 1803 Delhi was occupied and much of the United Provinces – the traditional centre of Muslim rule and culture in India – was within their control; the two Anglo-Sikh wars of 1846 and 1849 led to the British annexing the Punjab.

4. For works of such distinction and empathy as *Mystical Dimensions of Islam* (North Carolina, 1975), Annemarie Schimmel was awarded Pakistan's highest honour, the Star of Pakistan.

5. Margaret Smith, *Al-Muhasibi, an Early Mystic of Baghdad* (London, 1935, reprint Lahore 1980) p 243.

6. Nicholson, *Kashf al-Mahjub*, p 382.

7. Nicholson, *Kashf al-Mahjub*, pp 55 and 212. This latter tradition (*hadith*) belongs to a category known as divine tradition (*hadith qudsi*), ascribed to God on the authority of Muhammad. In an important study William Graham has challenged a scholarly consensus that such traditions were late fabrications made by mystics to validate their ecstatic experience. Graham contends that such traditions are well attested in early and genuine collections of hadith and thus belong to a primitive element in the Islamic tradition. 'Not only is the divine saying *not* a late blossom of … sufism … [but rather] a strong argument for the deep roots of Sufi piety in early Muslim spirituality and the prophetic-revelatory event itself.' William Graham, *Divine Word and Prophetic Word in Early Islam* (Paris, 1977) p 110.

8. Nicholson, *Kashf al-Mahjub*, p 338.

9. Nicholson, *Kashf al-Mahjub*, p 214.

10. For these similarities see, S.H. Nasr, *Living Sufism* (London, 1980) pp 89–105.

11. See Francis Robinson, 'Perso-Islamic culture in India from the seventeenth to the early twentieth century' in R.L. Canfield (ed.), *Turco-Persia in Historical Perspective* (Cambridge, 1990) pp 104–31.

12. Bruce Lawrence, *Notes from a Distant Flute, The Extant Literature of Pre-Mughal Indian Sufism* (Teheran, 1978) p 72.

13. Lawrence, *Notes from a Distant Flute*, p 72.

14. See S. Digby, 'Tabarrukat and Succession among the Chishti Shaykhs of the Delhi Sultanate' in R.E. Frykenberg (ed.), *Delhi Through the Ages: Studies in Urban Culture and Society* (Delhi, 1986) pp 63–103.

15. Lawrence, *Notes from a Distant Flute*, pp 41, 25.

16. Richard Eaton, 'The Political and Religious Authority of the Shrine of Baba Farid' in B.D. Metcalf (ed.), *Moral Conduct and Authority, The Place of Adab in South Asian Islam* (Berkeley, 1984) p 338.

17. *Sharafuddin Maneri, The Hundrd Letters*, introduction and translation by P. Jackson (New York, 1980) p 427.

18. See *Teachings of Khwaja Farid*, translated by C. Shackle (Multan, 1978).

19. Eaton, 'The Political and Religious Authority of the Shrine of Baba Farid', p 355.

20. Annemarie Schimmel, *Islam in the Indian Sub-continent* (Leiden, 1980) pp 34, 134.

21. Y. Friedmann, *Shaykh Ahmad Sirhindi* (Montreal, 1971) p 70.

22. B. Lawrence, 'Islam in India: the function of institutional sufism in the islamization of Rajasthan, Gujarat and Kashmir', in R.C. Martin (ed.) *Islam in Local Contexts* (Leiden, 1982) p 33.

23. See L.M. Fruzetti, 'Ritual status of Muslim women in rural India' in J.I. Smith (ed.) *Women in Contemporary Societies* (London, 1980) pp 186–208; and A. Roy, *The Islamic Syncretistic Tradition in Bengal* (New Jersey, 1983).

24. L. Massignon, *The Passion of al-Hallaj* (New Jersey, 1982) vol 2. p 20.

25. See P. Jeffery 'Creating a scene: the disruption of ceremonial in a sufi shrine', in I. Ahmad, *Ritual and Religion among Muslims in India* (Delhi, 1981); D. Gilmartin 'Shrines, Succession and Sources of Moral Authority' in Metcalf (ed.) *Moral Conduct and Authority* pp 221–40; and E. Mann, 'Religion, Money and Status: competition for resources at the shrine of Shah Jamal, Aligarh' in C.W. Troll (ed.), *Muslim Shrines in India* (Delhi, 1989) pp 145–71.

26. Although the term 'sect' was a category developed by the sociologists Max Weber and Ernst Troeltsch to define a religious association over and against the 'church' and thus, like 'orthodox', belongs to a Western cultural tradition, its use is not so limited. An Urdu equivalent to sect and sectarian exist in common usage, e.g. *firqa* and *firqaparast*. In Urdu the word *maslak*, 'path', is used for discrete schools of thought and practice, such as Barelwi and Wahhabi. Within contemporary Islamic discourse it is not uncommon for one *maslak* to refer to another in disparaging terms, e.g. Barelwis often use Wahhabi in this sense, where the term carries the pejorative overtones of 'sect' in English.

27. The phrase is taken from K.W. Jones, *Socio-religious Reform Movements in British India* (Cambridge, 1989).

28. Islamism is to be preferred to 'fundamentalism', a term derived from the American Protestant tradition. Etymologically there is neither an Arabic nor an Urdu term for 'fundamentalism', although there are terms for reform, revival, renewal and modernity. A recent study reminds us that, 'the term "Islamism", which apparently originated in both Arabic and French in North Africa, and has begun to be used in English … has the great practical value of being the term most acceptable to Muslims.' See N.R. Keddie, 'Ideology, society and the state in post-colonial Muslim societies', in F. Halliday and H. Alavi (eds) *State and Ideology in the Middle East and Pakistan* (London, 1988) p 13.

29. In a context where Islam is a minority tradition or feels itself threatened by other developed religions, Islamic law has always been emphasized as the decisive marker of religious identity. There are four extant schools of Islamic law within the majority Sunni tradition – Hanafi, Hanbali, Maliki and Shafi'i – all named after famous scholars in early Islam. In South Asia the Hanafi school predominates.

30. M. Saroha, *Heavenly Ornaments, Being an English Translation of Maulana Ashraf Ali Thanawi's Bahishti Zewar* (Lahore, 1981) p 23.

31. B.D. Metcalf, 'The madrasa at Deoband: a model for religious education in modern India', *Modern Asian Studies* 12:1 (1978) pp 132–4.

32. B.D. Metcalf, *Islamic Revival in British India: Deoband 1860–1900* (New Jersey, 1982) pp 162–63.

33. See Saroha, *Heavenly Ornaments*, pp 18–19 and 393.

34. See Z.H. Faruqi, 'The Tablighi Jama'at', in S.T. Lokhandwalla (ed.), *India and Contemporary Islam* (Simla, 1971) pp 60–69.

35. M. Asad, *The Message of the Qur'an* (Gibraltar, 1980) p 83.

36. (1) *The profession of faith* – a reminder of God's Oneness and His Lordship; (2) *The five daily prayers*; (3) *Knowledge and remembrance* – knowledge of God's

commands and remembrance, *zikr*, a technical term for sufi devotional practices; (4) *Respect for every Muslim* – an attempt to transcend the sectarianism of
Islam in South Asia; (5) *Sincerity of intention* – to prefer the Hereafter and divine approval to the luxuries of the present, transitory world; (6) *To spare time*
– for training and revivalist activities. The six points and the interpretation
are taken from S.A. Ansari, *Six Points of Tabligh* (New Delhi, 1978).

37. Faruqi, 'The Tablighi Jama'at', p 68.

38. M.A. Haq, *The Faith Movement of Muhammad Ilyas* (London, 1972) p 133.

39. M. Ahmad, 'Islamic Fundamentalism in South Asia: The Jamaat-i-
Islami and the Tablighi Jamaat of South Asia' in M.E. Marty and R.S.
Appleby (eds) *Fundamentalism Observed* (Chicago, 1991) p 510.

40. Ahmad, 'Islamic Fundamentalism in South Asia', p 515.

41. Ahmad, 'Islamic Fundamentalism in South Asia', p 517.

42. In Urdu to be without a pir – *be-pir* – has the connotation of being
vicious, cruel and pitiless. See J.T. Platts, *A Dictionary of Urdu, Classical Hindi
and English* (London, 1974/1884).

43. For further details see Metcalf, *Islamic Revival in British India*.

44. Metcalf, *Islamic Revival in British India*, pp 309–11.

45. Ahmad, 'Islamic Fundamentalism in South Asia', p 523.

46. See H. Alavi, 'Pakistan and Islam: Ethnicity and Ideology' in Halliday
and Alavi, *State and Ideology*, p 86.

47. S. Saulat, *Maulana Maududi* (Karachi, 1979) p 143.

48. A. Maududi, *A Short History of the Revivalist Movement in Islam* (Lahore,
1972/1940) pp 112–13.

49. E. Sivan, *Radical Islam: Medieval Theology and Modern Politics* (New Haven, 1985) pp 22–3.

50. F. Robinson, *Varieties of South Asian Islam*, Research Papers in Ethnic
Relations 8 (Coventry, 1988) pp 17–18.

51. Maulana Maududi was a consultant in 1960 when the syllabus for the
new Medina University was drawn up – intended to rival the venerable Azhar
in Egypt, probably the most famous centre for Islamic studies in the Sunni
community world-wide; in 1962 he was elected a founder member of the
Muslim World League based at Mecca, an organization intended to mobilize
opinion against Nasser's Arab socialism. Both Maududi and one of his influential Pakistani successors, Professor Khurshid Ahmad, have been recipients
of King Faisal International Prizes for services to Islam. Maududi won the
first such prize in 1979 and Ahmad in 1990.

52. I.M. Lapidus, *A History of Islamic Societies* (Cambridge, 1988) p 890.

53. See Ahmad, 'Islamic Fundamentalism in South Asia', pp 498–9.

54. K. Mumtaz and F. Shaheed, *Women of Pakistan, Two Steps Forward One
Step Back?* (Lahore, 1987) p 158.

55. Educated Muslims critical of 'Islamism' are invariably accused of being culturally inauthentic and infatuated by the West. The Iranian intellectual Jalal Al-e Ahmad coined the term 'Euromania' – the Persian literally
means 'West-stricken-ness' – in a widely read work, translated by R.
Campbell, *Occidentosis. A Plague from the West* (Berkeley 1984).

56. A. Syed, *Pakistan, Islam, Politics and National Solidarity* (Lahore, 1984) pp
144–5.

57. Ahmad, 'Islamic Fundamentalism in South Asia', p 529.

58. In European history a useful parallel with Islamism viewed, in part, as a cultural phenomenon, is the German revolt against France and French materialism in the eighteenth century. See I. Berlin, 'The Apotheosis of the Romantic Will', in his *The Crooked Timber of Humanity* (London, 1991 edition) pp 218–25.

59. J.M.S. Baljon, *Religion and Thought of Shah Wali Allah Dihlawi, 1703–1762* (Leiden, 1986) p 167. Shah Wali Allah is one of the few South Asian writers whose works have been read in the Arab world.

60. C.W. Troll, *Sayyid Ahmad Khan, A Reinterpretation of Muslim Theology* (Karachi, 1979) p xix.

61. Fazlur Rahman, *Islam and Modernity: Transformation of an Intellectual Tradition* (Chicago, 1982) p 2. Rahman is one of a handful of distinguished South Asian Muslims to be mentioned in the late Albert Hourani's magisterial *A History of the Arab Peoples* (London, 1991). Hourani considered that Rahman's work represents perhaps 'the most carefully reasoned attempt to state the principles of a new jurisprudence ... a method of Qur'anic exegesis which would, he claimed, be true to the spirit of Islam but provide for the needs of modern life', p 447.

62. Muhammad Abduh (d. 1905) (the influential Egyptian modernist) sought to reinterpret Qur'anic texts to conform to democratic ideals, institutions and nineteenth-century scientific views. However, such scholarship depended 'on an epistemological *legerdemain*, which operates by assuming the scriptures do not mean what they say'. See Aziz Al-Azmeh, *Islams and Modernities* (London, 1993) p 33.

63. A. Wahid (ed.) *Thoughts and Reflections of Iqbal* (Lahore, 1964) pp 81–3.

64. Fazlur Rahman, *Major Themes of the Qur'an* (Chicago, 1980) p 31.

65. Jones, *Socio-religious Reform Movements*, p 83.

66. D. Lelyveld, *Aligarh's First Generation: Muslim Solidarity in British India* (New Jersey, 1978) pp xvi and 324.

67. Lelyveld, *Aligarh's First Generation*, p 207.

68. A. Iqbal, *My Life A Fragment: An Autobiographical Sketch of Maulana Mohamed Ali* (Lahore, 1966/1942) p 22.

69. See M. Munir, *From Jinnah to Zia* (Lahore, 1979); A. Syed, *Pakistan, Islam, Politics and National Solidarity* (Lahore, 1984); and H. Alavi, 'Pakistan and Islam: Ethnicity and Ideology'.

70. See Rahman, *Islam and Modernity*.

71. Mumtaz and Shaheed, *Women of Pakistan*, p 73.

72. Mumtaz and Shaheed, *Women of Pakistan*, p 159.

73. K.A. Faruki, 'Pakistan, Islamic Government and Society' in J. Esposito, *Islam in Asia* (Oxford, 1987) p 75.

74. A.S. Ahmed, *Discovering Islam, Making Sense of Muslim History and Society* (London and Lahore, 1988) p 11.

3. Bradford: Britain's 'Islamabad'

1. Richard Burghart (ed.), *Hinduism in Great Britain, The Perpetuation of Religion in an Alien Cultural Milieu* (London, 1987) p 2.

2. Burghart, *Hinduism in Great Britain*, p 2.

3. Burghart, *Hinduism in Great Britain*, p 3.

4. For Muslim minorities in the West today, exercised by the question of how to express their self-identity in a non-Muslim polity, Muslim scholars point to two earlier episodes in Islamic history as models for living in a non-Muslim environment, free to express their religious identity, without the necessity of a further *hijra* or recourse to *jihad*. The first is the migration to Abyssinia, a Christian country, between 615 and 622 AD and the second, the pact of Hudaybiyyah, 628 and 630 AD, a written pact between Muslims and non-Muslims. See M.K. Masud, 'Being Muslim in a non-Muslim Polity: Three Alternative Models', *Journal of Institute of Muslim Minority Affairs*, 10/1 (1989) pp 118–29.

5. M.K. Masud, 'The obligation to migrate: the doctrine of Hijra in Islamic law', in D.F. Eickelman and J. Piscatori (eds), *Muslim Travellers: Pilgrimage, Migration and the Religious Imagination* (London, 1990) p 32.

6. Exemption from both categories was allowed to anyone who was defined as weak – women, children and the infirm. These categories of flight and fight are still part of Islamic discourse in Britain. At the height of the Rushdie Affair Shabbir Akhtar, a Muslim scholar and apologist from Bradford, could write an article entitled 'Whose light? Whose darkness?', in which he insisted that, 'those Muslims who find it intolerable to live in a United Kingdom contaminated with the Rushdie virus need to seriously consider the Islamic alternatives of emigration (*hijra*) to the House of Islam or a declaration of holy war (*jihad*) on the House of Rejection.' See *The Guardian*, 27–2–1989.

7. H. Enayat, *Modern Islamic Political Thought* (London, 1982) p 6.

8. 'The People of the Book' as bearers of a 'revealed book' – Jews and Christians – are categorised in Islamic law as distinct from the heathen and enjoy certain rights within a Muslim polity as a 'protected minority'. See *Shorter Encyclopaedia of Islam* (Leiden, 1953) pp 16–17.

9. P. Hardy, *The Muslims of British India* (Cambridge, 1972) pp 109–10.

10. Masud, 'The obligation to migrate', p 40.

11. *Dar al-Islam* and the related *dar* categories are now being defined more frequently with reference to the question: from where does one not need to migrate? Answers to this question have produced categories such as *dar al-'ahd* (the land of pact), *dar al-sulh* (the land of truce), and *dar al-aman* (the land of peace), in which the freedom of Muslims to practise their religion is protected by covenant. See Masud, 'The obligation to migrate', p 44. Muslim scholars in Bradford use these categories along with *dar al-ahl al-Kītāb* (the land of the People of the Book).

12. Z. Badawi, *Islam in Britain* (London, 1981) p 27.

13. See A. Ahmed, *From Samarkand to Stornoway, Living Islam* (BBC Books, London, 1993). In this accessible study Dr Ahmed considers the shared dilemmas of Muslim minorities world-wide.

14. Speech delivered at St George's Hall in Bradford, 8–8–91.

15. This is also the burden of the writings of Syed Abul Hasan Ali Nadwi (b. 1914), a distinguished Indian scholar, secretary of the pretigious Nadwat al-Ulama academy, Lucknow, and a recipient of the prestigious Saudi Arabian Faisal Award for services to Islam in 1980. See particularly his book of talks, *Muslims in the West*, especially chapter 10, 'Main Duty of Muslim Immi-

grants' (Leicester, 1983) pp 125–33. This book is published in Britain by The Islamic Foundation, Leicester, the publishing and research wing of Jama'at-i Islami.

16. S. Akhtar, *Be Careful with Muhammad!* (London, 1989) p 89.

17. Video recording of opening of the 'Muslim Parliament' 4–1–92, for which I am indebted to a Bradford participant and member.

18. I. Ahmed, 'The Muslim factor in Britain and Europe', unpublished paper presented at 'Racial Equality in Europe' conference held in Birmingham in the autumn of 1991.

19. See the excellent oral history with pictorial commentary, *Here To Stay, Bradford's South Asian Communities*, Bradford Heritage Recording Unit (Bradford, 1994).

20. B. Dahya, 'The Nature of Pakistani Ethnicity in Industrial Cities in Britain' in A. Cohen (ed.), *Urban Ethnicity* (London, 1974) p 84.

21. See V. Waughray, *Visit to Bradford* (unpublished, Bradford Central Library, 1959). The figures were 65 Pakistani and 36 Indian conductors.

22. See *Here To Stay*.

23. *Here To Stay*, p 23.

24. *Here To Stay*, p 27.

25. *Here To Stay*, p 31.

26. Figures and reference in A. Shaw, *A Pakistani Community in Britain* (Oxford, 1988) p 51, footnote 15.

27. These figures are estimates based on such local authority figures as are available, census data, discussions with community leaders who run associations for different regional and linguistic groups, and the guestimates of earlier researchers.

28. *Here To Stay*, p 49.

29. S. Barton, *The Bengali Muslims of Bradford*, Monograph Series, Community Religions Project, Department of Theology and Religious Studies (University of Leeds, 1986) p 177.

30. See Dahya, 'The Nature of Pakistani Ethnicity', pp 77–95.

31. Ahl-i Hadith, the followers of the (prophetic) tradition, are a late-nineteenth-century Indian reformist sect. They accepted the classical collections of traditions in their totality as genuine and gave them priority over the four schools of Islamic law, whenever the latter seemed at variance with the traditions. See A. Ahmed, *Islamic Modernism in India and Pakistan, 1857–1964* (London, 1967) pp 113–22.

32. To argue that one regional group *controls* a mosque means just that rather than implying that no one outside that community can belong to the mosque committee.

33. The proliferation of mosques and supplementary schools mirrors the rising curve of Muslim children in the city. The following are council percentages for children of Pakistani and Bangladeshi origin of school age, 5–15 years old: in 1971, 4 per cent of all school children; in 1981, 11 per cent; and in 1991, 22 per cent. There are no separate figures for Indian Muslims. These figures include Keighley, 10 miles from the city, which has a small Muslim population of some 4,000 plus. However, the number of mosques and supplementary schools enumerated are those in the city of Bradford – the focus of research – excluding the few in Keighley.

34. The Gujaratis from East Africa (Khalifa) belong to an artisan caste of barbers, etc., while the majority of those from India belong to a landowning caste, the *vohra jat*. The East African Khalifa are usually professional, urban and bilingual – including English – while the majority of those migrating from India are rural with little English. It is not surprising that it is the Khalifa community which provided the first Muslim woman councillor in 1992. For the meaning of caste in a South Asian Muslim context see Chapter 1, footnote 22.

35. Both the Shah Bano case in 1985 and the continuing Babri mosque saga in Ayodhya, Uttar Pradesh, feeds Muslim insecurity and contributes to the sharply rising curve of religious communalism in India, so marked a feature of India in the 1980s. See I. Talbot, 'Politics and religion in contemporary India', in G. Moyser (ed.), *Politics and Religion in the Modern World* (London, 1991) pp 135–61. Shah Bano Begum is a divorced Muslim woman whose right to maintenance from her husband was upheld by the Indian Supreme Court. This ran contrary to Islamic law, which limits the obligations of the husband to a waiting period of three to four months between separation and final divorce – *'iddat* – during which time it can be established whether she is carrying a child by her former husband, for whom he is responsible. A perceived attack on Muslim personal law has always been considered in South Asia as tantamount to an assault on the very foundations of Muslim identity. Babri mosque is a mosque built on a site of a Temple, destroyed by the Mughal Emperor, Babur (d. 1530). It is one of a series of sacred Hindu sites targeted for liberation from Muslim 'occupation' by the Vishwa Hindu Parishad, an umbrella organization for various Hindu groups. The first attempt was made in October 1984. See P. Van der Veer, '"God must be liberated!" A Hindu liberation movement in Ayodhya', *Modern Asian Studies*, 21/2 (1987) pp 283–301.

36. The UK Islamic Mission is a vehicle for the Jama'at-i Islami tradition in Britain. The Bangladeshi community has one mosque in this tradition but is organized under a separate association in Britain, *Dawat-ul-Islam*, Invitation to Islam.

37. The term 'Asian' is used when statistics do not distinguish between Muslim, Sikh and Hindu and functions as a shorthand for all these communities. The 1991 census gave a figure of 11,713 for those of 'Indian' descent in the city. The majority are Hindus and Sikhs but they also include Muslims.

38. M. Rafiq, *Asian Businesses in Bradford: Profile and Prospects*, City of Bradford Metropolitan Council (Bradford, 1985) p 4.

39. *Bradford 1993, Facing the Future*, City of Bradford Metropolitan Council, p 9.

40. M. Anwar, *Muslims in Britain: Census and other Statistical Sources*, Centre for the Study of Islam and Christian–Muslim Relations, CSIC Papers 9 (Birmingham, September 1993) p 17.

41. Rafiq, *Asian Businesses in Bradford*, pp 5–8.

42. V.S. Khan, 'The Pakistanis: Mirpuri Villagers at Home and in Bradford', in J.L. Watson (ed.), *Between Two Cultures, Migrants and Minorities in Britain* (Oxford, 1977) p 76.

43. Promotional literature, n.d.

44. Ibn Sina (d. 1037), known to the West in the Latinized form Avicenna,

was hugely influential. 'His main medieval work, the *Canon* (Qanun) became a kind of bible of medieval medicine ... It was printed in Rome in the original as early as 1593, shortly after the introduction of Arabic printing into Europe'. M. Plessner, 'The Natural Sciences and Medicine' in J. Schacht and C.E. Bosworth (eds), *The Legacy of Islam* (Oxford, 1979) p 449.

45. B.D. Metcalf, *Islamic Revival in British India: Deoband 1860–1900* (New Jersey, 1982) p 192.

46. A. Moinuddin, *The Book of Sufi Healing* (New York, 1991) p 5.

47. Promotional literature, n.d.

48. W. Lyon, 'Competing doctors, unequal patients: stratified medicine in Lahore' in H. Donnan and P. Werbner (eds), *Economy and Culture in Pakistan* (London, 1991) p 145.

49. D.J. Matthews, C. Shackle, and S. Hussain (eds), *Urdu Literature* (London, 1985) p 121.

50. Fazal Mahmood, born in Gujar Khan, in the Punjab, Pakistan, came to Britain as a 15-year-old in 1972. Before starting his own business he was a community worker in the city.

51. The station changed hands in 1991 and became part of the Southall 'Sunrise Radio' group. This has generated some criticism by Muslims in the local press claiming that this has led to a bias towards non-Muslim, Indian perspectives and language (Hindi). See *Telegraph & Argus*, 10–5–91. It has fuelled support for a local pirate radio station, run by Muslims, Paradise City Radio (*Telegraph & Argus*, 6–11–91).

52. *Telegraph & Argus*, 24–5–91.

53. This is not to ignore the incidence of racial exclusion but simply to point out that for such professionals bilingualism can be a marketable asset.

54. Khan, 'The Pakistanis', pp 85–7.

55. Khan, 'The Pakistanis', p 74.

56. See Hiro, *Black British White British*, pp 172–5; and T. Mehmood, *Hand on the Sun* (Harmondsworth, 1983) pp 126–32.

57. Indicative of the consolidation of allegiances around religious identity is the emergence in the 1980s of three umbrella organizations for the three religious communities: in 1981 the Bradford Council for Mosques, and in 1984 both the Federation of Sikh Organizations and the Vishwa Hindu Parishad. For the limited social interaction and tensions between these three communities see R. Singh, *Immigrants to Citizens, the Sikh Community in Bradford*, The Race Relations Unit, Bradford and Ilkley Community College, 1992.

58. Promotional literature, n.d.

59. M. Le Lohe, 'The effects of the presence of immigrants upon the local political system in Bradford, 1945–77', in R. Miles and A. Phizacklea (eds), *Racism and Political Action* (London 1979) p 197.

60. Le Lohe, 'The effects of the presence of immigrants', pp 195–6.

61. *Telegraph & Argus*, 1–2–92.

62. Le Lohe, 'The effects of the presence of immigrants', p 197.

63. Khan, 'The Pakistanis', p 83.

64. C. Richardson, *A Geography of Bradford* (University of Bradford, 1976) pp 175–6.

65. See M. Halstead, *Education, Justice and Cultural Diversity: An Examination of the Honeyford Affair, 1984–85* (Falmer, Sussex, 1988) pp 37–9.

66. Halstead, *Education, Justice and Cutural Diversity*, p 27.

67. D. Shepherd, 'The accomplishment of divergence', *British Journal of Sociology of Education*, 8/3 (1987) p 265.

68. Halstead, *Education, Justice and Cultural Diversity*, p 38.

69. I have excluded reference here to the three schools which serve Keighley, 10 miles from the city.

70. Dahya, 'The nature of Pakistani Ethnicity', p 95.

71. P. Werbner, 'The fiction of unity in ethnic politics: aspects of representation and the state among British Pakistanis', in P. Werbner and M. Anwar (eds), *Black and Ethnic Leaderships in Britain: The Cultural Dimensions of Political Action* (London, 1991) p 141.

72. Halstead, *Education, Justice and Cultural Diversity*, p 113.

73. The Rajput are a landowning caste, originally high caste Hindu converts to Islam. In South Asia castes are usually ranked according to one of three categories: *ashraf* (noble), *zamindar* (landowner) and *kami* (artisan/servant). *Ashraf* castes trace their descent back to foreigners, whether *sayeds*, who claim to have the Prophet's blood in their veins, Pathans from Afghanistan, Mughals from Central Asia, or Shaikhs, descendants of the Quraish, the Prophet's tribe. The *zamindar* include the Rajputs, Jats, a farming caste, and Arains, market gardeners and vegetable growers. The *kami* include barbers, potters, tailors, blacksmiths, carpenters, shoemakers etc. The higher castes, many originating from outside the Indian sub-continent, are often lighter skinned. Indeed, 'fairness of skin is coveted ... [with] dark skins associated with low caste status and inferior origins', Shaw, *A Pakistani Community*, p. 140. This, in part, explains why so many South Asian Muslims did not naturally identify with the anti-racist category 'black', used as a political label for all non-whites.

74. *Telegraph & Argus*, 26-3-92.

4. Islamic Institutions in Bradford

1. T. Modood, 'British Asian Muslims and the Rushdie Affair', *Political Quarterly*, 61/2 (1990) p 145.

2. E. Rose, *Colour and Citizenship, A Report on British Race Relations* (London, 1969) p 59.

3. A.S. Ahmed, *Discovering Islam, Making Sense of Muslim History and Society* (Lahore, 1988) p 201. The extent of padding is clearly substantial, with Pakistan claiming a 26 per cent literacy rate. However, an 'Action Plan for Educational Development, 1983–1988', itself acknowleged: a dropout rate of 50 per cent between the ages of five and nine; the phenomenon of ghost schools, which do not exist but inflate government figures, and large discrepancies in school attendance between one province and another, and within provinces between urban and rural, male and female. See L. Butler, 'Basic Education in Pakistan: Policies, Practice and Research Directives', *Journal of South Asian and Middle Eastern Studies*, 9/4 (1988) pp 91–4.

4. W.J. Ong, *Orality and Literacy, The Technologizing of the Word* (London, 1988) p 34.

5. Ong, *Orality and Literacy*, pp 41 and 60.

6. W.A. Graham. 'Qur'an as Spoken Word', in R.C. Martin (ed.),

Approaches to Islam in Religious Studies (Tucson, 1985) p 40.

7. Graham, 'Qur'an as Spoken Word', p 35.

8. Graham, 'Qur'an as Spoken Word', p 214, footnote 63.

9. F. Robinson, 'Technology and Religious Change: Islam and the Impact of Print', *Modern Asian Studies*, 27/1 (1993) p 236.

10. R.B. Qureshi, *Sufi Music of India and Pakistan: Sound, Context and Meaning in Qawwali* (Cambridge, 1986) p 1. The phenomenon of *sama'* remains controversial. Islamic theological opinion has prohibited it as dangerous and unlawful. An introduction to Islam, *Lessons in Islam*, written by a distinguished Indian scholar, Maulana Mufti Muhammad Kifayatullah (d. 1952), widely used in Bradford's Deobandi mosques in both its original Urdu and English translation, lists as a sign of the Day of Judgment, *inter alia*, 'the abundance of singing, dancing and revelries' (Delhi, n.d.) Book 2, p 13. Naqshbandi and Suhrawardi orders prohibit its use or permit it without the use of musical instruments. Islamic tradition recognizes and cultivates the chanting of religious texts, especially the Qur'an. Cantillation of *zikr*, remembrance of God, has qur'anic warrant (sura 33:40 and 13:28) since, 'in religious cantillation ... musical features are subordinated to the religious text and function and thereby legitimized. Singing on the other hand, is characterized by the presence of independent musical features which exist for their own sake, most of all the sound of musical instruments ... *sama'* has normally included the use of instruments, particularly of percussion, to reinforce the element of *zikr* repetition which is considered to be inherent in it.' See Qureshi, *Sufi Music of India and Pakistan*, p 82.

11. B.D. Metcalf, *Perfecting Women: Maulana Ashraf 'Ali Thanawi's Bihishti Zewar*, partial translation and commentary (Berkeley, 1990) p 20.

12. Robinson, 'Technology and Religious Change', p 242.

13. Metcalf, *Perfecting Women*, p 21.

14. Ong, *Orality and Literacy*, p 41.

15. See F. Rahman, 'Some Islamic Issues in the Ayyub Khan Era' in D.P. Little (ed.), *Essays on Islamic Civilizations Presented to Niyazi Berkes* (Leiden, 1976) pp 284–302.

16. M. Ahmad, 'Islamic Fundamentalism in South Asia: The Jamaat-i-Islami and the Tablighi Jamaat of South Asia', in M.E. Marty and R.S. Appleby (eds), *Fundamentalism Observed* (Chicago, 1991) p 473.

17. Robinson, 'Technology and Religious Change', p 249.

18. Ong, *Orality and Literacy*, p 80. The phrase 'community of anonymity' is taken from B. Anderson, *Imagined Communities: Reflections on the Origin and Spread of Nationalism* (London, 1987).

19. Ong, *Orality and Literacy*, p 136.

20. To put these differences in perspective two observations drawn from Ong are helpful. First, 'standard English has accessible for use a recorded vocabulary of at least a million and a half words ... a simply oral dialect will commonly have resources of only a few thousand words'; second, 'the restricted linguistic code can be at least as expressive and precise as the elaborated code *in contexts which are familiar and shared by speaker and hearer*. For dealings with the unfamiliar, expressively and precisely, however, the restricted linguistic code will not do; an elaborated linguistic code is absolutely needed.' See his *Orality and Literacy*, pp 8 and 106 (emphasis mine). Such comments provide a

context for a widespread anxiety voiced by religious and community leaders that there is little communication between parents and children in many homes.

21. There is considerable interaction between these orders in South Asia, not least in valuing treasured works such as Abu Hafs 'Umar Suhrawardi (d. 1234), *'Awarif al ma'arif*, The Benefits of Knowledge, which sought to regulate sufi corporate life. Pir Maroof listed this as one of the key works for understanding sufism. The main differences turned on attitudes to the state – many of the Chishti sufis kept their distance, while at the other extreme Naqshbandi sufis were reformists, who sought to infuence those in power. See P. Lewis, *Pirs, Shrines and Pakistani Islam* (Rawalpindi, 1985) pp 44–7 and 74–7.

22. *Ta'wiz* belong to a religious landscape troubled by the evil eye and spirits, often malevolent (the Qur'anic *jinn*) which cause human misery. The Qur'an refers to itself as 'a healing and a mercy' (17:82 and 10:57); two chapters of the Qur'an, suras 113 and 114, are known as the *mu'awwizatan*, the two who preserve. There is a prophetic tradition that recounts that the Prophet used 'to seek refuge in God from jinn and the evil eye until the *mu'awwizatan* came down, after which he made use of them and abandoned everything else'. See J. Robson, *Mishkat al-Masabih, English translation and explanatory notes* (Lahore, 1975) vol. 2, pp 951–2. Thus amulets containing Qur'anic verses have long been part of the high Islamic tradition of healing. Maulana Thanawi in his celebrated reformist *Bihishti Zewar*, Heavenly Ornaments, devotes a section to appropriate amulets for a range of complaints ranging from the desire of a woman for a son, stomach ache, depression and the removal of poverty. For depression the Qur'anic verse 37:47 – Wherein there is no headache nor are they made mad thereby – is to be written in Arabic on a piece of paper, placed within an amulet and worn around the heart. M. Saroha, *Heavenly Ornaments, Being an English Translation of Ashraf Ali Thanawi's Bihishti Zewar* (Lahore, 1981) pp 480–83.

23. The founders of the Deobandi seminary were also skilled interpreters of dreams. It has to be remembered that, 'medicine was widely understood to be not an objective science but an ancillary dimension of religion ... the efficacy of cures was understood to depend on the will of God, not on principles tested by experimentation and observed results. Hence the piety of the practitioner, who was close to God, was considered of great importance.' See B.D. Metcalf, *Islamic Revival in British India, Deoband 1860–1900* (New Jersey, 1982) pp 191–2. Here was a holistic view of healing with the shaikh/*pir* combining the confessional with the psychiatrist's chair.

24. G.D. Qureshi, an English translation of *Salaam* (World Islamic Mission, Bradford, 1981) p 29–31. Mustafa, the Arabic for the Chosen, refers to the Prophet. Such devotion has seemed excessive to some modernists, who consider it tantamount to the 'mythification of the person of the Prophet Muhammad', F. Rahman, *Islam and Modernity* (Chicago, 1982) p 41.

25. A. Schimmel, *And Muhammad is His Messenger, The Veneration of the Prophet in Islamic Piety* (North Carolina, 1985) p 148.

26. I owe this information to Malise Ruthven, who covered this event for the BBC World Service.

27. E. Zaheer, *Bareilawis: History and Beliefs* (Lahore, 1985) pp 26–7.

28. *Jang*, 14–10–88.

29. For a brief characterization of this order, founded in Egypt, see A. Schimmel, *Mystical Dimensions of Islam* (North Carolina, 1975) pp 249–51.

30. *Jang*, 31–10–88.

31. *The Islamic Times*, December, 1985, p 20.

32. *Telegraph & Argus*, 27–9–79.

33. Suffat ul Islam takes its name from a group of companions of the Prophet, models of piety, poverty and renunciation of the world, whose home was the *suffa* or veranda of the mosque at Medina. Since 1985 this mosque has also organized a public procession through the streets of the city on the occasion of the Prophet's birthday. Its route is different from that of Pir Maroof. Sultan Bahu is a famous seventeenth-century Indian sufi poet born in the Jhang district of the Punjab, in present day Pakistan. See L.R. Krishna, *Panjabi Sufi Poets, A.D. 1460–1900* (Karachi, 1977) pp 27–39.

34. P. Werbner, *The Migration Process, Capital, Gifts and Offerings among British Pakistanis* (New York, 1990) p 46.

35. This was the view communicated to me by the general-secretary of the association, Mr Liaqat Hussain.

36. *Zikr* means remembrance (of God), and is part of Islamic devotional practices, involving the repetition of the divine names or other religious phrases, often accompanied by a prescribed discipline of movement and breathing, intended as a vehicle for religious experience and recollection of God.

37. M.M. Khan, *Hamara Islam* (Urdu) (Lahore, n.d.) pp 20, 105, 118, 119–20, 194.

38. *The Islamic Times*, November 1990, p 4.

39. *The Islamic Times*, February 1989, p 2.

40. Twaqulia is the focus of a recent monograph by S.W. Barton, *The Bengali Muslims of Bradford*, Monograph Series, Community Religions Project (University of Leeds, 1986).

41. From the autumn of 1991 such local authority discretionary grants were only to be awarded for a maximum of four years.

42. Metcalf, *Islamic Revival In British India*, p 133.

43. M.S. Agwani, *Islamic Fundamentalism in India* (Chandigarh, 1986) p 119.

44. This was one of the anxieties expressed to me by Mr Minhas, who had advised both institutions on setting up such schools. He also worried that, since there was a reluctance to pursue 'A' level studies and the Islamic qualifications of both *dar al-'ulum* were not accredited by any British University, the career prospects of 'graduates' from both centres who did not want to work in a mosque would be blighted.

45. M. Kifayatullah, *Lessons in Islam/Ta'lim al–Islam* (Urdu) (Delhi, n.d.) Book 3, p 27. The distinguished eighteenth-century Indian scholar Shah Wali Allah of Delhi (d. 1762) dissented from such literalism and cited another scholar's opinion to the effect that: 'This phenomenon was occasioned by a cohesion of small particles of water into, so to speak, one plane. Behind it there was a mountain or a dense cloud. Together these produced the effect of a mirror. When the moon was reflected in it, people observed two moons in the sky. Since a part of the reflected and part of the real moon was concealed, two halves were seen in the sky.' See J.M.S. Baljon, *Religion and Thought of Shah Wali Allah Dihlawi, 1703–62* (Leiden, 1986) p 105.

46. Department of Education and Science, *Report by HM Inspectors on the Institute of Islamic Education, Dewsbury* (Crown Copyright, 1986) p 8.

47. *Report by HM Inspectors*, pp 3, 11 and 8.

48. M. Zakariyya, *Tablighi Nisab* (Urdu) (Lahore, n.d.) p 18.

49. Zakariyya, *Tablighi Nisab*, pp 85; and 'Blessings of zikr', in *Tablighi Nisab*, p 37.

50. Zakariyya, *Tablighi Nisab*, pp 5 and 23.

51. Zakariyya, *Tablighi Nisab*, pp 6 and 19.

52. Zakariyya, *Tablighi Nisab*, pp 22, 28 and 34.

53. Five Bradford mosques were listed as affiliated to the JUB in 1988. Omitted from that list was Twaqulia, which hosted a regional JUB gathering in 1988. These constitute all the large Deobandi centres in the city, including Gujarati, Bangladeshi and Pakistani mosques.

54. Two useful and accessible works on the Shi'ite tradition in South Asia are, D. Pinault, *The Shiites, Ritual and Popular Piety in a Muslim Community* (London, 1992) and M.D. Ahmed, 'The Shi'is of Pakistan', in M. Kramer (ed.), *Shi'ism, Resistance, and Revolution*, (London, 1987) pp 275–87.

55. Ahmad, 'Islamic Fundamentalism in South Asia', pp 516 and 529.

56. M.M. Nomani, *Khomeini, Iranian Revolution and the Shi'ite Faith* (Lucknow, 1985) pp 4–8, 191–2. My copy was bought in September 1987 from Bury, at the opening of the new mosque and teaching block. The opening ceremony was to have been conducted by Dr Abdullah Omar Naseef, the secretary-general of the Muslim World League, and prayers conducted by the imam of the great mosque in Mecca, but internal political tension within Saudi Arabia meant both were unable to attend.

57. See M. Munir, *From Jinnah to Zia* (Lahore, 1979). This is an important study by a retired Chief Justice of Pakistan, who presided over a committee of inquiry investigating the civil disturbances in Pakistan in 1953 targeting the Ahmadiyya community, which triggered the first period of martial law.

58. Documented in harrowing detail in the report by an International Commission of Jurists, *Pakistan: Human Rights after Martial Law* (Karachi Study Circle, 1987) pp 103–15.

59. *Millat*, 23-8-88.

60. *Telegraph & Argus*, 6–10–86 and 7–10–86. The Barelwi *'ulama* have no more sympathy for the Ahmadiyyas than do the Deobandis. However, they are less critical of the Shi'ite tradition since they share with them a devotion to 'Ali, through whom many orders trace their spiritual ancestry. Many Muslim scholars have identified striking parallels between devotion to sufis, organised into a spiritual hierarchy, and Shi'ite devotion to their imams. The famous North African scholar, Ibn Khaldun (d. 1406), drew attention to these in his famous Muqaddimah. See F. Rosenthal, *Ibn Khaldun, The Muqaddimah* (London, 1967), vol 3, p 93.

61. Kifayatullah, *Lessons in Islam*, Book 4, pp 22–8.

62. *Telegraph & Argus*, 3–4–92.

63. *The Independent*, 4–9–91.

64. Saroha, *Heavenly Ornaments*, p 424.

65. *The Independent*, 9–9–91.

66. Bradford Council for Mosques hand-out, 24–4–90.

67. Maulana Ahmed, Presidential Address at 25th Annual Conference, UK

Islamic Mission, 1988.

68. S.T.M. Wasti, *Report on the 25 years of the U.K. Islamic Mission*, 1988.

69. The *mi'raj*, the ascent, tells of a mysterious journey in which the Prophet was spirited away to Jerusalem and thence, with the angel Gabriel, ascended to heaven. It is an elaboration of a statement in sura 17:1 of the Qur'an. It is hugely important in the devotional life of ordinary Muslims, as well as sufis. See Schimmel, *And Muhammad is His Messenger*, pp 159–75.

70. Thirty years ago an historian of Islam, Wilfred Cantwell Smith, perceptively remarked that Maulana Maududi, was: 'the most systematic thinker of modern Islam; one might even wonder whether his chief contribution, in the realm of interpretation, has not been for good and ill his transforming of Islam into a system.' See W.C. Smith, *Islam in Modern History* (New Jersey, 1957/1977) p 234.

71. G. Sarwar, *Islam, Beliefs and Teachings* (Muslim Educational Trust, London, 1980) p 171.

72. K. Bahadur, *The Jama'at-i Islami of Pakistan* (Lahore, 1978) p 149.

73. *The Islamic Foundation: Objectives, Activities and Projects* (Leicester, n.d.).

74. *Twenty-Fifth Annual Report*, UK Islamic Mission, 1988.

75. 1984 Constitution of The Young Muslims UK, paragraph 23.

76. This decision must have been very difficult for UK Islamic Mission, since like the Jama'at-i Islami movement in general, it focuses on the transnational identity of Muslims, and is very critical of linguistic and regional differences institutionalizaed in different mosques.

77. A.Y. Andrews, 'Jamaat-i-Islami in the U.K.', paper delivered at a conference on 'Religious Minorities and Social Change', University of Bristol, 1991.

78. *Trends*, 2/4 (1988).

79. Modood, 'British Asian Muslims and the Rushdie Affair', p 150.

80. M. Halstead, *Education, Justice and Cultural Diversity: An Examination of The Honeyford Affair, 1984–85* (Sussex, 1988) p 232.

81. *The Movement*, January 1977, p 1.

82. *The Movement*, January, pp 5 and 7.

83. One of the most distinguished Muslim scholars of this century, the late Fazlur Rahman, had from the first worried that the activist stance of Jama'at-i Islami was not wedded to serious scholarship. Dr Rahman spoke of an illuminating meeting with Maududi in Lahore, after he had passed his MA and was about to pursue his Ph.D. studies. Maududi remarked, 'the more you study, the more your practical faculties are numbed ... It was no matter of surprise to me that, when [Maududi] decided to retire ... his successor was ... an obviously well-meaning lawyer ... without any pretensions whatever to Islamic scholarship.' Rahman, *Islam and Modernity*, p 117.

84. Modood, 'British Asian Muslims and the Rushdie Affair', p 152.

85. *Trends*, 3/4 (1989).

86. K. Murad, *Muslim Youth in the West, Towards a New Education Strategy* (Leicester, 1986) p 6.

87. Murad, *Muslim Youth in the West*, p 7.

88. *Trends*, 3/7 (1990) p 30.

89. *Trends*, 3/7 (1990) p 7.

90. *Trends*, 3/6 (1990) p 11.

5. The 'Ulama: The Making and Influence of a British Muslim Leadership

1. See G. Kepel, *The Revenge of God, The Resurgence of Islam, Christianity and Judaism in the Modern World* (Oxford, 1994) pp 23–32; and F. Rahman, *Islam and Modernity, Transformation of an Intellectual Tradition* (Chicago, 1982).

2. A.S. Ahmed, *Postmodernism and Islam, Predicament and Promise* (London, 1992) p 43.

3. I. Kandhalwi, 'Muslim Degeneration and its Remedy', in M. Zakariyya, *Tablighi Nisab* (Lahore, n.d.) pp 10 and 16.

4. A. Schimmel, *Mystical Dimensions of Islam* (North Carolina, 1975) p 362.

5. B.D. Metcalf, *Islamic Revival in British India: Deoband 1860–1900* (Berkeley, 1982) p 139.

6. S. Akhtar, *A Faith For All Seasons, Islam and Western Modernity* (London, 1990) p 160.

7. M.S. Raza, *Islam in Britain: Past, Present and Future* (Leicester, 1991) pp 32–3.

8. *Mulla* is a Persian transformation of the Arabic, *mawla*, which means, *inter alia*, master, patron, protector – in popular parlance it also carries pejorative overtones; *maulvi*, and *maulana*, mean respectively, 'my master' and 'our master'; *'allama* means 'very learned'.

9. See Chapter 1 for information on these two organisations.

10. S.M. Darsh, *Muslims in Europe* (London, 1980) p 40.

11. Imam Hasan would distinguish three categories: parents advised by a doctor to allow a space between children for reasons of health; parents worried about the economic implications of having more children and those newly married without children, wanting to delay parenthood. He would advise the latter not to use contraception, but would point out that *coitus interruptus* is Islamically licit. To those within the second category he would stress that economic anxiety is not an Islamic reason for indulging in contraception, since God has promised to provide: 'do not kill your children for fear of poverty; it is We who shall provide sustenance for them as well as you. Verily, killing is a great sin (sura 17:31)'. M. Asad, *The Message of the Qur'an* (Gibraltar, 1980) p 422. This verse is also used to oppose abortion. With regard to the first category, Imam Hasan is sympathetic to recourse to contraception, as a temporary measure, for health reasons.

12. See Metcalf, *Islamic Revival in British India*, pp 146–7.

13. Metcalf, *Islamic Revival in British India*, p 47.

14. Advertisement, n.d.

15. M. Kifayatullah, *Lessons in Islam* (Delhi, n.d.), Book 4, p 27.

16. This section excludes mention of the *pirs*, because they are employer of *'ulama* rather than the employed, and, in the person of Pir Maroof, their concerns and functions have already been reviewed in Chapter 4. However, it is worth recording that many *pirs*, indeed Pir Maroof himself, have also completed the training of an *'alim*.

17. A. Syed, *Pakistan, Islam, Politics and National Solidarity* (Lahore, 1984) pp 219–20. The fact that the village imam is paid in kind is probably at the root of the frequent criticism in South Asian literature that they are greedy and gluttonous. This accusation surfaces in the novel written by a Bradfordian,

Tariq Mehmood, and set in the city, *Hand on the Sun* (Harmondsworth, 1983) p 57.

18. *Islamia, National Muslim Education Newsletter*, July 1992, p 15.

19. *Bradford's Urban Programme Annual Report*, City of Bradford Metropolitan Council, 1989, pp 16, 35–6.

20. A. Shaw, *A Pakistani Community in Britain* (Oxford, 1988) p 130.

21. Raza, *Islam in Britain*, p 23.

22. Akbar Ahmed has cleverly coined the term 'occidentalism' to stand for that mood of angry rejection by many Muslims of 'orientalism' – Western study and cultural perspectives on the Muslim world – dismissed as merely a handmaid of Western colonial domination of the Muslim world. 'For many Muslim scholars working in Africa and Asia, imperfectly grasped bits of Marxist dogma, nationalism and religious chauvinism create incorrect images of the West ... [as] peopled by creatures whose sole purpose is to dominate, subvert and subjugate them ... there are many in whose work paranoia and hysteria pass for thought and analysis.' Ahmed, *Postmodernism and Islam*, p 177.

23. It is worth recalling that the distinction between church and state is foreign to Islam, and with it the vocabulary this distinction generated. Thus, 'in classical Arabic, as well as other languages which derive their intellectual and political vocabulary from classical Arabic, there were no pairs of words corresponding to spiritual and temporal, lay and ecclesiastical, religious and secular. It was not until the nineteenth and twentieth centuries, and then under the influence of Western ideas and institutions, that new words were found, first in Turkish and then in Arabic, to express the idea of the secular ... [even today] there is no equivalent to the term "laity", a meaningless expression in the context of Islam.' B. Lewis, *The Political Language of Islam* (Chicago, 1991) p 3.

24. *The Muslim Manifesto – A Strategy for Survival* (The Muslim Institute, London, 1990) pp 30–31.

25. Professor Vatikiotis reminds us that the Islamist, 'in arguing the case and calling for the construction of an Islamic society and political order, guided by the word of God and governed by His revealed law ... oppose secular political orders ... as belonging to the "age of ignorance" (*jahiliyya*) and as having an infidel provenance from the West and East alike.' See P.J. Vatikiotis, *Islam and the State* (Beckenham, 1987) p 85.

26. Ahmed, *Postmodernism and Islam*, p 173.

27. D.H. Khaled, 'Muslims and the purport of secularism', *Islam and the Modern Age*, 5/2 (1974) p 34.

28. *Dawn*, 21-1-83.

29. F. Robinson, 'Scholarship and mysticism in early 18th century Awadh', in A.L. Dallapiccola and S.Z. Lallemant (eds), *Islam and Indian Regions*, Vol 1: Texts (Stuttgart, 1993) pp 381–2.

30. F. Robinson, 'Perso-Islamic culture in India from the seventeenth to the early twentieth century', in R.L. Canfield (ed.), *Turko-Persia in Historical Perspective* (Cambridge, 1990) p 115.

31. See Rahman, *Islam and Modernity*.

32. Professor Robinson pertinently observed that, 'The heirs to the scholars of the rational sciences, as far as there were any, were the Islamic modernists, who learned the skills of the new imperial civilization, and who, from Saiyid

Ahmad Khan to Fazlur Rahman, sometime head of Pakistan's Institute of Islamic Research, have striven to reconcile Islamic revelation with modern knowledge.' F. Robinson, 'Perso-Islamic culture in India', p 126.

33. M. Iqbal, *The Reconstruction of Religious Thought in Islam* (Lahore, 1982/1934) p 169.

34. C. Hamilton, *Hedaya*, edited by S.G. Grady (Lahore, 1987) p 66. An abbreviated edition of an eighteenth-century translation into English by Charles Hamilton was published in 1870 by Standish Grove Grady, since 'this work has been made a text-book by the Council of Legal Education, for the examination of students of the Inns of Court, who are qualifying themselves for the call to the English Bar, with a view of practising in India'. Sections such as those rendered obsolete with the abolition of slavery were omitted. In the preface Grady entertained the hope that the work would be 'found useful in promoting the study of the (Islamic) law in universities in India'. Such has proved the case with the work reprinted in Pakistan. My copy is dated 1987 and printed in Lahore, Pakistan.

35. Iqbal, *The Reconstruction of Religious Thought in Islam*, p 168.

36. *Ijma'*, consensus, one of the sources of Islamic law, is an elusive concept, since there is neither agreement as to who should be consulted nor mechanisms for formulating it. It can usually only be detected retrospectively. Thus Bernard Lewis argues that it is tantamount to, '"the climate of opinion" among the learned and powerful ... there may be differing *ijma's* influenced by different traditions and circumstances in different parts of the Islamic world.' See B. Lewis, *Islam in History* (London, 1973) p 226.

37. Maulana Mufti Shafi based such a judgement on sura 4:115: 'And whosoever acts hostilely to the Messenger after guidance has become manifest to him and follows other than the way of the believers, We ... make him enter hell ... and the *hadith*, "My communtiy will never unite in error" ... [thus] the *ijtihad* ... of individual jurists were to be considered as based on surmise ... [until] a verdict is confirmed through *ijma'* or consensus of all jurists ... [then it can] attain almost as much sanctity as the Revealed Commandments.' K.A. Faruki, *Islam, Today and Tomorrow* (Karachi, 1974) p 49.

38. Rahman, *Islam and Modernity*, p 2.

39. See S.J. Malik, 'Islamization in Pakistan 1977–85: the ulama and their places of learning', *Islamic Studies*, 28/1 (1989) pp 8–9.

40. Malik, 'Islamization in Pakistan 1977–85', pp 7–8.

41. Malik, 'Islamization in Pakistan 1977–85', p 10.

42. S.J. Malik, *Islamisierung in Pakistan 1977–84* (Stuttgart, 1989) pp 231, 238 and 243.

43. Rahman, *Islam and Modernity*, p 122.

44. See S. Lateef, *Muslim Women in India* (London, 1990) pp 192–201.

45. Cited in Rahman, *Islam and Modernity*, p 111.

46. Z.H. Fauqi, *The Deoband School and the Demand for Pakistan* (Lahore, 1963) p 29.

47. See J.M.S. Baljon, *Religion and Thought of Shah Wali Allah Dihlawi, 1703–1762* (Leiden, 1986) p 10.

48. Abul Hasan Ali Nadwi, an Arabist, has been an important bridge between the South Asian Muslim communities and the Arab world. See E. Sivan, *Radical Islam: Medieval Theology and Modern Politics* (New Haven, 1985)

pp 26 and 36.

49. Hamilton, *Hedaya*, p 353.

50. Sura 2:282, Asad, *The Message of the Qur'an*, p 63.

51. F. Rahman, *Major Themes of the Qur'an* (Chicago, 1980) pp 48–9.

52. See K. Mumtaz and F. Shaheed, *Women of Pakistan, Two Steps Forward One Step Back?* (Lahore, 1987) pp 106–10.

53. Provisional Prospectus (n.d.) p 5.

54. Islamic Missionary College prospectus (1974) pp 3–4.

55. S. Barton, *The Bengali Muslims of Bradford* (Leeds, 1986) p 158.

56. M.A.K. Cheema, 'Education and the Muslims', a paper presented at the National Conference of British Muslims held in Bradford, 24–9–90, p 5.

57. *Telegraph & Argus*, 28–8–86.

58. *The Muslim News*, 15–12–89.

59. L. Butler, 'Basic Education in Pakistan: Policies, Practice and Research Directives', *Journal of South Asian and Middle Eastern Studies*, 9/4 (1988) pp 102–3.

60. B. Din, 'Asian parents' views about their Middle School children's education', (unpublished) MA thesis, Department of Education, University of York, 1986, p 77. His research involved questioning 100 Muslim parents (all male): 73 Pakistanis, 15 Bangladeshis and 12 Gujaratis.

6. Beyond Sectarianism:
The Role of the Council for Mosques

1. *Turning Points: A Review of Race Relations in Bradford*, City of Bradford Metropolitan Council (Bradford 1981) p 49.

2. *The Sunday Telegraph*, 5–1–92.

3. The other four members, along with Pir Maroof and Sher Azam, were Nazim Naqvi, president and founder of Anjuman-i Haideria, the earliest of the city's two Shi'a centres, Abdul Haq Pandor, president of the Gujarati-controlled Deobandi mosque at St Margaret's Road, Muhammad Ansari, president of the city's only Ahl-i Hadith mosque and Umar Warraich, president of the UK Islamic Mission mosque in Byron Street.

4. Sher Azam was recently profiled in the business section of the local press. He heads the Al Halal Supermarket and Cash & Carry (an Islamic co-operative), which has 'forty staff, a turnover topping £2.5 million and is on the city's tourist trail of attractions', a signal achievement for someone who, as a 19-year-old, had arrived in Bradford 30 years earlier without a word of English. *Telegraph & Argus*, 1–10–92.

5. The constitution made explicit that the Prophet Muhammad is 'the last prophet and there can be no new prophet till the Day of Judgement'. The inclusion of this phrase was clearly intended to exclude the Ahmadiyyas.

6. Councillors Hameed, Ajeeb, Amin and Nadeem Qureshi (father and son) and Riaz.

7. Councillor Hameed, when chairman of the Community Relations Council, was embroiled in a local controversy when he joined a Council for Mosques demonstration against the Ahmadiyya sect on 29 September 1986, which brought calls for his resignation.

8. *Local Administrative Memorandum, Education for a Multi-cultural Society: Pro-*

visions for Pupils of Ethnic Minority Communities, City of Bradford Metropolitan Council, 1982.

9. Cyclostyled report of the meeting supplied by the Bradford Council for Mosques.

10. M.A.K. Cheema, 'Islamic Education and the Maintained School', *Muslim Educational Quarterly*, 1/1 (1985) p 13.

11. *Telegraph & Argus*, 12–12–83.

12. *Telegraph & Argus*, 7–3–84.

13. *Telegraph & Argus*, 30–12–83.

14. M. Halstead, *Education, Justice and Cultural Diversity: An Examination of the Honeyford Affair, 1984–85* (Falmer, 1988) pp 246–7.

15. See Halstead, *Education, Justice and Cultural Diversity*, p 59.

16. *Hansard*, 16 April 1985, pp 234–6.

17. D. Murphy, *Tales from Two Cities: Travels of Another Sort* (London, 1987) pp 105–09. I owe the phrase 'Authorised Version' to this book.

18. Kureishi identified the following values as shared by C.M. Khan, the Council for Mosques and Ray Honeyford: 'the pre-eminent value of the family ... the importance of religion in establishing morality ... the innately inferior position of women ... [a dislike of] liberalism in all its forms, and ... an advocate of severe and vengeful retribution against law-breakers.' H. Kureishi, 'Bradford', in *In Trouble Again*, Granta 20 (Harmondsworth, 1986) p 160.

19. *Telegraph & Argus*, 26–11–85.

20. See Bradford Community Relations Council, *Annual Report*, 1984/85, p 2.

21. Murphy, *Tales from Two Cities*, p 124.

22. Murphy, *Tales from Two Cities*, p 127.

23. Halstead, *Education, Justice and Cultural Diversity*, p 107.

24. Bradford Community Relations Council, minutes of executive meeting, 22–10–85.

25. Halstead, *Education, Justice and Cultural Diversity*, p 64.

26. Taken from the service sheet.

27. See L. Appignanesi and S. Maitland (eds), *The Rushdie File* (London, 1989); and M. Ruthven, *The Satanic Affair: Salman Rushdie and the Rage of Islam* (London, 1990).

28. *Impact International*, 28 October–10 November 1988, p 14.

29. During the Rushdie affair Jami'at-i Tabligh al-Islam in Bradford published a pamphlet, *The Satanic Verses Affair: an Invitation to Blasphemy and Insult*, to explain the dismay and outrage the contents of the novel provoked. Verses from the *Salaam* were cited to illustrate the fact that to 'Muslims the Holy Prophet is more precious and closer than all the valuables they hold so dear'. Siddique (n.d.) p 7.

30. Cited in A. Schimmel, *And Muhammad is His Messenger, The Veneration of the Prophet in Islamic Piety* (North Carolina, 1985) p 4.

31. In 1938 a furore erupted in Britain and the Empire when Muslims became aware of the contents of H.G. Wells's *A Short History of the World*, which contained an unflattering picture of the Prophet, presented as a 'shifty character' and a man 'of very considerable vanity, greed, cunning, self-deception and quite insincere religious passion'. In certain particulars this

episode anticipated the Rushdie affair: 'an aroused Muslim sentiment extending beyond those who actually read the offending passages; the suggestion that the outrage was polit ically manipulated; demands that censorship be imposed; and the dilemma of a government that for strategic reasons must defuse an explosive situation of international proportions but must also oppose the suppression of expression.' J. Piscatori, 'The Rushdie Affair and the politics of ambiguity', *International Affairs*, 66/4 (1990) pp 767–8.

32. M. Ruthven, *The Satanic Affair*, p 87.

33. *Dawn Overseas Weekly*, 17–7–86. This legal amendment is part of the continued assault on the Ahmadiyya movement.

34. *New Statesman & Society*, 24–3–89.

35. Apostasy carries the death penalty for men in Islamic law. See the *Shorter Encyclopaedia of Islam* (Karachi 1981/53) p 413. Rushdie was also considered by some Muslims as guilty of *sabb al-nabi* or *shatm al-rasul*, insulting the Prophet, which involves a similar draconian punishment. See M.M. Ahsan and A.R. Kidwai (eds), *Sacrilege versus Civility, Muslim Perspectives on the Satanic Verses Affair* (Leicester, 1991) pp 52–3.

36. Ironically the visual media did not attend the book-burning and the only record of the incident was the video made by the Council for Mosques itself. Thus, whoever wanted to show it contributed to Council funds!

37. *Yorkshire Post*, 18–1–89.

38. *Telegraph & Argus*, 17–2–89.

39. See B. Parekh, 'The Rushdie Affair and the British Press', in D. Cohn-Sherbok (ed.), *The Salman Rushdie Controversy in Interreligious Perspective* (Lampeter, 1990).

40. *The Guardian*, 27–2–89.

41. S. Akhtar, *Be Careful with Muhammad!* (London, 1989) p 102.

42. *Telegraph & Argus*, 17–6–89. Such a display of vicious self-righteousness by some young men was hardly surprising when a scholar such as A. Kidwai, a member of the Islamic Foundation in Leicester, was prepared to endorse incitement to violence as a strategic tool against critics. In an article in *Trends*, the journal of *Young Muslims UK*, he wrote: 'Allah … has guaranteed the purity of the Holy Qur'an till the Day of Judgement and it is, therefore, our collective responsibilty to safeguard its authenticity by incitement to murder people like Salman Rushdie and his heinous supporters. This should serve as a lesson so that others will not dare innovate conjectures against Islam in the future.' *Trends*, 2:5 (1989) p 27.

43. *The Guardian*, 28–5–90.

44. Ruthven, *The Satanic Affair*, p 118.

45. See S. Lee and P. Stanford, *Believing Bishops* (London, 1990) and P. Lewis, 'Beyond Babel: An Anglican Perspective in Bradford, The Eighth Lambeth Interfaith Lecture', *Islam & Christian–Muslim Relations*, 4/1 (1993). The other institution which contributed, locally, to developing an informed awareness and debate about the issues was Bradford and Ilkley Community College, which sponsored a series of lectures and seminars led by Muslim and non-Muslim specialists, exploring the religious, literary, legal and educational dimensions of the Rushdie affair. The lectures were then published. See D. Bowen (ed.), *The Satanic Verses: Bradford Responds* (Bradford, 1992).

46. Bradford Community Relations Council, *Annual Report, 1988/89*, p 6.

47. Bradford Community Relations Council, *Annual Report 1988/89*, p 6.

48. Ahsan and Kidwai, *Sacrilege and Civility*, p 334.

49. *Bulletin UKACIA*, July 1989.

50. Akhtar, *Be Careful with Muhammad!*, pp 64 and 83.

51. *The Muslim News*, October 1989.

52. *The British Muslim Response to Mr Patten*, UK Action Committeee on Islamic Affairs (1989) pp 5–9.

53. *Yorkshire Post*, 30–4–90.

54. The phrase 'imagined community' was coined by Benedict Anderson to refer to nations. The members of the smallest of nations will 'never know most of their fellow-members, meet them, or even hear of them, yet in the minds of each lives the image of their communion ... all communities larger than primordial villages ... are imagined'. *Imagined Communities: Reflections on the Origin and Spread of Nationalism* (London, 1983) p 15. This seems an apt phrase to descibe the *umma*, which like a nation is difficult to describe, constantly re-imagined, yet remains the focus of devotion and fierce loyalty.

55. A.S. Ahmed, *Discovering Islam, Making Sense of Muslim History and Society* (Lahore, 1988) p 176.

56. *The Independent*, 23–2–91.

57. Press release, 12–8–90.

58. *Telegraph & Argus*, 20–8–90.

59. Press release, 1–9–90.

60. The other delegates were Yusuf Islam (Union of Muslim Organisations), Idris Mears (Murabitun European Muslim Movement), Bashir Maan (Islamic Council of Scotland), Ahmad Versi (Editor of *The Muslim News*) and Bassam Fattal (Protocol officer and translator). *The Muslim News*, 26 October 1990, p 1.

61. *The Guardian*, 21–1–91.

62. The Caliphate/*khilafat* has exercised a strange fascination for South Asian Muslims. An ill-starred *khilafat* movement was launched in India in 1919 to prevent the dismemberment of the Ottoman Empire, in the name of loyalty to the Caliph, at a time when Arabs and Turks themselves were wearying of this institution – indeed, in 1924 the Turks themselves abolished the caliphate. See A. Ahmad, *Islamic Modernism in India and Pakistan, 1857–1964* (London, 1967) pp 123–40. The fact that some 70 years after its abolition Muslims in Bradford can make quixotic references to its restoration points to its continuing imaginative appeal.

63. *The Guardian*, 21–1–91.

64. Bradford Council for Mosques press release, 13–2–91.

65. *Telegraph & Argus*, 14–2–91.

66. *Telegraph & Argus*, 16–2–91.

67. The ruling Labour group held 50 of the ninety seats in 1992. In addition to the 11 Muslim councillors there was one Sikh councillor. Muslim councillors were elected to the posts of deputy leader, vice chairman of the Labour group and chairman of the housing and environmental services committee (*Telegraph & Argus*, 12–5–92).

68. *Telegraph & Argus*, 3–8–90.

69. *Telegraph & Argus*, 7–8–90.

70. Despite the anger aroused by *The Satanic Verses* affair there were few

local incidents of violence and intimidation. The worst was an anonymous death threat to a local college lecturer, should a lecture go ahead which he had organized – to be addressed by Dr Badawi, the Principal of the Muslim College, in London. The college authorities thought it prudent to cancel (*Telegraph & Argus*, 1–3–90).

71. *The Independent*, 6–1–91.

72. *Telegraph & Argus*, 28–3–91.

73. An agreement of all Muslim sects on one date for the sighting of the moon, the beginning and ending of the month of fasting, has proved elusive. Often in Britain it is not visible to the eye – according to some hadith a precondition for starting the fast. How then is the date to be agreed? For some recourse to Morocco, the nearest Muslim country, is enough, for others Saudi Arabia or Pakistan is consulted, and there is a group who favour consulting the meteorological office in London. These issues are often interwoven with sectarian allegiance, with Barelwis suspicious of Saudi Arabian practice. Sometimes a precarious accord has been secured only to be undermined with the arrival of *'ulama* from South Asia not party to the earlier agreement.

7. Looking Forward: Muslim Communities in the 1990s

1. Race relations legislation in Britain is now shot through with inconsistencies. The Race Relations Act of 1976 criminalized discrimination on the basis of race/ethnicity. Definitions of race/ethnicity have been tested in the courts: the House of Lords delivered a judgement in 1983 (Mandhla v. Lee) which allowed Sikhs to be defined as an ethnic group and thus protected by the act. The recent industrial tribunal decision that Muslims were not an ethnic group (Commission for Racial Equality v. Precision, 26–7–91) meant that employers are 'liable to legal action for not employing turban-wearing Sikhs and *yamulka*-wearing Jews but may lawfully refuse employment to Muslim women who insist on wearing the *hijab*'. T. Modood, 'Establishment, Multiculturalism and Citizenship', *Political Quarterly*, 65/1 (1994) p 57.

2. *Telegraph & Argus*, 20–2–92.

3. The Islamic party of Britain was launched in September 1989 at London's Regent's Park Mosque. Its leader and general-secretary are converts, Daud Musa Pidcock and Mustaqim Bleher. This is seen as a partial explanation for their poor showing in elections, since they are unfamiliar with the *biradari* networks, the key to understanding how South Asian Muslims vote. In the 1992 general election they put up three candidates for Bradford constituencies. In all they lost their deposits. In Bradford West, with an estimated 16,000 Muslim votes, Pidcock canvassed 471 votes; in Bradford North with 7,000 Muslim votes their candidate won 304 votes.

4. *Telegraph & Argus*, 21–11–92.

5. W.C. Smith, *Islam in Modern History* (New Jersey, 1957/77) p 286.

6. *The Muslim News*, 27–4–90.

7. *The Guardian*, 26–3–90.

8. S. Vertovec, *Local Contexts and the Development of Muslim Communities in Britain: Observations in Keighley, West Yorkshire*, Centre for Research in Ethnic Relations, University of Warwick (forthcoming).

9. Alison Shaw's research on the Pakistani community in Oxford showed that where couples eloped this was not necessarily a result of exposure to Western liberal values but rather could be located within 'a distinctly Pakistani romantic idiom … [the stuff] of the Urdu and Hindi films avidly watched by east Oxford Pakistanis'. See *A Pakistani Community in Britain* (Oxford, 1988) p 170.

10. B. Din, 'Asian parents' views about their Middle School children', unpublished MA thesis, Department of Education, University of York (1986) pp 6 and 75.

11. *West Bowling Youth Report*, City of Bradford Metropolitan Council (1989) pp 4–14.

12. The Bangladesh Youth Organization, the Karmand Centre and Grange Interlink Community Association were set up in 1982; the Pakistan Community Centre in 1984, al-Falah in 1985, Frizinghall Community Centre and Saathi Centre were established in 1986 and the West Bowling Youth Organization in 1989. Most of these centres are not exclusively Muslim but the majority of their users are, given their location.

13. *Melody Maker*, 9–5–92.

14. *Jang*, 7–8–92.

15. *Telegraph & Argus*, 4–6–91.

16. *Telegraph & Argus*, 16–5–88.

17. *Trends*, 3/2 (1989) p 8.

18. *Sultan*, 3 (November–December 1989) p 16.

19. *Sultan*, 3, p 20.

20. See V.S. Khan, 'Asian women in Britain: strategies of adjustment of Indian and Pakistani migrants', in A. de Souza (ed.), *Women in Contemporary India* (Delhi, 1980) p 279.

21. This comment should not be interpreted as a justification for such procedures. It is evident from reading the annual reports of Himmat – a Bradford project set up in November 1989 to help young 'Asian' women caught up in domestic problems – that a pressing concern remains support and advocacy for those women who go to South Asia, marry, return home, often with a child, to find that their husband cannot get permission from the Home Office to join them or have to wait an interminable time for such permission to be granted.

22. As well as the community centres listed above there are a number of centres for women only, e.g. the Asian Women and Girls centre (1979), the Millan centre (1989) and a £160,000 training centre for 'Asian' women, Nur-e-Nisa (Urdu for Light of Women), opened in October 1992.

23. See Shaw, *A Pakistani Community in Britain*, pp 161–7; and P. Werbner, *The Migration Process, Capital, Gifts and Offerings among British Pakistanis* (New York, 1990) pp 149–50.

24. See T. Jones, *Britain's Ethnic Minorities* (London, 1993) p 88.

25. K. Knott and S. Khokher, 'Religious and ethnic identity among young Muslim women in Bradford', *New Community*, 19/4 (1993) pp 601–2.

26. Y. Ali, 'Muslim Women and the Politics of Ethnicity and Culture in Northern England', in G. Sahgal and N. Yuval-Davis (eds), *Refusing Holy Orders, Women and Fundamentalism in Britain* (London, 1992) pp 112–16.

27. Characteristic are comments from an interview with Imran Khan, in

which he asserted that British Muslims must understand that, 'Islam is a progressive religion. It's meant for all times. They shouldn't confine it to any period, era or a golden age. It should be developed all the time with new ideas. Islam is freedom of expression, it's debate. It should grow, it should evolve: the guidelines are in the Qur'an.' *Q News*, 31 July 1992, p 10.

28. K. Mumtaz and F. Shaheed, *Women of Pakistan, Two Steps Forward One Step Back?* (Lahore, 1987) pp 158–9.

29. S. Khanum, 'Education and the Muslim Girl', in *Refusing Holy Orders*, pp 125–26.

30. Promotional literature, n.d.

31. *The Independent*, 9–9–91.

32. *The Islamic Times*, 5/11 (1990) p 10.

33. See Mumtaz and Shaheed, *Women of Pakistan*, pp 106–10.

34. The science of Hadith classifies traditions as *sahih*, sound, *hasan*, good, *da'if*, weak, or *saqim*, infirm. All those in *Bukhari* and *Muslim* are considered sound. The sound and the good are recognized as valid bases for legal decisions. See J. Robson, *Mishkat al-Masabih, English Translation and explanatory notes* (Lahore, 1975), vol 1, introduction.

35. *Trends*, 3/3 (1989) pp 10–11.

36. *Trends*, 3/4 (1989) pp 4, 26–7. A recent pioneer study of just such hadith by a Moroccan sociologist and Islamic feminist indicates that the authenticity of such uncongenial hadith can be challenged by working with the very criteria established by famous Hadith scholars themselves. See F. Mernissi, *Women and Islam, An Historical and Theological Enquiry* (Oxford, 1991).

37. F. Rahman, *Islam and Modernity, Transformation of an Intellectual Tradition* (Chicago, 1982) p 150.

38. See A.S. Ahmed, *Postmodernism and Islam: Predicament and Promise* (London, 1992) p 163.

39. S. Akhtar, *A Faith For All Seasons, Islam and Western Modernity* (London, 1990) p 9.

40. A.S. Ahmed, *Discovering Islam, Making Sense of Muslim History and Society* (Lahore, 1988) p 205.

41. Ahmed, *Postmodernism and Islam*, p 168. Such organizations in Britain are the Islamic Academy in Cambridge, the Islamic Foundation in Leicester and the Muslim College and Muslim Institute, both in London. Jorgen Nielsen's assessment of such institutions is more sanguine. He contends that it is difficult to establish a 'direct correlation between funding source and subsequent policy'. See *Muslims in Western Europe* (Edinburgh, 1992) p 122.

42. Akhtar, *A Faith For All Seasons*, pp 17, 66–7, 112.

43. Akhtar, *A Faith For All Seasons*, pp 20, 150, 204.

44. Dr Akhtar's well-argued and deeply serious study earns him an astonishing rebuke from one Muslim reviewer, who dismisses it as a piece of self-indulgence, 'allowing full reins to an unsubmissive, un-Islamic, intellect ... [whereby] he strings together a series of often blasphemous but ever unorthodox, meditations.' See S. Parvez Manzoor, *The Muslim News*, 15–2–91, p 5.

45. *The Times*, 5–7–89.

46. Khanum, 'Education and the Muslim Girl', p 136.

47. *Trends*, 2/2 (1988) p 23.

48. *Trends*, 2/5 (1989) p 13.

49. *Trends*, 2/2 (1988) p 23.

50. In so far as it is possible to speak of a manistream Islamic position on religious freedom it approximates to that of the Roman Catholic Church *before* the Second Vatican Council; a position characterized by a historian thus: 'there cannot be liberty to teach error ... where Catholics are in a majority the government of the State has the duty to encourage them and to discourage Protestants and unbelievers. Where Catholics were in a minority, the government of the State had the duty to give them the freedoms of religion which they needed'. See O. Chadwick, *The Christian Church in the Cold War* (London, 1992) p 119.

51. S. Akhtar, *Be Careful with Muhammad!* (London, 1989) pp 76-7.

52. F. Rahman, 'Law and ethics in Islam' in R.G. Hovannisian (ed.), *Ethics in Islam* (California, 1985) p 15.

53. J.H. Brooke, *Science and Religion, Some Historical Perspectives* (Cambridge, 1991) pp 5 and 42.

54. According to the distinguished Pakistani nuclear physicist, P.A. Hoodbhoy, this work has been 'translated into numerous languages, hundreds of thousands of copies of the book have been printed and distributed free of cost by Muslim religious organizations throughout the world. At international airports and American campuses, it is the spearhead with which evangelical students seek to win conversion to Islam.' See *Muslims & Science, Religious orthodoxy and the struggle for rationality* (Lahore, 1991) p 79. Hoodbhoy's study is a damning indictment of this pseudo-scholarly book and the entire genre of so-called 'Islamic Science'.

55. M. Bucaille, *The Bible, The Qur'an and Science* (Indianapolis, 1979), introduction.

56. Z. Sardar, *Islamic Futures, The Shape of Ideas to Come* (London, 1985) p 168. The 'Islam and science' genre of apologetic first appeared in the nineteenth century, when Islamic thinkers such as Jamal al-Din Afghani (1839–97) sought to respond to the criticism of Ernest Renan. See A. Hourani, *Islam in European Thought* (Cambridge, 1991) pp 29–30. In India Sayyid Ahmad Khan (1817–98) sought to show that the Qur'an and modern science were perfectly compatible. See C. Troll, *Sayyid Ahmad Khan, A Reinterpretation of Muslim Theology* (Karachi, 1979) pp 144–70.

57. Sardar, *Islamic Futures*, pp 78 and 168.

58. See A.A. Powell, 'Maulana Rahmat Allah Kairanawi and the Muslim–Christian controversy in India in the mid-19th century', *Journal of the Royal Asiatic Society*, 1975/6, pp 42–63.

59. A. Deedat, *Is the Bible God's Word?* (Birmingham, 1985) p 62.

60. A. Deedat, *What Rushdie Says about the British* (Birmingham, 1989) pp 14–18.

61. *Telegraph & Argus*, 3–10–89.

62. A. Deedat, *Al-Qur'an, The Miracle of Miracles* (Birmingham, 1991) pp 14–29.

63. *Link International*, 4/1 (1989) p 2.

64. M. Raza, *Islam in Britain: Past, Prsent and the Future* (Leicester, 1991) pp 5 and 90–96.

65. Akhtar, *Be Careful with Muhammad!*, p 100.

66. Ahmed, *Discovering Islam*, p 185.

67. See J. Smith, 'Women, Religion and Social Change in Early Islam', in Y.Y. Haddad and E.B. Findly (eds), *Women, Religion and Social Change* (New York, 1985).

68. M. Saroha, *Heavenly Ornaments* (Lahore, 1981) pp 288, 304, 342 and 424.

69. R.Hassan, 'Made from Adam's Rib: the woman's creation question', *Al-Mushir*, 27/3 (1985) p 147.

70. Hassan, 'Made from Adam's Rib', p 145.

71. Hassan, 'Made from Adam's Rib', p 147.

72. See Saroha, *Heavenly Ornaments*, pp 463–5.

73. Rahman, *Islam and Modernity*, p 147.

74. See particularly F. Rahman, *Islam* (Chicago, 1979); *Major Themes of the Qur'an* (Chicago, 1980); and *Islam and Modernity* (Chicago, 1982).

75. Knott and Khokher, 'Religious and ethnic identity among young Muslim women in Bradford', p 605.

76. T. Gerholm, 'Three European intellectuals as Converts to Islam: Cultural mediators or social critics?', in T. Gerholm and Y.G. Lithman (eds), *The New Islamic Presence in Western Europe* (London, 1988) p 263.

77. K. Murad, *Da'wah Among Non-Muslims in the West: some conceptual and methodological aspects* (Leicester, 1986) pp 22–3.

78. See M.A. Haq, *The Faith Movement of Muhammad Ilyas* (London, 1972).

79. C. Troll, 'Five letters of Muhammad Ilyas (1885–1944), the founder of the Tablighi Jama'at, translated and introduced', in C. Troll (ed.), *Islam in India, Studies and Commentaries*, 2 (New Delhi, 1985) p 148.

80. *Trends*, 2/5 (1989) p 13.

81. See H. Ball, *Islamic Life: Why British Women Embrace Islam*, Muslim Community Survey Series, Occasional Paper 1 (Leicester, 1987).

82. *The Independent*, 26-8-91.

83. See F. Robinson, *Atlas of the Islamic World since 1500* (Oxford, 1982) pp 118–25.

84. P. Berger and T. Luckman, *The Social Construction of Reality: A Treatise on the Sociology of Knowledge* (New York, 1967) p 158.

85. For the Union of Muslim Organizations of the UK and Eire, see J. Nielsen, *Muslims in Western Europe*, p 47.

86. *Islamia*, July 1992, p 14.

87. See Ahmed, *Postmodernism and Islam*, pp 155–6.

88. *Telegraph & Argus*, 2–5–90.

Conclusion

1. Aziz Al-Azmeh accuses Islamists of being 'entirely inattentive to the historical experience of Muslims and to the historical character of their law', *Islams and Modernities* (London, 1993) p 13.

2. See Y. Qaradawi, *Islamic Awakening Between Rejection and Extremism* (Herndon, 1981).

3. Three in particular may be mentioned, one by an anthropologist, another by a philosopher and a third by an *'alim*: A.S. Ahmed, *Postmodernism and*

Islam, Predicament and Promise (London, 1992); S. Akhtar, *A Faith For All Seasons, Islam and Western Modernity* (London, 1990); and M.S. Raza, *Islam in Britain, Past, Present and Future* (Leicester, 1991). All are works by Muslims who are by origin from South Asia.

4. J. Nielsen, *Muslims in Western Europe* (Edinburgh, 1992) p 113.

5. I owe this information to a conversation with Dr J. Nielsen.

6. The Bradford Council for Mosques hosted a meeting on 29 January 1994 of 40 Muslim leaders from across the country to discuss the setting up a national consultative body. Sher Azam, once again president of the Council for Mosques, observed that, 'There are many local and national issues confronting the Muslim community which need to be tackled, and can only be effective if done by one national body.' *The Muslim News*, 25–2–94. External pressures are also pushing Muslims in this direction. The Home Secretary is reported to have told a group of Muslims in March 1994 that 'their demands would not be met unless they were put forward by a new, reconstituted Muslim body, representing all sections of the community'. See *Q News*, 25 March–1 April 1994.

7. Y. Ali, 'Muslim Women and the Politics of Ethnicity and Culture in Northern England', in G. Sahgal and N. Yuval-Davis (eds), *Refusing Holy Orders, Women and Fundamentalism in Britain* (London, 1992) p 123.

8. *The Runnymede Bulletin*, March 1993, p 5.

Glossary

Note: based in part on B. Metcalf, *Islamic Revival in British India: Deoband, 1860–1900*, (New Jersey, 1982); A. Schimmel, *Islam in the India Sub-continent*, (Leiden, 1980); and J.T. Platts, *A Dictionary of Urdu, Classical Hindi, and English*, (London, 1884/1974). Urdu speakers do not pronounce some of the letters their alphabet shares with Arabic as Arab speakers, these are then transliterated differently into English. Thus the Arabic word transliterated *dhikr* in English is transliterated *zikr* when the same word is used in Urdu. In the glossary I have included the Urdu word first and then added the Arabic transliteration, where both are used in the text. Where a bracket is included around a letter in a word this indicates a common variant used in transliteration of Urdu.

'alim (pl. *'ulama*), a learned man, particularly in one of the religious sciences. Also known as *mulla, maulvi, maulana.*

'alima, a learned woman (as above).

ashraf, the well-born, Muslims in India of foreign descent.

bai'at, vow of allegiance to a sufi by a devotee.

baraka(t), 'blessing', holiness inherent in holy persons or objects.

bid'a(t), (reprehensible) innovation, where something is added to or deviant from the Prophetic tradition.

biradari, literally 'brotherhood', localized intermarrying 'caste' group.

da'wa(h), 'invitation' to Islam.

dar al-Islam, 'House/domain of Islam' – lands under Muslim rule – in contrast to the *dar al-harb*, the domain of the enemy, war-zone.

dar al-'ulum, 'House of sciences', advanced Islamic seminary.

dars-i nizami, syllabus of religious education developed in India in the eighteenth century.

dhikr, see *zikr.*

durud, formulae of blessings for the Prophet.

fatwa, formal legal opinion pronounced by a *mufti* (q.v.).

fiqh, Islamic jurisprudence.

firqa/parast, sect/arianism.

hadis, Hadith, tradition from the Prophet containing his remarks on a given situation and based on a chain of transmitters.

hadith qudsi, divine tradition ascribed to God on the authority of the Prophet.

hafiz (pl. *huffaz*), one who has memorised the Qur'an.

hakim, a practitioner of the classical Muslim system of medicine.

haram, actions forbidden by Islamic law.

hijra, 'emigration' of the Prophet from Mecca to Medina in 622 AD, which begins the Muslim era, and by extension any migration from what has become an environment hostile to Muslims.

ijaza(t), permission, particularly for a student to teach a religious text he has successfully completed under the guidance of an accredited teacher.

ijma', 'consensus', one of the roots of Islamic jurisprudence, whereby there is general acceptance of a custom or decision by legal experts of a certain period within one of the schools of law.

ijtihad, 'striving', individual inquiry seeking to go back to the roots of Islamic jurisprudence, and thus by-passing *taqlid*, (q.v.), the solutions codified and accepted by one of the legal schools.

imam, (1) leader of the ritual prayers; (2) the leader of the Muslim community; (3) an honorific for a great scholar; (4) in the *Shi'ah* (q.v.) tradition the leader of their community in the line of 'Ali and Fatima, the Prophet's daughter.

jahiliyya, the time of 'ignorance', pre-Islamic paganism.

jihad, war against non-Muslims; in the sufi tradition the struggle against one's baser instincts.

jinn, creatures mentioned in the Qur'an, made from fire, and thought to be able to help or hinder human beings, who thus seek to control them.

kafir, a non-Muslim practising infidelity, therefore it has a pejorative meaning.

kalam, scholastic and apologetic theology.

kami, artisan 'castes'.

khalifa(h), in political theory the successor of the Prophet; in religious life the accredited successor of a *pir* (q.v.).

madrasa(h), institute for teaching *'ulama*.

manqulat, traditional sciences of Qur'an and Hadith.

ma'qulat, rational sciences of logic, philosophy, etc.

maslak, 'path', school of Islamic thought, e.g. Barelwi, named after the home town of their founder, Ahmad Raza Khan of Bareilly (d. 1921).

mazar, 'place of visitation', grave of holy man.

milad an nabi, the Prophet's birthday.

mi'raj, 'ascension', the Prophet's heavenly journey when he is considered to have come into God's presence.

mufti, an expert in the *shari'ah* (q.v.).

muhajir, migrant or refugee, often as part of a collective withdrawal from a situation which has become intolerable for Muslims unable to practise their faith.

murid, follower of a *murshid* (q.v.).

murshid, 'guide', a sufi able to lead devotees on the mystical path, also known as *pir and shaikh,* the Persian and Arabic, respectively, for 'elder'.

pir, see *murshid.*

purdah, 'veil', the seclusion of women.

qawwali, singing and playing devotional songs as part of certain sufi traditions, especially at the *mazar.*

sama', 'hearing', listening to music usually within a sufi circle.

shaikh, see *murshid.*

shari'a(h), the totality of rules guiding the individual and corporate lives of Muslims, covering law, ethics and etiquette.

Shi'a(h), shorthand for *shi'at 'Ali,* 'the faction of 'Ali', the minority tradition within Islam which considered that 'Ali, the Prophet's son-in-law, should have been his rightful successor. This trajectory of Islam developed variant understandings of authority, political and religious, compared with the *sunni* (q.v.) majority.

shirk, 'associating' someone or something with God, the greatest sin for Islam since it threatens His singularity.

silsila(h), the 'chain' of spiritual descent whereby a sufi traces his ancestry back to the Prophet.

Sunna(h), the tradition of the Prophet, the customs and norms which Muslims should emulate.

sunni, shorthand for *ahl al-sunnah wa'l-jama'ah,* 'the people of the custom and the community', the majority of the Muslims who accept the *sunna* and the authority of the first generation of Muslims which underwrites the integrity of the *sunna,* in contrast to the *Shi'ah* (q.v.).

tafsir, commentary on the Qur'an.

taqlid, 'imitation', following the rulings on the *shari'ah* arrived at by recognized authorities within the various schools of law.

tariqa, mystical 'way', referring to sufi orders, acknowledging a common *silsilah* (q.v.).

tasawwuf, sufism, the most common term for the mystical movement in Islam which began as asceticism and then developed theories and practices of mystical love and gnosis. The *tariqa* (q.v.) is the institutional expression of this movement.

ta'wiz, taviz, an amulet, often prepared at a *mazar,* containing qur'anic verses (etc.) for protection.

umma(h), community, especially the Prophet's community, the transnational world of all Muslims.

'urs, 'wedding', celebration of a sufi's death anniversary when his soul was considered to be united to God.

wali, 'friend' of God, a sufi deemed to be close to God.

zikr, dhikr, 'remembrance', the repetition of divine names, or religious formulae, intended to foster religious experience and recollection of God, an essential exercise for sufis and their devotees.

Index

Abduh, Muhammad, 138
Afzal, M., 77
Ahl-i Hadith tradition, 58, 62, 74, 85, 141
Ahmad, Khurshid, 102, 103–4, 105
Ahmad, Mirza Ghulam, 98
Ahmad Khan, Syed, 43, 44, 45, 47
Ahmadiyya movement, 12, 58, 62, 96, 99, 146; disparagement of, 98
Ahmed, Akbar, 47, 126, 190, 195, 197
Ahmed, Ishtiaq, 73
Ahmed, Maulana, 102, 198
Ahmed, Munir, 105, 109, 110, 125, 141, 175
Ahmed, Nadeem, 194
Ajeeb, Councillor, 69, 147, 153, 168, 169, 173
'Akhtar', Imam, 137, 142
Akhtar, Shabbir, 52, 114, 158, 159, 190, 191, 192, 195, 197
Alaud-Din, Nilofer, 188
alcohol, prohibition of, 118, 130
Ali, Muhammad, 45
Ali, Syed Ameer, 12, 13
Ali, Yasmin, 187
'alim see 'ulama
Ally, Mashuq, 105, 112, 173
Alvi, Maulana, 102
animal rights campaigners, and halal food, 148, 149
anti-racism, 2, 68, 159, 160
Arabic, 86, 87, 92, 94, 115, 116, 117, 128, 133, 135, 136, 137, 138, 176, 189, 193; learning of, 177, 178, 207
Arabs, in London, 14
Arya Samaj movement, 38
Asian Youth Movement, 68
assimilation, as government policy, 3
Association of British Muslims, 199
Awaz magazine, 189
Awliya, Nizan al-din, 31, 32

Azad Kashmir, 16, 77, 204
Azam, Muhammad, 178
Azam, Sher, 25–6, 90, 100, 101, 145, 147, 152, 157, 160, 161, 162, 163, 166, 167, 168, 172, 174
Azhar university, 135, 137, 138
Azmi, Maulana, 86, 88, 127

Badawi, Jamal, 109, 183
Badawi, Zaki, 123, 201
Baghdad, bombing of, 168
Bangladesh, 2, 14, 20, 178; cyclone disaster, 170
Bangladeshi community, 7, 15, 18, 21, 22, 23, 54, 56, 60, 63, 69, 89, 104, 106
al-Banna, Hasan, 5
Barelwi tradition, 36, 40, 43, 47, 73, 74, 82, 83, 84, 85, 86, 87, 88, 89, 95, 98, 99, 107, 109, 112, 114, 115, 122, 125, 126, 139, 146, 153, 154, 160, 162, 163, 166, 172, 176, 185, 186, 188, 199
Barq, Syed Abul Kamal, 83
'Bhangra Beat' programme, 66, 180
bhangra music, 180, 181
Bhutto, Benazir, 182, 187, 188
Bhutto, Zulfiqar, 108
Bihishti Zewar, 37, 79, 101, 195
bilingualism, 8, 21
biradari network, 73, 74, 86, 202, 206
Birmingham, 15, 24
Bishop of Bradford, 158, 163
Black Workers Collective, 73
blasphemy, law of, 158, 163
Bose, Mihir, 143, 144, 172
Bradford, 1–4; as city of Islam, 1, 49–75; Islamic institutions in, 76–112; Muslim community in, 24–6
Bradford City Radio, 66, 169, 170, 180
Bradford City Transport, 54
Bradford Council for Mosques, 8, 24,